CRC Press
Computer Engineering Series

Series Editor
Udo W. Pooch
Texas A&M University

Algorithms and Data Structure in C++
Alan Parker, Georgia Institute of Technology

Computer System and Network Security
Gregory B. White, United States Air Force Academy
Eric A. Fisch, Texas A&M University
Udo W. Pooch, Texas A&M University

Discrete Event Simulation: A Practical Approach
Udo W. Pooch, Texas A&M University
James A. Wall, Simulation Consultant

Distributed Simulation
John A. Hamilton, Jr., United States Military Academy
David A. Nash, United States Military Academy
Udo W. Pooch, Texas A&M University

Handbook of Software Engineering
· Udo W. Pooch, Texas A&M University

**Microprocessor-Based Parallel Architecture
for Reliable Digital Signal Processing Systems**
Alan D. George, Florida State University
Lois Wright Hawkes, Florida State University

**Spicey Circuits: Elements of Computer-Aided
Circuit Analysis**
Rahul Chattergy, University of Hawaii

Telecommunications and Networking
Udo W. Pooch, Texas A&M University
Denis P. Machuel, Telecommunications Consultant
John T. McCahn, Networking Consultant

John A. Hamilton, Jr.
United States Military Academy

David A. Nash
United States Military Academy

Udo W. Pooch
Texas A&M University

DISTRIBUTED SIMULATION

CRC Press

Boca Raton   New York

Acquiring Editor: *Jerry Papke*
Senior Project Editor: *Susan Fox*
Cover Design: *Denise Craig*
Prepress: *Gary Bennett*
Marketing Manager: *Susie Carlisle*
Direct Marketing Manager: *Becky McEldowney*

Library of Congress Cataloging-in-Publication Data

Catalog record is available from the Library of Congress.

Credits

The figures listed below were included with the kind permission of the publishers:

Figure 5.11: from *Power Programming with RPC*, 1991, p. 3, by J. Bloomer. O'Reilly and Associates, Sebastopol, California.

Figure 5.15: from *Design and Analysis of Fault Tolerant Digital Systems*, 1989, p. 39, by B. W. Johnson. Addison-Wesley, Reading, Massachusetts.

Figure 6.7: from *Object-Oriented Modeling and Design*, 1991, back cover, by J. Rumbaugh, M. Blaha, W. Premerlani, F. Eddy, and W. Lorensen. Prentice-Hall, Upper Saddle River, New Jersey.

Figure 9.1: from *Object-Oriented Programming With SIMULA*, 1989, p. 230, by Bjørn Kirkerud. Addison-Wesley, Reading, Massachusetts.

TABLE OF CONTENTS

Preface

Chapter 1   Fundamentals of Simulation   1

Chapter 2   Random Variable Distributions   31

Chapter 3   Statistical Inference   61

Preface

Distributed computer systems, software design methods, and new simulation techniques offer synergistic multipliers when joined together in a distributed simulation. Research journals have been the primary reference source for distributed simulation topics. Simulation is a multidisciplinary field and significant simulation research is dispersed across multiple fields of study.

Distributed Simulation brings together the many enabling technologies for distributed simulation. There is strong emphasis on emerging methodologies for distributed simulation including object-oriented simulation, multilevel simulation, and multiresolution simulation. The purpose of this volume is to provide a practical guide to distributed simulation for the simulation professional as well as serving as a textbook to support courses in simulation.

Systems of most interest to the simulation practitioner are often the most difficult to model and implement. Complex systems are the raison d'être for simulation. As the object-oriented paradigm has entered the mainstream of systems analysis and software engineering, a powerful new tool has become available for modeling complex systems. Object-oriented methodologies enable the systematic design of multilevel, multiresolution simulations.

Distributed simulation implies the use of multiple processors. Consequently, hardware characteristics of distributed systems are considered in this volume. The revolution in connectivity and computer networking has created numerous heterogeneous distributed environments. Distributed systems offer significant flexible capabilities as simulation platforms. Networking is an important enabling technology allowing the application of multiple processors to the execution of a simulation.

Parallel computer architectures continue to mature. However, parallel processors still face serial bottlenecks. The computing power of a multiprocessing environment may solve short-term performance problems. Currently, such an implementation is not likely to be easily extended or modified.

Any nontrivial, high-fidelity representation of a complex system requires significant effort to model and implement. Real systems change. A successful long-term simulation effort must also be able to change with it. A simulation infrastructure with well-defined interfaces is required to allow the use of multiple models as well as the use of existing models in new ways. An object-oriented simulation on a distributed system provides the hardware/software strategy that is best able to deliver acceptable, high-fidelity simulation performance with existing technology.

Distributed Simulation has utility for the researcher, the practitioner, and the classroom. In the university environment it is well suited for graduate students as well as upper division undergraduates who have strong backgrounds in simulation, statistics, and software engineering. *Distributed Simulation* is designed to provide a foundation for the development of high-fidelity simulations in a heterogeneous distributed computing environment.

The first four chapters of the text review the fundamentals of simulation. Strong emphasis is placed on the statistical tools needed to apply the power of simulation in a rigorous manner. An overview of probability, statistics, and simulation terminology is provided in Chapter 1. The use of random variables is highlighted in Chapter 2. Particular attention is paid to the use of continuous and discrete distributions. Chapter 3 covers statistical inference including random sampling, higher-order moments, and moment generating functions. Finally, system modeling as well as simulation verification and validation is presented in Chapter 4.

Chapter 5 discusses parallel and distributed systems with particular emphasis on the characteristics of distributed systems. The next four chapters establish the software and modeling foundations for distributed simulation. Chapter 6 covers the object-oriented paradigm and its use in simulation. Several methodologies are examined as well as their applicability to distributed simulation. Chapter 7 discusses event-driven and process-driven simulation. The resolution of a simulation can be dynamically changed by switching between event-driven and process-driven simulation. In a distributed environment, different parts of the simulation can be run simultaneously using either method. System modeling using a multilevel modeling strategy is discussed in Chapter 8. Emphasis is placed on modeling, to include abstraction. Aggregation and deaggregation are discussed. Chapter 9 surveys some of the available environments for implementing distributed simulation.

Chapter 10 discusses discrete simulation issues in distributed environments including synchronous and asynchronous distributed simulation. The logical process protocols to control distributed simulation are also covered in Chapter 10. Examples of distributed simulation enabling technologies are provided in Chapter 11, which covers communication networks and artificial intelligence methods. Chapter 12 details the design issues of a distributed, multilevel, multiresolution combat simulation.

We close this preface with an acknowledgment of those who have helped make this book possible. We are grateful to Lieutenant Colonel James A. Wall for his research in the field of multiresolution simulation. Many students in Professor Pooch's advanced simulation classes have helped contribute to this text and we would be remiss if we did not take the time to recognize them. We acknowledge the invaluable assistance of Willis F. Marti who was gracious enough to share his distributed systems expertise with us. Dr. Patricia K. Lawlis provided key insights in the use of object-oriented methods. Dr. David A. Cook contributed his observations on programming language issues for distributed simulation. Lieutenant Colonel Bruce D. Bachus provided an important review of the Force XXI-related simulation sections.

We also acknowledge the Department of Computer Science, Texas A&M University for its implicit support and for providing a stimulating environment in which to write this book. Our final acknowledgments go to the many researchers, practitioners, and colleagues who have contributed to the integration of several rapidly changing fields. A debt of thanks is owed to the many who helped us with this effort. However, it is our book and we acknowledge our responsibility for any errors or omissions.

John A. Hamilton, Jr.

David A. Nash

Udo W. Pooch

College Station, Texas

1

Fundamentals of Simulation

In the context of this book, *simulation* describes the field of study concerned with the use of a computer to duplicate the behavior of a system. The system of interest might have some actual physical analogue, such as a particular electric power plant, or it may be completely hypothetical, such as a simulation which models an airfoil whose geometry is known, but has not yet been built. In either case, the purpose of a simulation is to enable us to make useful conjectures regarding the model which are applicable to the system itself, without having to manipulate or observe the actual system.

Bringing the power of a computer to bear upon any problem of simulation is a logical extension of any modeling methodology. While the computer is at its heart a numerical manipulator, we can always come up with an encoding which allows us to use it to model symbols as well as numbers, and in this way obtain the ability to reproduce the behavior of nearly any system.

If we assume that the cost of preparing the simulation is much less than the cost of performing the corresponding analysis using the actual system, then it is in our interest to employ the simulation. In many cases, this cost-benefit determination is simple: when the analysis we desire is impossible to carry out using the actual system, we can say that the associated cost would be infinite. As an example, consider the problem of projecting the spread of a disease whose pathology is known, but whose method of transmission cannot be determined.

1.1 Systems analysis

Simulation inevitably involves the study of the *activities* of a particular system. Non-trivial systems are characterized by large numbers of inputs and outputs and a complex mechanism for converting inputs to outputs. The means by which that mechanism is communicated to interested persons (such as analysts, programmers, and management) is the province of *systems analysis*. It is generally concerned with the employment of a particular set of formalisms which simplify and clarify the characteristics and relationships of the processes involved.

The functions of simplification and clarification are each necessary and distinct. Simplification of the system to be analyzed is necessary because there is always a finite pool of resources (like time, computing power, or money) available to commit to the simulation. These constraints imply a limit to the feasible fidelity of the simulation. Thus, a competent authority must decide which elements of the system require explicit representation, and which may be safely discarded or subsumed by artifice. Clarification is needed because of the inherent ambiguity of the various modes of informal human communication. When human beings converse, for example, each is ideally taking advantage of a lifetime of culture and experience as well as various non-verbal cues such as facial expression, bodily posture, and gesticulation to make assumptions about the *real* meaning of what the other is saying. In systems analysis, a non-ambiguous method of communication must be adopted to prevent misunderstanding.

A plethora of analysis methodologies have been developed. Each depends upon a particular representational paradigm. Some techniques are better suited for particular problem domains than others because they incorporate devices for describing phenomena that are unique to that domain, or occur with high frequency. One of the methodologies that is well-suited to the domain of distributed simulation is surveyed in Chapter 4. Ideally, an analyst would use the methodology which yields the greatest insight concerning the function of the system being modeled; in practice, the ability of a particular technique to produce such insights is highly dependent upon the receptiveness of an individual analyst to its fundamental cognitive approach. Also, the analysis of non-trivial systems usually requires an automated tool. The cost of procuring different analysis packages to suit different modeling situations tends to minimize that practice as well. In the end, the techniques which are most familiar or most readily available to the analyst will probably suffice to characterize a problem domain.

1.2 Types of data

We can often simplify the task of analysis by characterizing the data we wish to simulate as belonging to one of three categories:

- *Discrete*: the data in question may take on any one of a finite or countably infinite set of values.

- *Continuous*: the data in question may take on any value in an interval of real numbers.

- *Categorical*: the data in question may take on any one of a finite, usually small set of values.

1.3 Probability and statistics

The study of *statistics* is the use of mathematics to discover patterns in, and draw inferences from data. It is important to simulation in a variety of contexts. Primarily, we rely on statistics to provide a means of describing the behavior of systems which cannot be adequately defined in terms of some small set of state variables. In most cases, either the set of defining variables is too large to handle easily, or there is no obvious set available at the outset of the investigation. In either case, statistical methods of analysis are powerful aids to the representation of a system.

The notion of *probability* goes hand-in-glove with any discussion of statistical analysis. Many systems which we would seek to model contain some sort of dynamic element. It is often the case that such systems incorporate a degree of variability concerning the behavior of interest that is infinite, or so great as to be considered infinite for all practical purposes. In such cases, the state of the system at a given juncture of time or space is subject to some uncertainty. A probability model gives us a means of articulating some assumptions about the nature of this uncertainty, and in this way gives us at least some power to tame the otherwise impossible chore of dealing with a system that is ever-changing, without any known mechanism of action.

To put the finest possible point on the subject, probability is the study of random events. Our main interest in employing probability will be for the purpose of describing or modeling a population. As an example, consider the problem of modeling the growth of a colony of micro-organisms. If we assume that the number of organisms existing at time $t_0 = A(0)$, and that the rate at which the colony is growing at any time t is proportional to the number of organisms present $A(t)$, then we could model the problem in the following way:

$$\begin{cases} A(0) = A_0 \\ \dfrac{dA}{dt} = kA(t) \end{cases}$$

where k is a constant of proportionality. Thus we have a first-order linear differential equation, which can be solved readily by a number of methods. But what if our original assumption regarding the rate of growth's dependency upon the number of organisms is an oversimplification? Suppose that a more accurate explanation is that for reasons unknown, an organism may or may not reproduce itself with some probability that is proportional to the number of organisms. In this case, we lose the ability to apply the techniques of differential equations to perform any intended analysis. As we will see though, all is not lost. We can still employ probabilistic methods to achieve our goal.

1.3.1 Notation and terminology

We shall develop an axiomatic understanding of the mathematics of probability by beginning with some definitions. As an example, suppose that we have a bag containing three marbles, colored red, white, and blue. We are interested in describing the probable result of drawing one or more marbles from the bag at random under various circumstances. An *outcome* is an indivisible, uniquely identifiable event, such as "drawing the red marble" or "drawing the white marble."

An *event* is a set of outcomes that is of particular interest. Suppose that instead of three marbles we had five black and five green marbles. In an experiment involving the selection of five marbles without replacement, one event of interest might be "an odd number of black marbles is selected." An equivalent description of the same event could be stated as "either one, three, or five black marbles is selected." We use the notation of braces from set theory to indicate the occurrence of an event. It is up to the analyst to ensure that the means used to describe an event is meaningful and consistent. In the example above, we might observe the event wherein three black balls are chosen consecutively, followed by a green, and finally another black. One way to describe the event would be:

```
{four black, one green}
```

An alternative might be:

```
{black, black, black, green, black}
```

This description is perhaps more meaningful than the previous one, since it allows the possibility of including information about the *order* in which each colored marble was drawn. Finally, note that we often use script capital letters to stand for a particular event. This is merely a notation of convenience, which allows one to avoid writing out event descriptions which might be long and cumbersome. We shall understand the notation $\mathcal{A}$ =

{green, green} to indicate that $\mathcal{A}$ will represent the event wherein two green marbles are drawn.

We usually associate probabilities with events, rather than outcomes, because they are the more general construct. We denote the *probability of an event occurrence* as $P\{\mathcal{A}\}$, where $\mathcal{A}$ is the event of interest.

The *sample space* is the set of all possible outcomes of an experiment conducted according to a particular protocol. For example, if an experiment is conducted such that two marbles are drawn at random from the bag containing five green and five black marbles without replacement, the sample space would be:

$S =$ {{green, green}, {green, black}, {black, green}, {black, black}}

It is worth emphasizing that depending upon the intended analysis, the events {black, green} and {green, black} might be considered to be the same event, in which case the sample space would have only three possible events.

1.3.2 The interpretation of probability

Through the years, several interpretations of the *meaning* of probabilistic results have arisen. The most often used interpretations are:

- *Classical*: The population of interest has a finite size of N distinct individuals. The mechanism of randomness involves a selection of individuals from the population, where each individual has the same chance of being chosen, namely $\dfrac{1}{N}$. Now consider two sets, A and P, where $|A| = n$. If $A \subseteq P$, then *the probability of A occurring* is the probability of choosing some x such that $x \in A$.

- *Long-term relative frequency*: An experiment is conceptually repeated an infinite number of times, such that each experiment is unaffected by previous ones. If we define the set A as being the set whose members are the possible results of the experiment, and a_n the number of times that some result in A occurs for the first n trials of the experiment, then $\hat{p}_n = \dfrac{a_n}{n}$ is the relative frequency of that result through trial n. Then *the probability of A occurring* is defined as $P\{A\} = \lim_{n \to \infty} \hat{p}_n$. Note that this interpretation is the common view of most statisticians.

- *Subjective*: Probabilities are obtained by a personal assessment, or expressed in terms of the risk one is willing to take under a particular set of circumstances.

Example 1.1

Consider a population which consists of a deck of ordinary playing cards. If we employ a selection technique that does not predispose us to selecting any particular one, then it's equally likely that we'll select each card. Thus we have the situation where $N = 52$, and P{selecting any particular card} = 1/52.

Define A as the subset of the population such that every member x of A is a club, and that A includes every club in the population. According to the classical interpretation of probability, we can calculate the probability of randomly selecting a club as $\dfrac{|A|}{52} = \dfrac{13}{52} = 0.25$.

Example 1.2

A fair, five-sided die is rolled and the resulting face upon which it rests is noted. According to the relative frequency interpretation, the probability of any one face being the one that the die ultimately rests upon is 1/5.

Example 1.3

An expert in the field of human behavior offers his opinion that there is a twelve percent probability that the human race will be extinct in the next hundred years. In that the probabilities of the alternative to extinction cannot be considered to be equally probable, and this is clearly an experiment which cannot be repeated numerous times, the expert is employing the subjective interpretation of probability.

1.3.3 The axioms of probability

The axiomatic definition of probability rests upon three truths:

I. $P\{\mathcal{A}\} \geq 0$ for any event $\mathcal{A}$.

II. $P\{S\} = 1$. That is, it is certain that something within the sample space occurs.

III. If $\mathcal{A}, \mathcal{B}, C, ...$ are mutually exclusive events in S, then $P\{\mathcal{A} \cup \mathcal{B} \cup C \cup J \} = P\{\mathcal{A}\} + P\{\mathcal{B}\} + P\{C\} + J +$.

Example 1.4

Consider a bag containing eight marbles, each of which has a different color. If we draw a single marble at random, what is the probability that it is either blue or white?

The sample space consists of eight events, each of which corresponds to the drawing of a marble with a different color. Since we are drawing at random, each color has an equal probability of being drawn, namely 1/8. Then the probability of drawing either a blue or a white marble is $P\{\text{blue} \cup \text{white}\} = P\{\text{blue}\} + P\{\text{white}\} = 1/8 + 1/8 = 1/4$.

1.3.4 Operations on events

In general, it is meaningful to think of any operation that is possible on sets to be possible with respect to events. This includes operations such as complementation, intersection, and union. As in set theory, we consider the *union* of two events $\mathcal{A}$ and $\mathcal{B}$, denoted $\mathcal{A} \cup \mathcal{B}$ (or often $\mathcal{A} + \mathcal{B}$), to be the event which occurs when either $\mathcal{A}$ or $\mathcal{B}$ occur. The *intersection* of $\mathcal{A}$ and $\mathcal{B}$, denoted $\mathcal{A} \cap \mathcal{B}$ is the event which occurs when both $\mathcal{A}$ and $\mathcal{B}$ occur. The *complement* of $\mathcal{A}$, denoted $\overline{\mathcal{A}}$, is interpreted as the set of events in which $\mathcal{A}$ does not occur. *Exclusion* is the set equivalent of algebraic subtraction: $\mathcal{A} - \mathcal{B}$ is the set which results when $\mathcal{B}$ is excluded from $\mathcal{A}$.

Many useful theorems can be derived from just the three axioms and set operations. For example, we claim that $P\{\overline{\mathcal{A}}\} = 1 - P\{\mathcal{A}\}$. The proof follows immediately from axioms II and III, as follows:

$$S = \mathcal{A} \cup \mathcal{B} \cup \cdots$$
$$P\{S\} = P\{\mathcal{A} \cup \mathcal{B} \cup \cdots\}$$
$$1 = P\{\mathcal{A}\} + P\{\mathcal{B}\} + \cdots$$
$$1 - P\{\mathcal{A}\} = P\{\mathcal{B}\} + P\{C\} + \cdots$$

$$\overline{\mathcal{A}} = S - \mathcal{A}$$
$$= \mathcal{B} \cup C \cup \cdots$$
$$P\{\overline{\mathcal{A}}\} = P\{\mathcal{B} \cup C \cup \cdots\}$$
$$= P\{\mathcal{B}\} + P\{C\} + \cdots$$

$$\therefore \quad 1 - P\{\mathcal{A}\} = P\{\overline{\mathcal{A}}\}$$

1.3.5 Independent events

Intuitively, we know that two events are *independent* if the occurrence of one does not influence the occurrence (or failure to occur) of the other. It is frequently useful to think of them as being widely dispersed in terms of space or time, although this doesn't necessarily imply independence. In terms of probabilities, we define independence in this way:

Definition 1.1 Independent random events

Two events $\mathcal{A}$ and $\mathcal{B}$ are independent if and only if $P\{\mathcal{A} \cap \mathcal{B}\} = P\{\mathcal{A}\}P\{\mathcal{B}\}$.

Since the probability of *any* event occurring is a value which is less than one, we note that this definition accounts for the idea that multiple events occurring simultaneously do so with lower probability than either one alone. Correspondingly, this quantifies our expectation that if one increases the number of independent events that are anticipated in a single observation, the probability of actually observing that set of events decreases.

1.4 Random variable distributions

A *random variable* is a variable which takes on values according to some random process. We usually categorize random variables further as being either *discrete* or *continuous*, depending on the type of data they represent. Random processes, by definition, are ill-suited to description by deterministic methods. Otherwise, we'd use the appropriate formula to duplicate the behavior of interest and carry on without difficulty. We are led to wonder, then, if there is *any* way that we can characterize such processes for the purpose of analysis. This is in fact the first of the two central questions of the study of statistics:

- What are the useful ways that a random process can be described?

- Having described the process, how can we perform useful analysis?

We shall answer the first question by applying some caveats to our intuitive ideas regarding the notion of randomness.

When we observe a random process and record the behaviors of interest, we accumulate a body of data which can be used to give us an *approximate* idea of the actual behavior of the process in its entirety. Note that in order to specify the process with complete accuracy, we would have to make an infinite number of observations – clearly an approach too costly to entertain. Therefore we must accept some degree of uncertainty regarding our understanding of the way that the process truly behaves for the sake of analytical tractability.

1.4.1 Statistical notation

Some standard terminology and notation have been developed to describe the processes associated with statistical analysis. At the highest level, we can consider statistics to be concerned with the description of and inference for the characteristics of two related groups: *populations* and *samples*. A population is a collection of all possible observations of a particular event or, alternatively, a collection of all possible instances of an object. It may be finite and well-defined (e.g., every bottle of a certain medicine produced in a single lot) or it may be infinite (e.g., all of the possible combinations of inputs that a user might supply to a certain computer program). A sample is a proper subset of a population that is observed.

Invariably, each object or event that is being studied has some characteristics which are of interest. A *parameter* is a numerical value which represents such a characteristic of a population; a *statistic* is the analogous value pertaining to a sample. Typically, the parameter's value is unknown and can never actually be observed (otherwise, we'd have no need of sampling). Therefore we employ a statistic to estimate a parameter. There are some statistics and parameters which are so commonly used that a common notation has developed:

Table 1.1 Common statistical notation.

Meaning	Sample	Population
Mean of X	$\bar{x}$	μ_x
Variance of X	S_x^2	σ_x^2
Standard deviation of X	S_x	σ_x
Number of observations	n	N

In situations where the specific random variable is clear from the context, the subscript is often dropped. A common notational convention is the use of a caret ($^\wedge$) to denote an estimate for some actual value; for example, we denote an estimated variance as $\hat{\sigma}_x^2$. Many other statistics are derived in some way from the ones listed here.

1.4.2 Visualizing a random process

A *histogram* is a helpful visualization technique which can be used to give us some indication of the overall behavior of a random process. It is a series of rectangles placed side by side on a graph, scaled in such a way that the horizontal width of each rectangle either represents the width of the sampling interval (in the case of continuous data) or is of some arbitrary unit width (for discrete data). The height of each rectangle is the *relative frequency*, which is the proportion of data in a specified category, divided by the interval length. Observe the following continuous-valued example:

Example 1.5

A chemist is interested in the time needed to complete a chemical reaction. He conducts an experiment in the following way: a catalyst is added to a solution containing a certain compound. The reaction converts this compound into a different, inert substance. The concentration of the original compound is continuously monitored, and when its overall concentration is determined to be less than 1% of the original, the reaction is considered to be finished. The chemist conducts several experiments, measuring the time needed to reach the threshold level of 1%, and observes the following:

Trial	Elapsed time (seconds)	Trial	Elapsed time (seconds)
1	10.7	6	10.7
2	11.1	7	10.1
3	6.7	8	11.0
4	8.7	9	10.0
5	10.6	10	12.1

As a general rule, it's useful to choose the number of categories (and hence the number of rectangles in the histogram) to be the square root of the

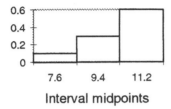

Figure 1.1. Example histogram.

number of data points. It's simplest to make the width of the intervals the same by dividing the range of the data by the number of intervals. In this case, we'd choose the width of the interval to be $\dfrac{12.1 - 6.7}{\left\lfloor \sqrt{10} \right\rfloor} \approx 1.8$. This results in a histogram which appears as shown in Figure 1.1.

We can tell at a glance how a random experiment will turn out: usually, the time elapsed will be in the 10.3 to 12.1 range. A simple expansion of this intuitive notion will lead us to an understanding of how probability distributions are formed.

Consider an arbitrary random variable. When we mention the word "random," we frequently bring to mind a picture of a chaotic activity, seemingly without pattern. Let us refine that notion somewhat, by the introduction of two characteristics of every random variable: *central tendency* and *variability*. The central tendency of a random variable describes its "preferred" behavior. Alternatively, we can define the central tendency as being a measure of which value (or values) the random variable takes on most often during a series of observations. In the same way, we can define a random variable's variability as its tendency to wander away from its preferred value. In some sense, the variability serves as an identifier of the "strength" of the central tendency: a small degree of variability would denote a variable with a marked preference for its central value; a larger variability would indicate a correspondingly lesser affinity. Consider the histograms associated with the two random variables in Figure 1.2:

The data set in Figure 1.2(b) displays a marked tendency toward a particular range of values, as indicated by its pronounced peaked shape. In contrast, the data set in Figure 1.2(a) shows a tendency for the data to distribute itself nearly equally across several of the intervals. Note that the idea of a data set's "tendency" is by definition somewhat vague. Therefore there is more than one way to express the central tendency and variability of a data set.

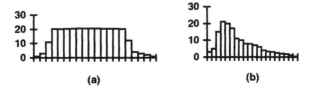

Figure 1.2. Two data sets.

1.4.3 Measures of central tendency

Mode: Location of the peak of the distribution. For discrete data, it is the value with the largest relative frequency. Consequently, its interpretation in terms of representing the central tendency is that it is the value which is most likely to be observed.

Median: The data point such that half of the data are less than or equal to it and at least half are greater than or equal to it. We can identify the median of a finite data set by inspection using the procedure described in Table 1.2.

Mean: The average value of the data. The sample mean, $\bar{x}$, is given by $\dfrac{1}{n}\displaystyle\sum_{i=1}^{n} x_i$.

Table 1.2 The median of a data set.

If the number of data elements is ...	... then the median will be the ...
even	((n+1)/2)<u>th</u> ordered value.
odd	average of the $(n/2)$<u>th</u> and $(n/2 +1)$<u>th</u> ordered values.

1.4.4 Measures of variability

Range: The largest data point minus the smallest data point.

Standard deviation: Our expectation of a "typical" deviation from the mean value. For the sample standard deviation, we calculate $S_x = \sqrt{\left(\dfrac{1}{n-1}\right)\sum_{i=1}^{n}(x_i - \bar{x})^2}$.

1.4.5 The continuous probability density function

In both example data sets above, the histograms illustrate the *distribution* of the data. In practical terms, knowledge of a data set's distribution allows us to make reasonable predictions about the outcomes of future experiments, so long as the conditions of those experiments are equivalent to the ones which gave rise to the original distribution. Intuitively, if we repeated such an experiment an enormous number of times, we would expect the resulting histogram to be very close to the actual population distribution. The actual distribution, usually represented as a function $f(x)$, is called the *probability density function*, or PDF. Geometrically, the PDF comes about as a result of a limiting process concerning the sample histogram, as shown in Figure 1.3.

If we increase the number of observations in the sample, we can increase the resolution of the histogram by making the widths of the interval smaller and increasing the number of intervals. As the number of intervals approaches infinity and their widths approach zero, the figure ultimately resolves to the continuous density, as shown. Since the histogram was originally constructed so that the area of one rectangle represented the relative frequency of values in that interval, the area under the probability density function curve between two points on the x-axis represents the probability that an observation will lie in that interval. This gives rise to the formal definition of a PDF.

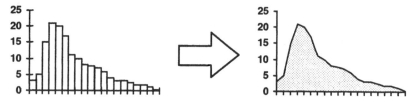

Figure 1.3. Formation of a distribution.

Definition 1.2 Continuous probability density function.

A function $f(x)$ is a probability density function (PDF) if and only if it possesses the following properties:

- $f(x) \geq 0 \ \forall x, \ -\infty \leq x \leq \infty.$

- $\int_{-\infty}^{\infty} f(x) \, dx = 1.$

- $P\{a \leq X \leq b\} = \int_{a}^{b} f(x) \, dx.$

By way of notation, we will usually use capital Roman letters (e.g., X) to represent random variables. Therefore, we interpret the third condition $P\{a \leq X \leq b\}$ as "The probability that the random variable X takes on a value between a and b." Note that, in general, not all density functions are defined over $(-\infty, \infty)$. In such cases, the normalization condition must be satisfied by whatever lower and upper bounds over which the function is defined.   Notice also that the definition precludes (that is, associates a zero probability with) the possibility of a *continuous* random variable assuming any *single* value, as opposed to some range of values. Intuitively, we can explain this by remembering that there are an uncountably infinite number of real numbers in any interval. The gamut of possibilities are distributed over every one of these real numbers. Since there is a finite total "amount" of probability, (namely 1), there must be an infinitely small bit of probability associated with any particular real number. It follows that since all probabilities must be greater than or equal to zero, this infinitesimal bit of probability is zero. Proving that this is true mathematically is trivial; evaluate the integral which defines the density with upper and lower limits equal to the real number of interest. By the definition of a definite integral, the result must be zero.

Example 1.6

Is the function $f(x) = e^{-x}$ a probability density function over the interval $(0, \infty)$?

Consider a plot of the density shown in Figure 1.4. Observing the function, we can guess that the area under the curve will be close to one. Since an exponential function is always positive, the first requirement is satisfied. Now one must examine

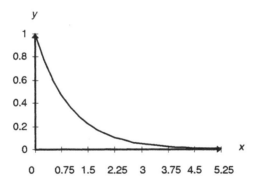

Figure 1.4. A plot of the function $y = e^{-x}$.

the normalization condition, which stipulates that the area under the density curve between its defining boundaries must equal one:

$$\int_0^\infty e^{-x}dx = \lim_{M\to\infty}\left(\int_0^M e^{-x}dx\right) = \lim_{M\to\infty}\left(-e^{-x}\Big|_0^M\right) = \lim_{M\to\infty}\left(-e^{-M} + e^0\right)$$

$$= \lim_{M \to \infty} 1 = 1$$

Since   the   function   satisfies   the   three   requirements   of

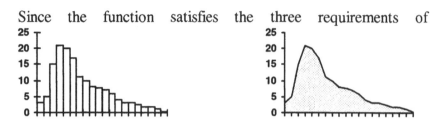

Figure 1.3. Formation of a distribution.

Definition 1.2, it is a density over the indicated interval.

1.4.6 Discrete distributions

As opposed to continuous random variables, a random variable with a discrete distribution takes on values which are of an integral type. This makes it possible to associate probabilities with a random variable taking on a single value, in addition to a range of values. Note that when one speaks of the probability that some discrete random variable is between *a* and *b* in value, it is understood that the values of interest are restricted to the discrete values in that range which it may take on. Contrast this with the continuous random variable, where the implication is that the probabilities apply to *every real number* in the interval [*a*, *b*]. Therefore we have the following complementary definition of the discrete probability function:

Definition 1.3 Discrete probability function

A function $f(x)$ is a discrete probability function if and only if it possesses the following properties:

- $f(x) \geq 0 \ \forall x, \quad -\infty \leq x \leq \infty.$

- $\sum_{x=-\infty}^{\infty} f(x) = 1, \quad x \in J.$

- $P\{X = x\} = f(x)$.

1.4.7 The cumulative distribution function

We are often interested in a special case of the more general probability that a random variable takes on a value between any two limits. For the purpose of decision-making, we frequently have a need to know the probability that a random variable is greater than, or perhaps less than, a certain value. This requirement occurs so often that it is usual to calculate the *cumulative distribution function*, or CDF, in the following way:

Definition 1.4 Cumulative distribution function

Consider the probability density function $f(x)$, associated with a random variable X, over the interval $a \leq x \leq b$. The cumulative distribution function $F(x)$ is defined as a function which maps a value x in the domain of the random variable X onto the probability that X is less than or equal to x, which is given by

$$F(x) = \int_a^x f(u)\, du$$

Thus when the PDF is known, the form of the CDF may be calculated in advance. Notice that in the continuous case, $F(x)$ is defined as a function which is a probability; $f(x)$, in contrast, is a function whose *integral* is a probability. When we pose the question, "What is the probability that X is less than g," we simply calculate $F(g)$.

Example 1.7

The function $f(x) = 1/2$ is a density for the random variable X over the interval $-1 \leq x \leq 1$. Find the CDF, and the probability that X is less than or equal to 0.7.

To find the CDF, we integrate, obtaining:

$$F(x) = \int_{-1}^{x} \frac{1}{2} du = \frac{u}{2}\Big|_{-1}^{x} = \frac{x}{2} + \frac{1}{2} = \frac{x+1}{2}$$

Therefore $P\{\, X \le 0.7 \,\} = F(0.7) = \dfrac{0.7+1}{2} = 0.85$ The probability density function is depicted graphically in Figure 1.5.

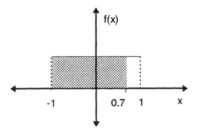

Figure 1.5. Probability that $X \le 0.7$ is shaded.

A closely related idea is the notion of a *percentile*:

Definition 1.5 Percentile

The *100p*th *percentile* of a probability density function $f(x)$ is the value x_p such that

$$\int_{-\infty}^{x_p} f(x)\, dx = p$$

Example 1.8

If Ξ has the probability density function $f(\xi) = \dfrac{3}{4}(1 - \xi^2)$ over the interval $-1 \le \xi \le 1$, what is the 75th percentile of the distribution?

$$\int_{-1}^{x_p} \frac{3}{4}(1 - \xi^2)\, d\xi = \frac{3}{4}\left(\xi - \frac{\xi^3}{3}\right)\Bigg|_{-1}^{x_p} = 0.75 \Rightarrow x_p \approx 0.3473$$

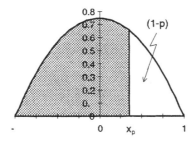

Figure 1.6. An example 0.75th percentile.

1.4.8 Expected value

Definition 1.6 Expectation

The expectation of $h(x)$, denoted $E[h(x)]$, is given by

$$E[h(x)] = \int_{-\infty}^{\infty} h(x) f(x) \, dx,$$

where $f(x)$ is a density function of interest.

The significance of expectation becomes apparent when we consider a special case of the general definition, such that $h(x) = x$. We have already seen that the mean value of a sample is the sum of the sample values divided by the sample size. If we have a continuous random variable's density function at hand, we can calculate the mean as $E[X]$:

Definition 1.7 Mean of a continuous random variable

The *mean*, also known as the *expected value* of a continuous random variable X is given by

$$\mu_x = \int_{-\infty}^{\infty} x f(x) \, dx,$$

where $f(x)$ is the associated density function.

This definition of expectation has some important ramifications. In particular, expectation is a *linear operator*. This implies that the following are valid theorems of expectation:

- If c is any constant, then $E[c\,h(x)] = c\,E[h(x)]$. This is easily demonstrated by virtue of the expectation's definition. Since expectation is an integral, and an integral is an infinite sum, the distributivity of multiplication over addition tells us that the theorem must hold.

- If c is any constant, then $E[c] = c$. The proof is as follows: $E[c] = \int_{-\infty}^{\infty} c\,f(x)\,dx = c\int_{-\infty}^{\infty} f(x)\,dx$, according to the definition of expectation and the preceding theorem. Since $f(x)$ is a density function, $\int_{-\infty}^{\infty} f(x)\,dx = 1$, therefore $E[c] = c(1) = c$, and the proof is complete.

- $E[h(x) + g(x)] = E[h(x)] + E[g(x)]$. Proof of the theorem again follows from the realization that integration is an infinite sum and application of the law of associativity of addition.

Therefore we are free to use expectation as if it were any other unary operator, such as negation, for example. We will see that in the analysis of performance, being able to take the expectation of both sides of an equation will be a useful algebraic device.

Example 1.9

Consider the random variable Ξ. If Ξ has the probability density function $f(\xi) = (3/4)(1 - \xi^2)$ over the interval $-1 \le \xi \le 1$, what is the expected value of Ξ?

$$E[\Xi] = \int_{-\infty}^{\infty} \xi\, f(\xi)\, d\xi = \int_{-1}^{1} \xi\left(\frac{3}{4}\right)\left(1-\xi^2\right) d\xi = \frac{3}{4}\int_{-1}^{1} \xi\left(1-\xi^2\right) d\xi$$

$$= \frac{3}{4}\left[\int_{-1}^{1} \xi\, d\xi - \int_{-1}^{1} \xi^3\, d\xi\right] = \frac{3}{4}\left[\frac{\xi^2}{2}\bigg|_{-1}^{1} - \left(\xi - \frac{\xi^4}{4}\right)\bigg|_{-1}^{1}\right]$$

$$= \frac{3}{4}\left[\left(\frac{1}{2}-\frac{1}{2}\right)-\left(1-\frac{1}{4}-1+\frac{1}{4}\right)\right] = 0$$

1.4.9 Moments

Take note of the structure of the formula for the mean in terms of the definition of expectation. The integral is the product of two components, x and $f(x)$. Consider a physical analogy. If a plot of the density function was actually a solid mass, it would have some "center of balance," that is, some point on the x-axis such that equal amounts of its mass would be on either side of that point. Now think of this mass as being composed of an infinite number of particles, each infinitely small, and having a weight equal to the value of the density function at that point. Further suppose that the body is supported from below at a single point. Then each particle in the body which does not lie on a line perpendicular to and passing through the support tends to make the figure want to rotate about an axis passing through the support and perpendicular to the surface of the page. The strength of this rotating force exerted by each particle depends upon its weight and upon the particle's distance from the point about which the rotation takes place. This is the well-known phenomenon of a *moment force* in mechanics, which is any force that causes a body to rotate. This analogy gives rise to the mean being known as the *first moment*.

Continuing the analogy of mechanics, we determine a body's centroid by summing all the moment forces and dividing by the body's weight. In our example, we would sum the moments by integrating according to the formula given for the mean. Since the body's total weight is the area under the density function between plus and minus infinity, we know by the normalization condition that this value must be equal to one. Therefore, Definition 1.7 gives exactly what we seek: a formula to find the point in the distribution which equally divides the total probability of the distribution. Figure 1.7 describes this analogy.

The mean represents our *expectation* of values in the sample, since it is the point that divides the distribution into equal areas of probability. (Paradoxically though, as we saw earlier, the probability that the random variable actually assumes the mean value, or any other value, is zero).

In mechanics, the first moment is the center of balance of a body. There are higher-order moments, and these find analogies in identifying characteristics of distributions as well. It is common to refer to two different types of moments in statistics: the *standard* and the *central* moment. Actually, one is just a special case of the other. The preferred definition depends upon the point of reference that one wishes to take.

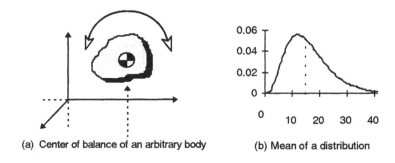

(a) Center of balance of an arbitrary body   (b) Mean of a distribution

Figure 1.7. The moment interpretation of the mean.

Definition 1.8 Standard moment

The k*th standard moment*, or k*th moment* of a distribution is defined as:

$$m_k = E\left[X^k\right] = \begin{cases} \int_{-\infty}^{\infty} x^k f(x)\, dx, & \text{for continuous distributions} \\ \sum_{x=-\infty}^{\infty} x^k f(x), & \text{for discrete distributions} \end{cases}$$

Definition 1.9 Central moment

The k*th central moment* of a distribution is defined as:

$$\mu_k = E\left[(X - \eta)^k\right], \text{ where } \eta \text{ is the distribution mean.}$$

1.4.10 Variance as expectation

Let us return for a moment to the second descriptive characteristic of a random variable: the variance. We said earlier that the variance was used to measure a random variable's tendency to depart from the average, or mean, value. Consider a random variable Y. Suppose we could sample each member of some population and measure the characteristic which Y describes. Then we could calculate the actual population average, μ_Y, from this data. If the variance is intended to measure deviation from the mean, we might be tempted to define the average of the quantity $(x_i - \mu)$ as the variance, as this quantity certainly describes the deviation from the mean in the most precise possible terms. However, our experience tells us that it is likely that some observations will be larger than the mean, and some smaller. This implies that any averaging process will tend to dilute the true value of the variable's tendency to wander away from the mean. In fact, $E[X - \mu] = E[X] - E[\mu] = \mu - \mu = 0$. Since our interest is mainly in the magnitude of this quantity, we can remove the influence of directional differences by squaring it.

The final question to consider then is: What is our expectation of the magnitude of this deviation? This is the very thing that the expectation operator addresses. If we apply the operator to the quantity $(X - \mu)^2$, we have:

$$E\left[(X - \mu)^2\right] = \int_{-\infty}^{\infty}(x - \mu)^2 f(x)\ dx = \int_{-\infty}^{\infty}(x^2 - 2\mu x + \mu^2)f(x)\ dx$$

$$= \int_{-\infty}^{\infty} x^2 f(x)\ dx - 2\mu \int_{-\infty}^{\infty} x\ f(x)\ dx + \mu^2 \int_{-\infty}^{\infty}(1)f(x)\ dx$$

$$= E\left[X^2\right] - \left\{E[X]\right\}^2$$

The term $\{E[X]\}^2$ is often written $E^2[X]$, and we will adopt this notation for the remainder of the text.

Example 1.10

If M has the probability density function $f(m) = (3/4)(1 - m^2)$ over the interval $-1 \le m \le 1$, what is the variance of M?

$$E[M^2] = \int_{-\infty}^{\infty} m^2 \left[\frac{3}{4}(1 - m^2) \, dm \right] = \frac{3}{4} \int_{-\infty}^{\infty} (m^2 - m^4) \, dm = \frac{1}{5}$$

$$Var[M] = E[M^2] - E^2[M] = E[M^2] - \mu^2 = \frac{1}{5} - 0 = \frac{1}{5}$$

1.5 Summary

We have introduced the fundamental ideas of probability and statistical analysis and described the ways in which these branches of mathematics are relevant to the practice of simulation. We now have at our disposal the notion of a random variable for use as a means of modeling uncertain or stochastically varying phenomena. We introduced the ways that the distribution of a random variable may be characterized, namely, in terms of its central tendency and variability. In the following chapters, we will see how knowledge of a random variable's distribution enables us to make inferences regarding the values which it takes on during a simulation.

1.6 Exercises

1.1   Suppose that we have a fair three-sided die. Each face is painted either blue, green, or red. An experiment is conducted in which the die is tossed and the face upon which it rests is observed. If the die is tossed twice, what is the sample space associated with the experiment?

1.2   It is proposed that 1 in every 12,000 adult males has a particular genetic characteristic. If we choose 10 men at random, what is the probability that one or more of them possess the characteristic?

1.3   A random sample of 50 cardiac pacemakers from a particular manufacturer reveals that four of them have a wiring defect. Under the relative frequency interpretation of probability, what is the probability that *any* single pacemaker (not just the ones considered in the sample) has the defect?

1.4   Determine whether or not the following functions can be probability distribution functions over the given interval:

a) $f(x) = \sin(x), \quad 0 \le x \le \dfrac{3\pi}{2}$

b) $f(x) = \sin(x), \quad 0 \le x \le \dfrac{\pi}{2}$

c) $f(x) = x + 2x, \quad \sqrt{1/3} \le x \le 1$

1.5   Find the probability density function associated with each cumulative distribution function:

a) $F(x) = e^x \cos(x)$

b) $F(x) = \dfrac{\pi x^2}{2} - x$

c) $F(x) = \dfrac{1}{x} + xe^x$

1.6   Given the definition of a probability density function, is it conceivable that a function that is only piecewise continuous could be a PDF? Why or why not?

1.7   Prove that for the family of functions $f(x) = ae^{bx}$, $a > 0$, there exists at least one interval on the real line for any choice of b such that $f(x)$ will be a satisfactory PDF.

1.8   A random sample of the lifetime of a particular light bulb results in the following data:

133.2	145.7	139.8	141.2	151.3
155.2	133.3	121.9	124.6	134.2
135.5	133.9	150.2	122.9	151.0
135.2	145.4	149.7	132.1	128.6

Find the mean, standard deviation, and median of the data set.

1.9   Consider the function $f(x) = 10xe^{x} - \sin(x)$.

   a) Find an interval over which the function is a density.

   b)   Find the mean and standard deviation of the distribution.

   c) Find the 90th percentile of the distribution.

1.10 Calculate the first and second standard moments of the distribution whose PDF is given by $f(x) = e^{-x}, 0 \le x < \infty$.

1.7 Suggested further reading

American Mathematical Society, *Operations Research: Mathematics and Models*, American Mathematical Society, Providence, RI, 1981.

J. H. Durran, *Statistics and Probability*, Cambridge University Press, London, 1970.

A. Hughes, *Statistics: A Foundation for Analysis*, Addison-Wesley, Reading, MA, 1971.

J. J. Hunter, *Mathematical Techniques of Applied Probability*, Academic Press, New York, NY, 1983.

P. A. W. Lewis, *Simulation Methodology for Statisticians, Operations Analysts, and Engineers*, Wadsworth & Brooks/Cole, Pacific Grove, CA, 1989.

W. Medenhall, *Statistics for Engineering and Computer Sciences*, Dellen Publishing Co., San Francisco, CA, 1984.

P. Z. Peebles, *Probability, Random Variables, and Random Signal Principles*, McGraw-Hill, New York, NY, 1993.

B. D. Ripley, *Stochastic Simulation*, John Wiley & Sons, New York, NY, 1987.

R. E. Walpole, *Probability and Statistics for Engineers and Scientists*, Macmillan, New York, NY, 1972.

R. S. Witte, *Statistics*, Holt, Rinehart and Winston, New York, NY, 1980.

S. J. Yakowitz, *Computational Probability and Simulation*, Addison-Wesley, Reading, MA, 1977.

2

Random Variable Distributions

One important reason that we would want to simulate a process is that it may be too expensive to model with full generality. Therefore we are interested in ways to simplify the representation of a system's behavior. In fact, finding ways to perform this simplification without compromising the accuracy of the simulation is the chief engineering concern of simulation design, because it is generally (though not always) true that there is a positive correlation between the number of variables considered in a model and the accuracy with which the model can predict real-world behavior.

If an investigator had to develop completely new ways to model variable data from simulation to simulation, the process would become very time-consuming indeed. Instead, one usually looks for patterns in the data which suggest that the process of interest can be modeled by a distribution which has been previously derived. It is a fortunate thing that most processes that have a stochastic element can be described in terms of just a few different kinds of random variable distributions. Thus if we know the details of these, we have a standardized methodology that may be used to simplify the problem of simulating many types of stochastic processes.

This chapter is primarily concerned with *describing* the characteristics of several different kinds of distributions. By itself, this would enable one to simulate the behavior of processes for which the distribution of events was known in advance. Even though this is not generally the case in simulation, it will not hurt to defer consideration of how to associate data with the distribution from which it came until a later chapter.

A number of distributions have qualities that make them especially well-suited for particular applications. The qualities themselves may be symmetry of the distribution, flexibility in defining the distribution's shape, or simply ease of computation. In any event, the overriding factor in choosing any particular distribution is the fidelity with which it represents the events being modeled. Often only previous experience suffices to know in advance what distribution will yield good results in some specific domain. The following sections describe probability distributions which have been used in numerous applications with satisfactory results.

2.1 Continuous distributions

Where the random variable of interest can assume values that are constrained only at the extrema (if at all), a continuous distribution is most appropriate. In such distributions, the PDF exhibits mathematical continuity, or at least a finite number of discontinuities, and thus permits the use of integral calculus to evaluate probabilities associated with events.

2.1.1 The Weibull distribution

Definition 2.1 The Weibull(α, β) distribution

A distribution is said to be *Weibull with parameters α and β* if it has a probability density function of the form:

$$f(x) = \alpha\beta x^{\beta-1} e^{-\alpha x^{\beta}}, \ x \geq 0 \text{ and } \alpha \text{ and } \beta \geq 0.$$

The Weibull distribution is often used to model reliability, lifetime, and mean time between failure (MTBF). The α parameter controls the horizontal scale of the distribution; the β parameter influences its symmetry. The availability of two parameters makes for a very flexible distribution. As well, both of the parameters appear as linear coefficients and exponents, which allows for a wide variety of possible distribution shapes indeed. Figure 2.1 shows a representative example of the Weibull distribution.

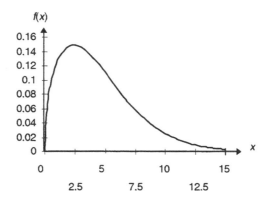

Figure 2.1. A Weibull(1.5, 5.0) distribution.

2.1.2 The gamma distribution

Definition 2.2 The gamma(α, β) distribution

A distribution is said to be *gamma with parameters* α *and* β if it has a probability density function of the form:

$$f(x) = \frac{x^{\alpha-1}e^{-(x/\beta)}}{\beta^{\alpha}\Gamma(\alpha)}, \text{ where } \Gamma(\alpha) \equiv \int_0^{\infty} u^{\alpha-1}e^{-u}\,du, x > 0, \alpha > 0, \beta > 0.$$

The gamma distribution, so named because of the presence of the *gamma function* $\Gamma(\alpha)$ in the denominator, is used to model data which is positive, unimodal, and tends to be right-skewed. A representative sample of a portion of a gamma distribution is shown in Figure 2.2. Note that due to the multiplicity of exponents, there are numerous algebraically equivalent forms of the definition. The gamma function by itself may be thought of as a non-integral form of the factorial function, since it is defined for all $x \in \mathbb{R}$, and additionally for all natural numbers t greater than 0, $\Gamma(t) = (t-1)!$.

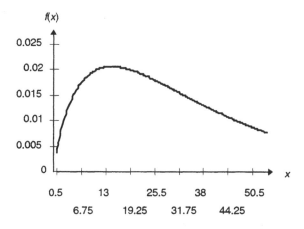

Figure 2.2. A gamma(1.7, 20.7) distribution.

An important computational theorem which may be proven by straightforward integration is that for $t > 1$, $\Gamma(t) = (t - 1)\,\Gamma(t - 1)$. In general, probabilities for the gamma distribution must be calculated numerically. An exception is the case where α is an integer, in which case if m is a positive integer and X has gamma(m, β),

$$P\{X \le x\} = 1 - \left[1 + \frac{x}{\beta} + \cdots + \frac{(x/\beta)^{m-1}}{(m-1)!}\right]e^{-(x/\beta)}$$

We have seen that values of the gamma distribution must in general be calculated numerically, due to the difficulty of evaluating its defining integral in closed form. But what about its mean, or, expected value? Suppose that some random variable T has distribution gamma(α, β). Then the mean of T, by the definition of expected value, is given by:

$$\mu_T = \int_{-\infty}^{\infty} t f(t)\,dt = \frac{1}{\beta^\alpha \Gamma(\alpha)} \int_{-\infty}^{\infty} t^\alpha e^{-(t/\beta)}\,dt$$

The distribution is defined only for values greater than zero, so the lower limit of integration becomes 0. Now let $y = t/\beta$.

Differentiation with respect to t yields $dt = \beta dy$. Making these substitutions leads to:

$$\mu_T = \frac{\beta}{\beta^\alpha \Gamma(\alpha)} \int_0^\infty (\beta y)^\alpha e^{-y} dy = \frac{\beta^{\alpha+1}}{\beta^\alpha \Gamma(\alpha)} \int_0^\infty y^\alpha e^{-y} dy$$

$$= \frac{\beta \Gamma(\alpha+1)}{\Gamma(\alpha)} = \alpha\beta$$

The gamma's variance may be obtained similarly. The second moment is calculated as:

$$E[T^2] = \int_{-\infty}^\infty t^2 f(t)\, dt = \frac{1}{\beta^\alpha \Gamma(\alpha)} \int_0^\infty t^2 t^{\alpha-1} e^{-(t/\beta)} dt$$

$$= \frac{1}{\beta^\alpha \Gamma(\alpha)} \int_{-\infty}^\infty t^{\alpha+1} e^{-(t/\beta)} dt = \left[\frac{1}{\beta^\alpha \Gamma(\alpha)} \right] \left[\frac{\Gamma(\alpha+2)}{(1/\beta)^{\alpha+2}} \right]$$

$$= \left[\frac{1}{\beta^\alpha \Gamma(\alpha)} \right] \left[\beta^{\alpha+2} \Gamma(\alpha+2) \right] = \frac{\beta^2 (\alpha+1)\Gamma(\alpha+1)}{\Gamma(\alpha)}$$

$$= \frac{\beta^2 (\alpha+1)\alpha\, \Gamma(\alpha)}{\Gamma(\alpha)} = \beta^2 \alpha(\alpha+1)$$

Since $Var[T] = E[T^2] - \mu^2_T$, we have $Var[T] = \beta^2\alpha(\alpha + 1) - \alpha^2\beta^2$, which reduces to $\alpha\beta^2$. Having proven the form of the mean and variance for the gamma distribution, we now can see that knowledge of a phenomenon's central tendency and variability alone allows one to specify a model which accommodates those characteristics.

Example 2.1

A large convenience store chain estimates that, on average, three out of ten of their stores will be robbed in a year's time, with a variance of 0.4. Derive the parameters needed to model the probability of a randomly selected store being robbed using a gamma distribution.

From our knowledge of the gamma distribution's mean, we have that $\bar{x} = \alpha\beta = 0.3$, therefore $\alpha = 0.3/\beta$. Also, $s^2 = 0.4 = \alpha\beta^2$. Substituting for α and solving for β gives:

$$0.4 = (0.3/\beta)\beta^2 = 0.3\beta \Rightarrow \beta = 1.33\overline{3}$$

Substitution for β yields the conclusion that a gamma(0.225, 1.333) distribution would model the probability of this event.

A gamma(m, β) is in fact the *Erlang* distribution. A special case of the Erlang is the *exponential* distribution, which is gamma($1, \beta$):

2.1.3 The exponential distribution

Definition 2.3 The exponential(β) distribution

A distribution is said to be *exponential with parameter* β if it has a probability density function of the form:

$$f(x) = \left(\frac{1}{\beta}\right)e^{-(x/\beta)}, x > 0, \alpha > 0.$$

The exponential distribution appears frequently in simulation. One commonly encountered use involves the *Poisson process*. Such a process involves the distribution of discrete random events over time or space such that the elapsed time between the ith and $(i+1)$th events (over a time continuum) or the distance between the ith and $(i+1)$th events (over a space continuum) has an exponential distribution. In such processes, the reciprocal of the parameter β has the useful interpretation of being the long-term average of events per unit time or space.

As well, a Poisson process has the computationally desirable characteristic that the time from zero to the mth event has gamma(m, β) distribution. This fact is helpful in the respect that one frequently wishes to know the probability of the passage of a particular interval prior to the observation of some number (often just 1) of events.

Example 2.2

Suppose that the diagram shown in Figure 2.3 is representative of a Poisson process which describes the existence of flaws in a length of fiber optic cable. If the production of such a cable is known to produce on average one flaw with every 400 meters' length, and the distance between these flaws is exponentially distributed, what is the probability that we will encounter at most four flaws in a cable 5000 meters long?

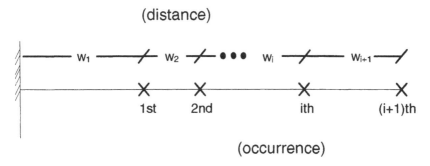

Figure 2.3. A space continuum Poisson process.

The occurrence of these flaws is a Poisson process. If we let L_m represent the distance from the beginning of the cable until the mth flaw, we can say that L_m has gamma(m, 400). Then the probability of encountering four or fewer flaws in the first 5000 meters of cable is

$$P\{T_4 \leq 5000\} = 1 - \left[1 + \frac{(5000/400)^1}{1} + \frac{(5000/400)^2}{2} + \frac{(5000/400)^3}{6}\right]e^{-(5000/400)}$$

$$\doteq 0.9984$$

An oft-mentioned characteristic of the exponential distribution is that it is "memoryless." This description arises from the fact that the probability of an event occurring at some time or space in the continuum does not depend on the existence or non-existence of events which precede it. Practically, this has the important consequence that having observed a great many events in the recent past does not imply any expectation of a reduced incidence of events in the future – there is no "memory" of the preceding events, and no compensation for their having occurred. Conversely, just because a long interval has elapsed since the last observance of an event does not imply any increased expectation that the event will occur in the future. This somewhat counter-intuitive behavior actually finds application in many models. Consider, for example, the classic example of a queue of customers at a bank teller's window. As the vast majority of customers have not coordinated the timing of their business with one another, we can say that the inter-arrival times of any particular customer will be independent of the number of customers which have gone before.

Mathematically, the memoryless property may be expressed as

$$P\{W > w_1 + w_2 \,|\, W > w_1\} = P\{W > w_2\}$$

We interpret the above as meaning that the probability of having to wait longer than $(w_1 + w_2)$ time units before observing an event, given that we have waited w_1 units already, is the same as the probability that we will have to wait w_2 time units. Assume that w_1 and w_2 are any two real numbers. The Bayesian statement of conditional probability holds that:

$$P\{W > w_1 + w_2 \,|\, W > w_1\} = \frac{P\{W > w_1 + w_2 \cap W > w_1\}}{P\{W > w_1\}}$$

The form of the exponential distribution tells us that it is monotonic. Therefore,

$$P\{W > w_1 + w_2 \cap W > w_1\} = P\{W > w_1 + w_2\}$$

Substituting,

$$\frac{P\{W > w_1 + w_2 \cap W > w_1\}}{P\{W > w_1\}} = \frac{P\{W > w_1 + w_2\}}{P\{W > w_1\}}$$

Using the definition of the exponential distribution to evaluate the numerator and denominator leads to:

$$P\{W > w_1 + w_2\} = 1 - P\{W \le w_1 + w_2\} = 1 - \int_0^{w_1 + w_2} \frac{1}{\beta} e^{-(x/\beta)} dx$$

$$= 1 - \frac{1}{\beta}\left(-\beta e^{-(x/\beta)}\Big|_0^{w_1 + w_2}\right) = 1 - \frac{1}{\beta}\left[-\beta e^{-\left(\frac{w_1 + w_2}{\beta}\right)} + \beta\right]$$

$$= e^{-\left(\frac{w_1 + w_2}{\beta}\right)}$$

Similarly, $P\{W > w_1\} = e^{-(w_1/\beta)}$. Thus,

$$P\{W > w_1 + w_2 \,|\, W > w_1\} = \frac{e^{-\left(\frac{w_1 + w_2}{\beta}\right)}}{e^{-(w_1/\beta)}} = e^{-\left(\frac{w_1 + w_2}{\beta}\right) + \frac{w_1}{\beta}} = e^{-(w_2/\beta)}$$

$$= P\{W > w_2\}$$

2.1.4 The chi-squared distribution

Definition 2.4 The $\chi^2(\gamma)$ distribution

A distribution is said to be *chi-squared with γ degrees of freedom* if it has a probability density function of the form:

$$f(x) = \frac{x^{\frac{\gamma-2}{2}} e^{-\frac{x}{2}}}{2^{\gamma/2} \Gamma\left(\frac{\gamma}{2}\right)}, \quad \gamma \in \mathbb{N}, x > 0.$$

Notice that the chi-squared distribution is simply a gamma($\gamma/2$, 2). The observation that a χ^2 is just a special case of the more general gamma distribution should give some indication of its overall shape. Like the gamma, a χ^2 distribution is unimodal and right-skewed. Its mean is readily calculated from the density as:

$$\mu_{\chi_\gamma^2} = \int_0^\infty \frac{x\, x^{\frac{\gamma-2}{2}} e^{-\frac{x}{2}}}{2^{\gamma/2}\,\Gamma\!\left(\dfrac{\gamma}{2}\right)}\, dx = \frac{1}{2^{\gamma/2}\,\Gamma\!\left(\dfrac{\gamma}{2}\right)} \int_0^\infty x^{\frac{\gamma}{2}} e^{-\frac{x}{2}}\, dx$$

$$= \frac{1}{2^{\gamma/2}\,\Gamma\!\left(\dfrac{\gamma}{2}\right)} \int_0^\infty \left(2\frac{x}{2}\right)^{\frac{\gamma}{2}} e^{-\frac{x}{2}}\, dx$$

$$= \frac{2^{\gamma/2}}{2^{\gamma/2}\,\Gamma\!\left(\dfrac{\gamma}{2}\right)} \int_0^\infty \left(\frac{x}{2}\right)^{\frac{\gamma}{2}} e^{-\frac{x}{2}}\, dx = \frac{2^{\gamma/2}}{2^{\gamma/2}\,\Gamma\!\left(\dfrac{\gamma}{2}\right)} \int_0^\infty \left(\frac{x}{2}\right)^{\frac{\gamma+2}{2}-1} e^{-\frac{x}{2}}\, dx$$

$$= \frac{1}{\Gamma\!\left(\dfrac{\gamma}{2}\right)} \int_0^\infty 2u^{\frac{\gamma+2}{2}-1} e^{-u}\, du = \frac{2\Gamma\!\left(\dfrac{\gamma+2}{2}\right)}{\Gamma\!\left(\dfrac{\gamma}{2}\right)} = \frac{2\Gamma\!\left(\dfrac{\gamma}{2}+1\right)}{\Gamma\!\left(\dfrac{\gamma}{2}\right)}$$

$$= \frac{2\left(\dfrac{\gamma}{2}\right)\Gamma\!\left(\dfrac{\gamma}{2}\right)}{\Gamma\!\left(\dfrac{\gamma}{2}\right)} = \gamma$$

This derivation employs the substitution $u = x/2$, which implies that $dx = 2du$. Alternatively, we could have made use of the fact that the mean of any gamma distribution is the product of its parameters, which in this case is $\gamma/2 \times 2 = \gamma$.

The χ^2 introduces the idea of a distribution with associated *degrees of freedom*. This terminology is intended to alert us to the fact that γ is a special kind of parameter. It turns out that a χ^2

random variable with γ degrees of freedom is actually the sum of the squares of γ random variables, each of which is independent, and is *normally* distributed with a mean of zero and standard deviation of one. (Hopefully this clarifies why γ must be a positive integer – it certainly makes no sense to speak of non-integral numbers of random variables.)

2.1.5 The normal distribution

Definition 2.5 The normal(μ, σ) distribution

A distribution is said to be *normal with parameters μ and σ* if it has a probability density function of the form:

$$f(x) = \frac{1}{\sigma\sqrt{2\pi}} e^{-\left[\frac{(x-\mu)^2}{2\sigma^2}\right]}, \quad -\infty < x < \infty, \ -\infty < \mu < \infty, \ \sigma > 0.$$

The normal distribution is perhaps the most important of the continuous distributions in statistics. It is useful in modeling many different kinds of data, as it permits arguments of positive and negative value. It is also referred to as the *Gaussian* distribution (even though it was first described decades before it reached Gauss' attention). Figure 2.4 shows the unimodal, symmetric nature of the normal distribution that marks it as the quintessential "bell-shaped" curve, familiar to anyone with even a passing acquaintance with statistical analysis.

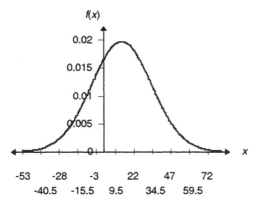

Figure 2.4. A normal(14.0, 20.25) distribution.

One very desirable characteristic of the normal distribution is that its parameters, μ and σ, have a directly interpretable meaning independent of any applied notion of probability. As the choices of their symbols imply, μ and σ are the mean and standard deviation, respectively, of the data which the distribution models. Recall that with the gamma distribution, we could derive the corresponding parameters, given the mean and standard deviation of the data. With the normal distribution, the mean and standard deviation are the very parameters we seek; no further manipulation is required to obtain a usable model.

2.1.6 The standard normal distribution

An important special case of the normal distribution is the *standard normal*.

Definition 2.6 The standard normal distribution

A distribution is said to be *standard normal* if it has a normal distribution with mean 0 and standard deviation 1.

The ubiquity of the normal distribution, coupled with the impossibility of evaluating the integral of its density function in closed form leads commonly to the use of tables to evaluate its probabilities. However, a small problem still remains. The parameters μ and σ which define a normal distribution may take on real values. This implies that there are infinitely many such distributions. One might think that this would severely limit the usefulness of the tabular approach to calculating probabilities, unless we had a large number of tables calculated for different values of the parameters. It is a fortunate thing that *every* normal distribution is in a sense equivalent to a primal normal distribution: the standard normal. This fact enables us to derive any normal probability from a single table. Thus any question about probabilities from a normal distribution may be stated equivalently in terms of the standard normal distribution.

The fundamental observation which allows us to articulate statistical inferences about any normal distribution as though it were standard normal is this: If X is a normally distributed random variable with mean μ and standard deviation σ, then $Z = \dfrac{X - \mu}{\sigma}$ is also a normally distributed random variable with mean 0 and standard deviation 1, which is to say that Z is standard normal. (Note: A convenient notation to indicate a random variable's distribution, which we will adopt here, is $X \sim N(\mu, \sigma)$. In general, the letter or word outside the parentheses identifies the distribution type; the first term within the parentheses will be the distribution mean; and the second term the standard deviation.) We will postpone the proof of the claim that Z is standard normal for any $X \sim N(\mu, \sigma)$ until our discussion of moment-generating functions. The transformation of X into Z is known as *standardization*.

We discussed the usefulness of the cumulative distribution function previously. In general, we find the probabilities for a standard normal distribution expressed as a table of its CDF. One consequence of the normality of a standardized normal random variable is that we can express cumulative probabilities of the non-standardized random variable in terms of the cumulative standard normal distribution. If $X \sim N(\mu, \sigma)$, then:

$$P\{X \le x\} = F(x) = \phi\left(\frac{x - \mu}{\sigma}\right), \text{ where } \phi(z) = \frac{1}{\sqrt{2\pi}} \int_{-\infty}^{z} e^{-\left(u^2/2\right)} du$$

We see that the definition of $\phi(z)$, the *cumulative standard normal distribution*, follows directly from the general definition of a CDF, substituting the PDF for a normal distribution with mean of zero and standard deviation 1.

Example 2.3

The random variable $X \sim N(60.0, 2.915)$ models the life expectancy in minutes of an attack helicopter pilot in a particular engagement scenario. What is the chance that a randomly selected pilot:

- Lives longer than 65 minutes?

- Lives between 58 and 61 minutes?

The probability that a pilot's life expectancy exceeds 65 is calculated as:

$$P\{X > 65\} = 1 - P\{X \leq 65\} = 1 - \phi\left(\frac{65-60}{2.915}\right) = 1 - \phi(1.7153)$$

$$\doteq 0.431$$

The chance that a pilot will live between 58 and 61 minutes may be calculated by considering that since the standard normal is symmetric about zero, $\phi(-z) = 1 - \phi(z)$:

$$P\{58 \leq X \leq 61\} = P\{X \leq 61\} - P\{X \leq 58\}$$

$$= \phi\left(\frac{61-60}{2.915}\right) - \phi\left(\frac{58-60}{2.915}\right)$$

$$= \phi(0.3430) - \phi(-0.6861) \doteq 0.3878$$

Since percentiles are essentially value points in the cumulative distribution, we can easily calculate percentiles via standardization as well. Continuing the previous example, what is the 95th percentile for pilot life expectancies? In the original distribution, this would be the value x which satisfies

$$P\{X \leq x\} = 0.95 = \phi\left(\frac{x-60}{2.915}\right)$$

From the standard normal tables, we find that the value z for which $\phi(z) = 0.95$ is 1.645. Then we have

$$\frac{x-60}{2.915} = 1.645 \Rightarrow x \doteq 55.2 \text{ minutes.}$$

One final point is in order regarding this example. Intuitively, a normal model seems appropriate for this random variable, as in the absence of better information to the contrary, most would agree that it is reasonable to assume that there is exactly equal probability attributable to data points lying at the same distance from, and on either side of, the mean. Thus, we would have no reason to expect that the distribution would not be very symmetric. But what about the allowable range of values? The normal distribution assigns non-zero probabilities to *any* interval of real numbers within $(-\infty, \infty)$. This implies that the random variable may take on negative values – clearly an impossibility in the context of this example. It is customary, then, to assume that if we use a normal distribution to model the behavior of a process, it is implied that the distribution holds only for the physically meaningful values that the system can accommodate. The probabilities associated with the impossible values are presumed to be so small as to be insignificant.

2.1.7 The log-normal distribution

The previous paragraph discussed an implied assumption regarding the use of the normal distribution to model phenomena that are strictly positive. In some cases, this assumption may not hold very well. As an example, consider a sample data distribution with mean close to zero, and a modest variance. If the normal distribution is employed, its symmetry will require that a substantial part of such a density be to the left of the x-axis. If the modeling situation is such that negative values are physically impossible, then the normal distribution will be ill-suited.

Often, a simple transformation of variables will improve matters. If we begin with a random variable Y that takes on values in the interval $(0, \infty)$, and define the random variable X such that $X(t) = \ln(Y(t))$ for all t, then X takes on values in the interval $(-\infty, \infty)$. (Actually, we wouldn't necessarily have to use e as the base of the logarithm in this transformation; any positive base would do. However, the mathematics which follow are greatly simplified by this choice.) Thus, we have regained the possibility of using the normal distribution to model the data by mapping the data onto a range of numbers on the entire number line. It now becomes necessary to develop a means of making inferences concerning the transformed distribution.

To find the density of Y in terms of X's known density, we make use of a transformation theorem. To avoid confusion, we return to the slightly more cumbersome notation of subscripted density functions, where the subscript indicates the random variable to which the density applies. For example, $f_Y(\alpha)$ represents the PDF of the random variable Y, evaluated in terms of the variable α. Suppose that the relation $X = g(Y)$ is defined over n contiguous intervals and that it is monotonic (i.e., either strictly increasing or decreasing) in each of these intervals. Note that the function need not be increasing across all intervals, nor decreasing across all intervals – it is only required that it be piece-wise monotonic. If g is differentiable, then in general

$$f_Y(y) = \sum_{j=1}^{n} f_X\left(g_j^{-1}(y)\right) \left| \frac{d}{dy} g_j^{-1}(y) \right|,$$

where $g_j^{-1}(y)$ is the inverse function mapping Y to X in the jth interval.

We outline a proof of the theorem for a single interval and leave the extension to n intervals as an exercise. The proof proceeds from the basis that we may describe the probabilities associated with the transformed variable in terms of the original variable by substitution in the original variable's cumulative distribution function:

$$P\{Y \le y\} = P\{g(X) \le y\} = P\{X \le g^{-1}(y)\}$$

Recalling some simpler notation for the CDF, remember that $F_X(x) = P\{X \le x\}$. Substitution into the previous equation gives us

$$F_Y(y) = F_X(g^{-1}(y))$$

Differentiation of a variable's CDF yields the PDF. Applying the differentiation operator to both sides of the foregoing equation and applying the chain rule for differentiation completes the proof:

$$\frac{d}{dy}F_Y(y) = \frac{d}{dy}F_X\big(g^{-1}(y)\big) = F_X'\big(g^{-1}(y)\big)\left|\frac{d}{dy}g^{-1}(y)\right|$$

$$f_Y(y) = f_X\big(g^{-1}(y)\big)\left|\frac{d}{dy}g^{-1}(y)\right|$$

We will often be interested in the case where $n = 1$, i.e., there exists a unique mapping from Y to X for all values of their arguments. This is the case in the situation at hand, as there is a single solution of the equation $\ln(Y) = X$, namely $Y = e^X$. Then $g^{-1}(y) = \ln(y)$; $\frac{d}{dy}g^{-1}(y) = \frac{1}{y}$, for $0 < y < \infty$. Substituting into the definition above, we have

$$f_Y(y) = f_X\big(g^{-1}(y)\big)\left|\frac{d}{dy}g^{-1}(y)\right| = \frac{1}{\sigma\sqrt{2\pi}}e^{-\left\{\frac{[\ln(y)-\mu]^2}{2\sigma^2}\right\}}\left(\frac{1}{y}\right)$$

$$= \frac{1}{\sigma\,y\sqrt{2\pi}}e^{-\left\{\frac{[\ln(y)-\mu]^2}{2\sigma^2}\right\}}$$

Suppose now that the mean and standard deviation of the transformed random variable Y are μ and σ, respectively. Then we come finally to the definition of the log-normal distribution:

Definition 2.7 The log-normal(μ, σ) distribution

A distribution is said to be *log-normal with parameters μ and σ* if it has a probability density function of the form:

$$f(x) = \frac{1}{\sigma\,x\sqrt{2\pi}}e^{-\left\{\frac{[\ln(x)-\mu]^2}{2\sigma^2}\right\}}, \quad -\infty < x < \infty, -\infty < \mu < \infty, \sigma > 0.$$

It is important to note that the parameters μ and σ are most definitely *not* the mean and standard deviation of a log-normal distributed random variable; rather, they are the mean and standard deviation of the transformed random variable, which has $N(\mu, \sigma)$ distribution.

2.2 Discrete distributions

When modeling phenomena that are constrained to occupy a countably infinite set of states, a discrete random variable is often appropriate. In contrast to the continuous case, recall that the PDF for a discrete random variable can associate a non-zero probability with the occurrence of an event which is described by the random variable taking on a single value in the interval over which the PDF is defined. Consequently, in the evaluation of probabilities for such distributions, the various probabilities involved must be summed via term-wise addition, as opposed to integration. This implies that in the discrete case, the possibility of evaluating the cumulative distribution (or any other interval of probabilities) in closed form depends upon the convergence of a series in the interval of interest.

In order to reinforce the idea that a discrete PDF associates probabilities with discrete values rather than a continuous range of values, we will use the notation $P\{X = x\} = f(x)$ to define the discrete PDF.

2.2.1 The discrete uniform distribution

Unlike most continuous distributions, the uniform distribution has a discrete analogue. Its density function assumes that it is equally likely that the random variable will assume any of the values in the defining interval.

Definition 2.8 Discrete uniform distribution

A distribution is said to be *uniform* if it has a probability density function of the form:

$$P\{X = x\} = 1/n \, , x \in \{x_1, x_2, \dots , x_n\}$$

The mean and variance of such a distribution is calculated as:

$$E[X] = \sum_{i=1}^{n} x_i f(x) = \sum_{i=1}^{n} x_i (1/n) = (1/n) \sum_{i=1}^{n} x_i$$

$$Var[X] = E[X^2] - E^2[X] = (1/n)\sum_{i=1}^{n} x_i^2 - (1/n^2)\left(\sum_{i=1}^{n} x_i\right)^2$$

2.2.2 The geometric distribution

Suppose that the phenomenon that we are modeling involves the observation of independent events, each of which is equally likely. If these events are independent, then it is possible to observe more than one event at the same time. The probability of observing more than one such event simultaneously is the product of their individual probabilities, i.e., if a single event occurs with probability p, then x such events occur with probability p^x. What conditions are necessary to form a density under these circumstances? As any probability must be positive, p^x will be positive for all x. The normalization condition requires that the sum of the possible probabilities must be 1. Therefore,

$$\sum_{i=1}^{\infty} p^{i-1} = 1, \, 0 < p \le 1$$

The choice of index and limits is made by noting that the notion of a negative number of observations has no physical meaning. The series produced by the summation above is the sum of a *geometric progression*, where each term in the series is related to the immediately preceding term by a constant ratio, namely, p. In the trivial case where $p = 1$, a density would be formed only in the case where a single observation comprises the entirety of possible probabilities. It hardly makes sense to discuss such a phenomenon in terms of probabilities, as the occurrence of the event is certain to begin with. For the more interesting scenario, it is well known that when $|p| < 1$, the infinite series converges to $\dfrac{a_1}{1-r}$, where a_1 is the first term of the series, and r is the common ratio between terms. In this case, convergence is at $\dfrac{p}{1-p}$. Since $0 < p < 1$, this implies that a distribution is formed only when $p = 1/2$.

We may also discover the requirements for the finite density by noting that the sum of the first n terms of a geometric series is $p\left(\dfrac{p^n - 1}{p-1}\right)$. For this to be a density,

$$p\left(\frac{p^n - 1}{p-1}\right) = 1 \Rightarrow \frac{p^n - 1}{p-1} = \frac{1}{p}$$

$$p^n - 1 = 1 - \frac{1}{p}$$

$$p^{n+1} - 2p = 1$$

An extension of the distributions which might be formed according to the previously discussed parameters that occurs often in simulation leads to the following definition.

Definition 2.9 The geometric(p) distribution

A distribution is said to be *geometric with parameter p* if it has a probability density function of the form:

$$P\{X = x\} = p(1 - p)^{x-1}, x \in \{1, 2, \dots n\}, 0 < p < 1, x \in \{1, 2, 3, \dots\}$$

The proof that this is indeed a density proceeds by noting first that the exponential nature of the function guarantees that it is positive, and that the infinite sum $\sum_{x=1}^{\infty} p(1 - p)^x$ is a geometric series whose first term is p and whose subsequent terms are related by the ratio $(1 - p)$. Thus the sum converges to

$$\frac{a_1}{1-r} = \frac{p}{1-(1-p)} = 1$$

The geometric distribution finds application in random variables that model processes having the following characteristics:

- The process consists of observations of one of two possible outcomes. Often it makes sense within the context of the model to denote one of the outcomes as *success* and the other as *failure*.

- The observation of a particular outcome does not influence any other observation, which is to say that the observations are independent.

The success/failure characteristic marks such systems as being in a class of phenomena that are often referred to as *Bernoulli* processes, which are modeled by Bernoulli trials. If the probability of observing a success in a single trial is p, and failure is $(1 - p)$, then the probability that success will be observed on the nth trial is given by $p\prod_{i=1}^{n-1}(1-p)$. This must be true, because the sequence of events leading to the first observation of success on the nth trial must be $(n - 1)$ failures, followed by one success:

$$\text{fail}_1, \text{fail}_2, \dots \text{fail}_{(n-1)}, \text{success}$$

Therefore, a random variable that describes the number of trials needed to observe the first success has a geometric(p) distribution.

Example 2.4

A certain highly unstable catalyst produces the desired chemical reaction in only thirty-five percent of the experiments attempted. What is the probability that exactly four attempts will be necessary before the first successful reaction is observed? How about the probability that four or fewer trials will be needed?

Let X be a random variable that assumes values according to the number of trials needed to produce success in this case. As noted, X follows a geometric distribution with parameter $p = 0.35$. Therefore,

$$P\{X = 4\} = f(4) = 0.35(1 - 0.35)^3 = 0.09612$$

Finding the probability $P\{X \leq 4\}$ may be accomplished in two ways. The straightforward approach is simply to calculate $\sum_{i=1}^{4} f(i)$. A more elegant and less computationally intensive approach is to remember that the first n terms in a geometric series may be calculated in closed form as

$$F(n) = a_1 \left(\frac{1 - r^n}{1 - r}\right) = p\left[\frac{1 - (1 - p)^n}{1 - (1 - p)}\right] = 1 - (1 - p)^n$$

Therefore, this is the formula for the CDF of the discrete geometric distribution, and the question may be answered as

$$F(4) = 1 - (1 - 0.35)^4 = 0.1328.$$

2.2.3 The binomial distribution

An extension of the ideas which gave rise to the geometric distribution allows one to model a slightly different class of commonly encountered phenomena. Consider the question of characterizing the sampling phenomenon, that is, describing the characteristics of a sample from a population. Imagine the existence of a population of size N, and that of these N individuals, M of them exhibit an attribute that is of interest to us. By the long-term relative frequency interpretation, the probability of choosing any single individual at random having the attribute is M/N.

Let us choose a subset of the entire population to form a sample of size n. If we sample at random *with replacement* (i.e., having selected one individual, that same individual is eligible to be chosen again), then there are N^n such samples possible. Some proportion of the individuals in these samples exhibit the characteristic of interest. This proportion may be found according to the formula $\dfrac{A_1 \times A_2 \times A_3}{N^n}$, where

A_1 = the number of ways to select j individuals from the n in any one sample.

A_2 = the number of samples (with replacement) of size j individuals from the M having the attribute of interest.

A_3 = the number of ways to select the $(n - j)$ individuals from the $(N - M)$ not having the attribute of interest.

From counting theory, we know that

$$A_1 = \binom{n}{j} = \frac{n!}{j!(n-j)!}; \ A_2 = M^j; \ A_3 = (N - M)^{(n-j)}$$

Then we observe that the probability that any random sample will include exactly j elements having the attribute of interest is

$$P\{X = j\} = \frac{\binom{n}{j} M^j (N-M)^{(n-j)}}{N^n} = \frac{\binom{n}{j} M^j (N-M)^{(n-j)}}{N^j N^{(n-j)}}$$

$$= \binom{n}{j} \left(\frac{M^j}{N^j} \right) \left[\frac{(N-M)^{(n-j)}}{N^{(n-j)}} \right] = \binom{n}{j} \left(\frac{M}{N} \right)^j \left[\frac{(N-M)}{N} \right]^{(n-j)}$$

$$= \binom{n}{j} \left(\frac{M}{N} \right)^j \left(1 - \frac{M}{N} \right)^{(n-j)}$$

This leads us finally to the definition of the distribution:

Definition 2.10 The binomial(n, p) distribution

A distribution is said to be *binomial with parameters n and p* if it has a probability density function of the form:

$$P\{X = x\} = \binom{n}{x} p^x (1-p)^{n-x}$$

This PDF finds frequent use in applications involving interest in *the number of successes in k trials*, where the probability of success on any given trial is p and the probability of failure is $(1 - p)$. Contrast this with the discussion of the geometric distribution where our interest was in the *number of trials until the first observed success*. Think carefully about the differences between the two scenarios until it is clear that they are distinct. Keep in mind that in the binomial case, we suppose that each individual may be chosen more than once. This is the idea of sampling "with replacement" – so named because of the apt analogy of choosing an object from a group and replacing it in the group before choosing the next.

Example 2.5

There are 317 birds in the apiary of a community zoo: 121 of them are species that are indigenous to the United States; the remainder are found naturally only in countries outside the U.S. Testing is done periodically for the presence of disease. Suppose that a sample of birds is collected, one per day, in the following manner: a bird is chosen at random, tested, and returned to the apiary. At the end of ten days, what is the probability that exactly four birds that are not native to the U.S. have been tested?

Let X be a random variable which takes on values according to the number of non-U.S. birds that are tested. We have a case of sampling with replacement, where there is a $(1 - 121/317) = 0.6183$ probability that a non-U.S. bird is included in the selection. In this instance, X follows a binomial $(10, 0.6183)$ distribution. Therefore, the probability that we seek is given by:

$$P\{X = 4\} = f(4) = \binom{10}{4}(0.6183)^4 (1 - 0.6183)^{(10-4)}$$

$$= (210)(0.1461)(0.003093) = 0.09492$$

2.2.4 The hypergeometric distribution

The previous section discussed a distribution that arises under conditions of sampling with replacement. Suppose that we decide to sample *without* replacement. How will this affect the probabilities of individuals in a sample having the attribute of interest? We can apply the same technique as was used for the binomial distribution by considering the situation in terms of a counting problem.

Sampling without replacement prevents an individual from appearing more than once in the same sample. This implies that there will be fewer possible distinct samples overall, as well as fewer ways for a member object to have the attribute of interest in any given sample. In fact, there are $\binom{N}{n}$ different ways to choose n objects from a population of size N. Then the equation for the probabilities becomes

$$P\{X = x\} = \frac{\binom{M}{x}\binom{N-M}{n-x}}{\binom{N}{n}}$$

Notice that since we are sampling without replacement, we discard the A_1 term from the numerator, since this would count samples with more than one instance of the same object. Then we have the definition of the hypergeometric density:

Definition 2.11 The hypergeometric(n, N, p) distribution

A distribution is said to be *hypergeometric with parameters n, N, and p* if it has a probability density function of the form:

$$P\{X = x\} = \frac{\binom{pN}{x}\binom{N(1-p)}{n-x}}{\binom{N}{n}}, \qquad \begin{array}{c} \max\left(0, n - N(1 - p)\right) \le x \le \min\left(n, pN\right) \\[2mm] pn,\ N(1-p),\ \text{and } n \in \mathbf{J}^{+} \end{array}$$

Notice that we made use of the same assumption regarding the probability of an individual object having the attribute of interest as was used for the binomial distribution: namely, that $p = M/N$.

Example 2.6

A group of scientists are studying the formation of skeletal structure in frogs from a certain region. To do this, they select a sample of 10 frog embryos from a group of 100. Each embryo is dissected to determine the rate at which certain key bones have grown since birth. The probability that any particular frog will exhibit normal growth rates is 0.4. What is the probability that of the 10 forming the sample, exactly 7 will be found to be normal?

The number of normal frogs in a sample of 10 has a hypergeometric ($N = 100$; $p = 0.4$; $n = 10$) distribution. Then the probability of 7 normal is given by:

$$P\{X = 7\} = \frac{\dbinom{(0.4)(100)}{7}\dbinom{100(1-0.4)}{10-7}}{\dbinom{100}{10}} = \frac{\dbinom{40}{7}\dbinom{60}{3}}{\dbinom{100}{10}}$$

$$= \frac{\left(\dfrac{40!}{7!33!}\right)\left(\dfrac{60!}{3!57!}\right)}{\dfrac{100!}{10!90!}} = \frac{\dfrac{\left(\dfrac{\prod\limits_{i=34}^{40} i}{7!}\right)\left(\dfrac{\prod\limits_{i=58}^{60} i}{3!}\right)}{\dfrac{\prod\limits_{i=91}^{100} i}{10!}}}{} = \left(\dfrac{\prod\limits_{i=34}^{40} i}{7!}\right)\left(\dfrac{\prod\limits_{i=58}^{60} i}{3!}\right)\left(\dfrac{10!}{\prod\limits_{i=91}^{100} i}\right)$$

$$= \frac{120\left(\prod\limits_{i=34}^{40} i\right)\left(\prod\limits_{i=58}^{60} i\right)}{\prod\limits_{i=91}^{100} i} = \frac{(120)(93963542400)(205320)}{6.281565095553e+019}$$

$$\doteq 0.0368$$

The tedious nature of evaluating the factorials in the above calculations leads one to wonder if there isn't an easier technique. Fortunately, as the next section shows, there often is.

2.2.5 The Poisson distribution

Recall that the definition of the binomial distribution is $P\{X = x\} = \binom{n}{x} p^x (1 - p)^{n-x}$. The first term, which is the number of n things taken x at a time, may be rewritten as:

$$\binom{n}{x} = \frac{n!}{x!(n-x)!} = \frac{n(n-1)(n-2)\cdots(n-x)(n-x-1)\cdots 1}{x![(n-x)(n-x-1)(n-x-2)\cdots 1]}$$

$$= \frac{n(n-1)(n-2)\cdots(n-x+1)}{x!}$$

If we have the situation where $x \approx np$, then for modest n it must be the case that $x \ll n$ and $xp \ll 1$. Using these assumptions, we can simplify the calculation of the binomial probability by noting that

- $n(n-1)(n-2)\cdots(n-x+1) \approx n^x$ (since x is small compared to n)

- $\lim_{p \to 0}(1-p) = 1$; $\lim_{p \to 0} e^{-p} = 1$; therefore since $xp \ll 1$, $1 - p \approx e^{-p}$.

- For the same reason as above, $(1-p)^{n-x} \approx (e^{-p})^{n-x} = e^{xp-np}$. Because $xp \ll 1$, $e^{xp} \approx e^0 = 1$. Thus, $(1-p)^{n-x} \approx e^{-np}$.

Making substitution for the simplified terms that were derived here and combining the product np into a single constant g leads to the definition of the Poisson distribution.

Definition 2.12 The Poisson(g) distribution

A distribution is said to be *Poisson with parameter g* if it has a probability density function of the form:

$$P\{X = x\} = \frac{e^{-g}g^x}{x!}, x \in \{0, 1, 2 \ldots\}$$

This distribution was mentioned briefly in the context of its relation to the exponential distribution. The significance of the parameter g becomes clear upon calculation of the distribution mean:

$$E[X] = \sum_{i=0}^{\infty} x\left(\frac{e^{-g}g^x}{x!}\right) = e^{-g}\sum_{i=0}^{\infty} x\left(\frac{g^x}{x!}\right) = e^{-g}\sum_{i=1}^{\infty}\frac{g^x}{(x-1)!}$$

$$= ge^{-g}\sum_{i=1}^{\infty}\frac{g^{x-1}}{(x-1)!} = ge^{-g}e^{g} = g$$

Thus, changes in g have the effect of changing the average value of the random variable in a linear way. We can think of this parameter then as being an average "rate" parameter of some sort, if we consider the random variable as describing a process which evolves over time.

2.3 Summary

The use of continuous and discrete probability distributions provides a convenient and in most cases mathematically tractable way to describe real systems. While there are many functions that are known to be distributions, only a handful are frequently used in simulations. We have endeavored in this chapter to cover the most commonly encountered forms and describe some scenarios where they often arise.

2.4 Exercises

2.1   Derive the formula for the cumulative distribution function of an exponential distribution with parameter β.

2.2   If T is a random variable with exponential (1.3) distribution, what is the probability that T is less than or equal to 0.5?

2.3   Prove that for $t > 1$, $\Gamma(t) = (t - 1)\ \Gamma(t - 1)$.

2.4   Explain the ramifications of the exponential distribution's memoryless property in terms of its usefulness in modeling various physical processes. When would this property *not* be a desirable feature?

2.5   It is noted that upon taking the natural log of a data set, the resulting data is normally distributed with mean equal to 2.05 and standard deviation 0.98. What is the probability that a random variable from this distribution takes on values between 2.67 and 2.9?

2.6   A random variable $X \sim N(2.1,\ 0.9)$ is transformed by the rule $Y = aX + b$. Derive the formula for the probability density function of Y, $f_Y(y)$.

2.7   A random variable $X \sim$ exponential (1.3) is transformed by the rule $Y = aX^2$. Derive the formula for the probability density function of Y, $f_Y(y)$.

2.8   Derive formulae for the mean and variance of a geometric(p) distribution.

2.9   Bottles of medicine are selected at random from lots of 250, tested, and then destroyed. It is known that each bottle has a 0.02 probability that it will not meet quality standards. If seven bottles are selected at random from a lot of 250, what is the probability that fewer than three of them will fail to meet quality standards?

2.10 The number of new TELNET (remote terminal) connections requested at a specific computer in an interval of one minute is modeled as a Poisson random variable with parameter g = 5.34 requests per minute. What is the probability that exactly six requests will be received in a particular minute?

2.5 Suggested further reading

H. Cramer, *Random Variables and Probability Distributions*, Cambridge University Press, London, 1970.

N. A. J. Hastings, *Statistical Distributions: A Handbook for Students and Practitioners*, John Wiley and Sons, New York, NY, 1975.

N. L. Johnson, *Discrete Distributions*, John Wiley and Sons, New York, NY, 1969.

G. P. Patil, *A Dictionary and Bibliography of Discrete Distributions*, International Statistical Institute, Edinburgh, 1968.

V. Rothschild, *Probability Distributions*, John Wiley and Sons, New York, NY, 1986.

3

Statistical Inference

The application of statistical models in simulation arises out of an inability to find more satisfactory analytical models. When a system behavior is encountered that cannot be adequately explained using known theories relevant to the subject matter, one option is to make a "reasonable guess" of the system's model, based upon previous observations. We now consider the mechanics of deriving estimates which will in some way approximate the actual values that govern the behavior of the system, keeping in mind that these actual values can never be known with complete certainty. This is the act of *statistical inference* – the generation of conclusions about the characteristics of the population through an analysis of the corresponding characteristics in a sample.

3.1 Random sampling

We have previously discussed various methods to describe datasets and are nearly ready to make use of them in the performance of statistical inference. One important element remains – to describe the notion of *random sampling*. We most often make use of statistics as a means of drawing conclusions about large numbers of related objects on the basis of having observed a subset of the whole group. The process of selecting which items will form the observed subset is referred to as *sampling*. On its face, it might seem odd that any rigor in defining the mechanism by which this is accomplished would be necessary. After all, we recognize in advance that we will not be able to observe the population in its entirety, and so it would seem that one element would do just as well as another as a member of the observed subset. In fact precisely the opposite is true. Primarily, we employ random sampling to avoid bias in our conclusions, and to provide a measure of precision for those conclusions in terms of the risk of arriving at an erroneous result. In most cases, the use of random sampling will guarantee the existence of error bounds on estimated quantities.

There are two approaches to random sampling:

- *Controlled* random sample: The sample is a result of a mechanism with a *known* probability model. The classic example is a pseudo-random number generator.

- *Observational* random sample: The sample is obtained and accepted as having come from some probability model, which is not known. As an example, observations of the behavior of animals when exposed to certain stimuli could be interpreted as having come from a normal distribution.

Many situations are combinations of the two approaches. For example, suppose an experiment is conducted to measure the strength of a composite material after having been treated in four different ways. A supply of the material comes to the investigator through laboratory supply channels, over which he has no control. In the sense that the investigator does not know the true probability model which governs the production of each piece of material he receives, this will be an observational random sample. However, the sample may be randomly divided into four subsamples, and different treatments applied to each. This technique establishes a known probability model for the experiment.

The most straightforward model assumes *simple random sampling*: every possible sample has the same chance to be the one which is ultimately selected. In cases where the population is infinite, each individual in the population has the same chance to be in the sample, and observations are independently selected. Independence in this context implies that the selection of a particular item does not affect the probability that any other item will or will not be selected. Note that it can be hard to verify independence, but there are commonly encountered situations where the assumption routinely fails. One such scenario arises whenever selection proceeds by a mechanism which picks items that are *consecutively available*, e.g., ten consecutive components from a factory production line. It is commonly the case that production processes exhibit small slippages in tolerances, due to mechanical wear of machinery, or cumulative numerical errors in control circuits. Thus, items which are adjacent to one another in the production process tend to be more similar than items which are far apart. The case of *repeated measures* also violates independence axiomatically. For example, a common technique for estimating the proportion of a person's body composition that is attributable to fat is to average several measurements of the thickness of folds in the subcutaneous fat at various places on the body. Assuming that the measurements are made at the same place on the body each time, they will necessarily be correlated, as their observations are not random.

In a well-defined finite population, we usually have the notion of a *frame* − an implicit or explicit list of the population. Ideally one can identify the N individuals of the population with the numbers 1, 2, ... N. For example, consider a record in a database of many records. Each one typically has some value which identifies it uniquely among all of the other records in the database. Assuming that we can associate a unique number in the interval [1, N] with each element of the population, an easy way to obtain a simple random sample is:

- Generate random variables $\{U_1, U_2, ... \} \sim U(0, 1)$ using any suitable random number generator.

- Let $L_i = \texttt{int}(NU_i) + 1$, where $\texttt{int}(x)$ is the number formed by truncating any decimal portion of x to zero, i.e., it is the integral portion of the number. Each such L_i will be a number in the interval $[1, N]$, and each will have equal probability.

- Select as the sample the first n distinct values from L_1, L_2, ... The objects which correspond to those identifying values constitute the sample.

A bit of possibly confusing terminology is necessary before proceeding. Our interest in this section is in looking at ways to estimate parameters. To do so, we will make use of *estimators*, which are algebraic representations derived in a certain way that are used to estimate parameters. In contrast, an *estimate* is an actual value (or range of values) calculated according to the rules by which its estimator was defined. Thus there may exist several distinct kinds of estimators for a single parameter, each of which define a sort of "recipe" for calculating an estimate. We shall see that some estimators are more useful than others.

3.1.1 Sampling behavior

Suppose the existence of a population exhibiting a parameter of interest, whose actual value we will refer to as θ. Let Y be an estimator; further, let it be a random variable which takes on values from samples that we observe. Our intention is to use our observations of the statistic Y to estimate the parameter θ. We will describe $E[Y]$ as the average value of the estimator Y among all possible samples from the population, and define the quantity $E[Y] - \theta$ as the *bias*. If for a particular estimator the bias is zero, then we have the case where $E[Y] = \theta$; in other words, the average value of the estimator equals the actual value which we wish to estimate. We call estimators with this very desirable property *unbiased*. Given its definition, we can see that the bias of an estimator is a measure of its accuracy. When we have values of bias which are large relative to the parameter of interest, the average value of that estimator among all possible samples is far away from the parameter's real value. Thinking of it this way, we can say that the bias is a measurement of the central tendency of the set of all samples from a population.

A related idea is the *standard error* of Y, which is the standard deviation of Y among all possible samples from a population of size N. We often denote this quantity as $SE[Y]$. Note that this is different from the standard deviation of a parameter in some population, in that the standard error describes how large a "typical" deviation is between the estimator and the actual parameter, considering every possible sample which could be generated. A large standard error implies that Y varies greatly from sample to sample. Thus the standard error is a measure of precision.

3.1.2 Sums of random variables

We need to digress for a moment to establish a few useful theorems regarding expectation and random variables. These will be employed later to demonstrate some of the characteristics of the estimators that we'll use. First, consider a group of n continuous independent random variables, W_1, W_2, ... W_n. Let c_1, c_2, .. c_n be arbitrary real-valued constants. Suppose that we want to know the expected value of a sum of these random variables:

$$S = E[c_1 W_1 + c_2 W_2 + \ldots + c_n W_n]$$

Invoking the definition of the expectation operator leads to the following realization:

$$S = \int_{-\infty}^{\infty} c_1 w_1 f(w_1) dw_1 + \int_{-\infty}^{\infty} c_2 w_2 f(w_2) dw_2 + \ldots + \int_{-\infty}^{\infty} c_n w_n f(w_n) dw_n$$

$$= c_1 \int_{-\infty}^{\infty} w_1 f(w_1) dw_1 + c_2 \int_{-\infty}^{\infty} w_2 f(w_2) dw_2 + \ldots + c_n \int_{-\infty}^{\infty} w_n f(w_n) dw_n$$

$$= c_1 E[W_1] + c_2 E[W_2] + \ldots + c_n E[W_n]$$

This is just what we would anticipate, since expectation is a linear operator. Calculating the variance of a sum of random variables yields a result which is similar in terms of the form of the result, but nonetheless distinct:

$$V = Var[c_1 W_1 + c_2 W_2 + \ldots + c_n W_n]$$

$$= E\left[(c_1 W_1 + c_2 W_2 + \ldots + c_n W_n)^2\right] - E^2[c_1 W_1 + c_2 W_2 + \ldots + c_n W_n]$$

Expanding the interior of the first term of V leads to:

$$E\left[(c_1 W_1 + c_2 W_2 + \ldots + c_n W_n)^2\right] = E\left[\sum_{t=1}^{n} c_t^2 W_t^2 + \sum_{\substack{i,j\in[1,n]\\ i\neq j}} c_i c_j W_i W_j\right]$$

$$= E\left[\sum_{t=1}^{n} c_t^2 W_t^2\right] + E\left[\sum_{\substack{i,j\in[1,n]\\ i\neq j}} c_i c_j W_i W_j\right]$$

It may be shown using the definition of expectation and some straightforward calculus that the independence of each random variable implies that $E[c_i c_j W_i W_j] = c_i c_j E[W_i] E[W_j]$, $i \neq j$. Therefore, the previous equation becomes

$$E\left[\sum_{t=1}^{n} c_t^2 W_t^2\right] + \sum_{\substack{i,j\in[1,n]\\ i\neq j}} c_i c_j E[W_i] E[W_j].$$

The second term of the original expansion for V may be calculated directly from the preceding analysis of the expected value of a sum of random variables as:

$$E^2[c_1 W_1 + c_2 W_2 + \ldots + c_n W_n] =$$

$$\{c_1 E[W_1] + c_2 E[W_2] + \ldots + c_n E[W_n]\}^2$$

$$= \sum_{t=1}^{n} c_t^2 E^2[W_t] + \sum_{\substack{i,j\in[1,n]\\ i\neq j}} c_i c_j E[W_i] E[W_j]$$

Now subtracting the expanded versions of the first and second terms of the original expression for V gives the final result:

$$V = E\left[\sum_{t=1}^{n} c_t^2 W_t^2\right] - \sum_{t=1}^{n} c_t^2 E^2[W_t]$$

$$= c_1^2\left\{E[W_1^2] - E^2[W_1]\right\} + c_2^2\left\{E[W_2^2] - E^2[W_2]\right\} + \ldots +$$

$$c_n^2\left\{E[W_n^2] - E^2[W_n]\right\}$$

$$= c_1^2 Var[W_1] + c_2^2 Var[W_2] + \ldots + c_n^2 Var[W_n]$$

Thus we see that the variance of a linear combination of random variables can be easily calculated as the sum of the individual variances, each multiplied by the square of any associated coefficient. Many statistics are simply sums of other kinds of statistics, and so knowledge of the results just derived will prove useful in the general analysis of estimators.

3.1.3 Sampling distributions

We return now to the population from which we were interested originally in estimating the parameter θ. If this population has N elements, there are $\sum_{i=1}^{N}\binom{N}{i}$ different samples which may be taken. For each such sample, we could observe the statistic of interest and calculate a sample mean. In order to estimate the parameter of interest, we could obtain one set of n observations, calculate the average observed value, and call this our estimate. The massive number of possible samples, even for modest n, might cause us to wonder what would happen if a different sample were taken (either a different sample size or different individuals in a sample of the same size). This leads us to the notion of a *sampling distribution*.

A sampling distribution is a distribution formed by a random variable whose values are themselves random variables. We let $\overline{X}$ represent the random variable which takes on values according to the value of the sample mean of some population. To answer the very important question posed above, we need to know the same sorts of things about $\overline{X}$ that we use to characterize any other distribution: its central tendency and variability.

Note that for a random sample from a distribution of the random variable X_i, $E[X_i] = \mu$ and $Var[X_i] = \sigma^2$. $\mu_{\overline{x}}$, the mean of the population whose members are the sample means from every possible sample from a population, can be calculated as:

$$E[\overline{X}] = E\left[\frac{1}{n}(X_1 + X_2 + \ldots + X_n)\right]$$

$$= \frac{1}{n}\{E[X_1] + E[X_2] + \ldots + E[X_n]\}$$

$$= \frac{1}{n}(\mu + \mu + \ldots + \mu) = \mu$$

Since we see that $E[\overline{X}] - \mu = 0$, we conclude that $\overline{X}$ is an unbiased estimator for μ. Further, we notice that the bias is *independent of the sample size* – this implies that regardless of the size of the sample, $\overline{X}$ would still be an unbiased estimator for μ. This answers at least part of the original question. All that remains is to consider how intrinsically variable the samples are. We do so by calculating the estimator's standard error:

$$Var[\overline{X}] = E\left[(\overline{X})^2\right] - E^2[\overline{X}]$$

$$= E\left[\left\{\frac{1}{n}(X_1 + X_2 + \ldots + X_n)\right\}^2\right] - \left\{E\left[\frac{1}{n}(X_1 + X_2 + \ldots + X_n)\right]\right\}^2$$

$$= E\left[\frac{1}{n^2}\left(\sum_{i=1}^{n}X_i^2 + \sum_{\substack{i,j\in[1,n]\\i\neq j}}X_iX_j\right)\right] - \frac{1}{n^2}\{E[X_1 + X_2 + \ldots + X_n]\}^2$$

$$= \frac{1}{n^2} E\left[\sum_{i=1}^{n} X_i^2 + \sum_{\substack{i,j \in [1,n] \\ i \neq j}} X_i X_j \right] - \frac{1}{n^2}\left(\sum_{i=1}^{n} E^2[X_i] + \sum_{\substack{i,j \in [1,n] \\ i \neq j}} E[X_i]E[X_j] \right)$$

$$= \frac{1}{n^2}\left(\sum_{i=1}^{n} E[X_i^2] + \sum_{\substack{i,j \in [1,n] \\ i \neq j}} E[X_i]E[X_j] \right) -$$

$$\frac{1}{n^2}\left(\sum_{i=1}^{n} E^2[X_i] + \sum_{\substack{i,j \in [1,n] \\ i \neq j}} E[X_i]E[X_j] \right)$$

$$= \frac{1}{n^2}\left(Var[X_1] + Var[X_2] + \ldots + Var[X_n] \right) = \frac{n\sigma^2}{n^2} = \frac{\sigma^2}{n}$$

$$\therefore \ SE[\overline{X}] = \sqrt{Var[\overline{X}]} = \frac{\sigma}{\sqrt{n}}$$

Earlier, we observed that the bias of $\overline{X}$ was not dependent upon n. The standard error, on the other hand, is in fact a function of n. Fortunately, we have the case that as n becomes larger, the standard error becomes smaller:

$$\lim_{n \to \infty} SE[\overline{X}] = \lim_{n \to \infty} \frac{\sigma}{\sqrt{n}} = 0$$

We define the *mean squared error* of an estimator Y to be $MSE[Y] = bias^2[Y] + SE^2[Y]$. This will provide a way to characterize the overall power of Y in estimating θ. Estimators whose bias or standard error are large will have a correspondingly large MSE, compared to those with uniformly smaller bias and standard error. Consider the behavior of the MSE of $\overline{X}$ as n gets large:

$$\lim_{n \to \infty} MSE[\overline{X}] = \lim_{n \to \infty}\left(0 + \frac{\sigma^2}{n}\right) = 0$$

$\overline{X}$ therefore has the very useful property of *consistency*, which means that in the limit, as n grows large, the ability of $\overline{X}$ to estimate μ increases. We can take advantage of this fortunate fact by extending these observations to an analysis of *linear combinations* of $\overline{X}$ in the following way. By linear, we mean that the coefficients of each term in the sums of interest are constant, and that each term in the sum is a power of $\overline{X}$. Suppose that $\overline{X}_i$ is the average of a sample of size n_i. μ_i and σ_i^2 are the mean and variance of population i, respectively. We wish to compare μ_1 to μ_2. We can estimate $\theta = \mu_1 - \mu_2$ with a statistic $\hat{\theta} = \overline{X}_1 - \overline{X}_2$. For this case, the coefficients and powers of each term are each one. Using the same analysis employed for $\overline{X}$, we discover the following facts regarding this estimator:

$$E[\hat{\theta}] = E[\overline{X}_1 - \overline{X}_2] = E[\overline{X}_1] - E[\overline{X}_2] = \mu_1 - \mu_2$$

Therefore $\hat{\theta}$ is unbiased for $\mu_1 - \mu_2$. Also,

$$Var[\hat{\theta}] = Var[\overline{X}_1 - \overline{X}_2] = E[(\overline{X}_1 - \overline{X}_2)^2] - E^2[\overline{X}_1 - \overline{X}_2]$$

$$= E[\overline{X}_1^2 - 2\overline{X}_1\overline{X}_2 + \overline{X}_2^2] - E[\overline{X}_1 - \overline{X}_2]E[\overline{X}_1 - \overline{X}_2]$$

$$= E[\overline{X}_1^2] - 2E[\overline{X}_1\overline{X}_2] + E[\overline{X}_2^2] - E^2[\overline{X}_1] + 2E[\overline{X}_1]E[\overline{X}_2] -$$
$$E^2[\overline{X}_2]$$

$$= Var[\overline{X}_1] + Var[\overline{X}_2] = \frac{\sigma_1^2}{n_1} + \frac{\sigma_2^2}{n_2} \Rightarrow SE[\hat{\theta}] = \sqrt{\frac{\sigma_1^2}{n_1} + \frac{\sigma_2^2}{n_2}}$$

Evaluating this estimator's consistency, we find that

$$\lim_{n_i \to \infty} MSE[\hat{\theta}] = \lim_{n_i \to \infty}\left(0^2 + \frac{\sigma_1^2}{n_1} + \frac{\sigma_2^2}{n_2}\right) = 0,\text{ therefore it is consistent.}$$

Example 3.1

A machine shop employs lathes of two different types to perform the same milling operation during the construction of a particular part. Management is interested to know the difference between the average time necessary for each of the machines to complete the milling and the accuracy of the identified difference. In completing this task, it is found that lathe #1 exhibits a variance of 0.54 and lathe #2 has a variance of 0.23. A random sample of 20 observations is made for each lathe, and it is determined that lathe #1 finished the task in 1.17 minutes, on average. Lathe #2 finished in 1.89 minutes, on average.

Using the estimator described above, we can calculate the estimate of the difference as $\hat{\theta} = \overline{X}_1 - \overline{X}_2 = 1.17 - 1.89 = -0.72$. The standard error is given by $SE[\hat{\theta}] = \sqrt{\dfrac{\sigma_1^2}{n_1} + \dfrac{\sigma_2^2}{n_2}} = \sqrt{\dfrac{0.54}{20} + \dfrac{0.23}{20}} \approx 0.1962$. Thus we could report to management that the observed difference in average completion times was 0.72 minutes and that a typical deviation in estimates calculated in this fashion is 0.1962 minutes.

An estimate of this kind is a *point estimate*. As the name implies, it provides an estimate that is a unique real number for the parameter of interest. Knowledge of the standard error of the estimator can give us a clue as to how useful such an estimate might be. A large standard error relative to the likely range of the data would cause one to suspect that a different sample might yield a substantially different result. In the example above, the size of the standard error is about 27% of the size of the estimate. Depending on the goal of the analysis, this may or may not be considered "large." For example, if the intention was to determine whether or not a significant increment in total output could be gained by replacing the slower machine with the faster model, then a fairly coarse estimate would suffice. On the other hand, if the purpose was to tune the speed of conveyor systems servicing the two machines, a more precise estimate might be called for.

The notion that the standard error represents the size of a "typical" deviation from the actual parameter is quite vague. It would be desirable to be able to say something like, "this estimate is within ± 0.25 units of the actual parameter's value." Unfortunately, it is impossible to make such a statement, because the *actual* value of the parameter can never be known. (If this were not true, we wouldn't bother with estimating it at all – we'd just write it down and be done!) What we *can* say, however, is that estimates formed in a certain way capture the actual value of the parameter within some prescribed boundaries *with some known probability*. Finding a way to establish the size of the boundaries, and the corresponding probability with which those boundaries apply, is the heart of statistical inference. To develop the theory for doing so requires a more general means of describing a distribution than the characteristics that we've worked with so far.

3.2 Higher-order moments and moment generating functions

We referred earlier to the mean as being the first moment of a distribution and the variance being the difference between the second moment and the square of the first moment. The moments tell us the defining characteristics of a distribution. We ordinarily consider the first four moments as being most significant. The third and fourth moments are known as the *skewness* and *kurtosis*, respectively.

3.2.1 Skewness

The skewness is a measure of the symmetry of the distribution. Where the skewness is equal to zero, the areas under the probability density function curve on either side of the mean are exactly equal. When it is less than zero, there is less area under the PDF to the left of the mean than to the right. As shown in Figure 3.1, in such a distribution the peak of the distribution is to the right of the mean.

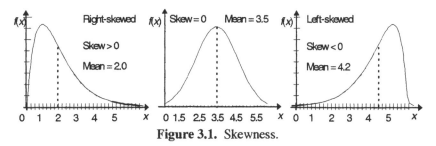

Figure 3.1. Skewness.

3.2.2 Kurtosis

The fourth moment measures the "pointedness" of the distribution. Higher values of kurtosis indicate that the bulk of the distribution's total area is closely packed about the mean and that the tails taper off rapidly. Smaller values indicate a "flat" distribution, where there are heavy tails on either side. Thus the kurtosis is related to the variance, in the sense that it measures dispersion about the mean, but it is nonetheless distinct. It is possible for a distribution with some specific variance to be either mesokurtic, leptokurtic, or platykurtic. The length of a unimodal distribution's tails is an important aspect of statistical analysis, because it is reflective of the information content of the mean. For the platykurtic case, for example, the inferential power of the distribution's mean is diluted by the fact that there is a high probability associated with observing values that are located fairly far away from it.

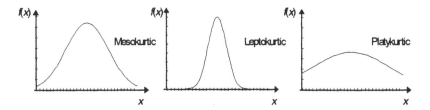

Figure 3.2. Kurtosis.

3.2.3 The moment generating function

Now that we know of the existence of the various moments, and the fact that each moment describes some aspect of a distribution, we're ready to discuss the *moment generating function*, or MGF. Consider an admittedly coarse analogy. We can characterize an automobile engine's performance in terms of attributes like number of cylinders, bore diameter, stroke length, and so on. For a given combination of these characteristics, we can predict generally how the engine will behave under certain circumstances. The same is true of a distribution: if we know what its moments are, we can describe the distribution's behavior in terms of central tendency, length of tails, and other significant descriptors.

The noted computer scientist R. W. Hamming described the MGF during a lecture as a means to "hold an entire distribution in one neat package." This is certainly an apt description, as the MGF is a function from which *every moment* of its corresponding distribution may be derived. It is in fact a function in the mathematical sense, in that it is a one-to-one mapping from the domain of PDFs to the range of real numbers. Since each moment "contains" a descriptor for the distribution, having the means to generate every one provides a convenient way to represent an entire distribution.

Definition 3.1 The moment generating function

If $f(x)$ is a probability density function for the random variable X, the *moment generating function* (MGF) of X is defined as:

$$m_X(t) = E\left[e^{tX}\right]$$

Note that this definition implies that in the case of a continuous random variable, $m_X(t) = \int_{-\infty}^{\infty} f(x)e^{tx}dx$; for a discrete random variable, it is $\sum_{all\ x} f(x)e^{tx}$.

The notation used here may seem a bit confusing at first. The expression $m_X(t)$ should be read as "the moment generating function of the random variable X in terms of the dummy variable t." The idea of a *dummy variable* is certainly not foreign, although this may be your first time seeing it used in this particular way. In general, a dummy variable appears in mathematical expressions whenever their use is convenient and necessary. For example, the variable i in the sum $\sum_{i=1}^{n} x_i$ serves no purpose other than to indicate the index of the term in the sum. It is a convenient way to represent the index and it accomplishes the necessary function of distinguishing terms from each other, but it has no intrinsic meaning that affects the calculation beyond this.

Also notice that when the random variable appears in the notation used for expectation it is capitalized, as in $E[e^{tX}]$; in the formulae that describe the calculation of expectation it is shown in lower case. This is because the random variable actually takes on a particular value in the process of integration or summation, whereas the capitalized form denotes a simultaneous reference to all of the values which the variable may assume.

We will show the need for a dummy variable in moment generating functions concurrently with the demonstration of the MGF's primary application, which is the generation of formulas for a distribution's moments. First, recall a bit of calculus. Suppose that we have a function f that is defined in terms of two variables, x and t. An example of such a function is:

$$f(x,t) = x^2 \ln(t)$$

The *partial derivative* of the above function is defined by taking the usual derivative, but treating every variable (except the one that the partial derivative is being taken with respect to) as constant. The notation for partial derivatives, and an example of the technique as applied to the previous bivariate example, is shown below:

$$\frac{\partial}{\partial t} x^2 \ln(t) = \frac{x^2}{t}$$

This results because the derivative of $\ln(t)$ with respect to t is just $1/t$. Treating x^2 as a constant and applying the chain rule yields the final answer.

We now have need of a result from the field of analysis, which tells us that so long as the partial derivative exists, the order of applying the differentiation and integration operators is immaterial. Symbolically,

$$\frac{\partial}{\partial t}\int_{-\infty}^{\infty} f(x,t)\,dx = \int_{-\infty}^{\infty}\left[\frac{\partial}{\partial t}f(x,t)\right]dx$$

Now consider the MGF. If $f(x,t) = f(x)e^{tx}$ for some PDF $f(x)$, then since the exponential function is known to be differentiable, the partial derivative discussed above exists so long as the derivative of $f(x)$ exists. Since the derivative is with respect to t, $(\partial/\partial t)f(x)$ will always exist and always be zero. Via the chain rule, then, we have:

$$\frac{\partial}{\partial t}\int_{-\infty}^{\infty} f(x)e^{tx}\,dx = \int_{-\infty}^{\infty}\left[\frac{\partial}{\partial t}f(x)e^{tx}\right]dx = \int_{-\infty}^{\infty} xf(x)e^{tx}\,dx$$

Applying this process n times, it follows that $\frac{\partial^n}{\partial t^n}m_X(t) = \int_{-\infty}^{\infty} x^n f(x)e^{tx}\,dx$, which is $E[X^n e^{tX}]$. Evaluating this expression at $t = 0$ gives the justification for the name "moment generating function":

$$\frac{\partial^n}{\partial t^n}m_X(t)\Big|_{t=0} = E[X^n]$$

In other words, if we evaluate the nth derivative of the MGF at zero, we have the nth moment of the associated distribution. The dummy variable t was used in this case to "wrap up" the moments via the device of repeated integration. As was mentioned, the name of the variable makes no difference, since our intent is to evaluate the derivative at $t = 0$, which causes it to disappear from the result. We could have used z for this purpose (which is a notation that is frequently employed for MGFs) just as easily.

The discrete case is also proven in a straightforward way. Consider the Maclaurin expansion of a function:

$$f(t) = \sum_{i=0}^{\infty}\left(\frac{t^i}{i!}\right)f^{(i)}(0) = f(0) + tf'(0) + \left(\frac{t^2}{2!}\right)f''(0) + \cdots$$

Here $f^{(i)}(0)$ is the ith derivative of f with respect to t, evaluated at zero. The 0th derivative of a function is just the function itself. If we let $f(x) = e^{tx}$, then we get:

$$e^{tx} = e^0 + txe^{0(x)} + \left(\frac{t^2 x^2}{2!}\right)e^{0(x)} + \left(\frac{t^3 x^3}{3!}\right)e^{0(x)} + \left(\frac{t^4 x^4}{4!}\right)e^{0(x)} + \cdots$$

$$= 1 + tx + \frac{t^2 x^2}{2} + \frac{t^3 x^3}{6} + \frac{t^4 x^4}{24} + \cdots$$

Therefore, the moment generating function is:

$$m_X(t) = E\left[e^{tX}\right] = E\left[1 + tX + \frac{t^2 X^2}{2} + \frac{t^3 X^3}{6} + \frac{t^4 X^4}{24} + \cdots\right]$$

$$= 1 + tE[X] + \frac{t^2}{2}E\left[X^2\right] + \frac{t^3}{6}E\left[X^3\right] + \frac{t^4}{24}E\left[X^4\right] + \cdots$$

Differentiating term by term with respect to t yields:

$$\frac{d}{dt}m_X(t) = E[X] + tE\left[X^2\right] + \frac{t^2}{2}E\left[X^3\right] + \frac{t^3}{6}E\left[X^4\right] + \cdots$$

Because powers of t appear as coefficients of every term except $E[X]$, it is clear that evaluating the derivative at $t = 0$ gives the expected value. By the power rule, each subsequent derivative will strip away the coefficient from the next higher moment, thus verifying the defining property of the MGF.

Example 3.2

Suppose that a random variable J has the following moment generating function, where α and β are constants:

$$m_J(t) = \frac{1}{(1 - \beta t)^\alpha}$$

What is the mean and variance of J's distribution?

The first derivative of the MGF is $\dfrac{\alpha\beta(1 - \beta t)^{\alpha-1}}{(1 - \beta t)^{2\alpha}} = \alpha\beta(1 - \beta t)^{-\alpha-1}$. Evaluating this expression at $t = 0$ gives the mean, which is $\alpha\beta$. To find the variance, we need the second moment. Taking the second derivative of the MGF gives $\alpha\beta^2(\alpha + 1)(1 - \beta t)^{-\alpha-2}$. Evaluating at $t = 0$ gives the second moment, which is $\alpha\beta^2(\alpha + 1)$. Then the variance is:

$$Var[J] = E[J^2] - E^2[J] = \alpha\beta^2(\alpha + 1) - \alpha^2\beta^2 = \alpha\beta^2$$

Notice that these values correspond to the mean and variance of a gamma (α, β) distribution. In fact, the MGF given applies to gamma-distributed random variables.

In summary, one very important consequence of this representation is that it can be used to show that two random variables are identically distributed. In fact, if any two random variables have the same moment generating function, then they have the same distribution. We will use this observation to our advantage in the next section, where the existence of identically-distributed random variables will be inferred by observation of their moment generating functions. This will, in turn, allow substantial algebraic simplification of the results which follow.

3.3 The distribution of $\overline{X}$

Now that moment generating functions have been explained, we can return to our discussion of how $\overline{X}$ is distributed. In Section 3.1.3, we calculated the mean and variance of its distribution, under the assumption that individual observations of $\overline{X}$ (i.e., elements of the population's power set) were independent, and that the mean and variance of the population were known. But the question still remains: What *particular* distribution does $\overline{X}$ follow? Is it gamma, uniform, or something else? The short answer is this:

- If the observations which formed $\overline{X}$ are normally distributed in the population, then $\overline{X}$ *itself* is normally distributed.

- If the observations which formed $\overline{X}$ are *not* normally distributed in the population, then $\overline{X}$ follows a distribution which may be approximated by a normal distribution, given a large enough sample size.

The second statement is known as the *central limit theorem*. We will examine the consequences of this theorem a little later. It will do well now to prove the first assertion in some detail, as the process is not difficult and highlights the significance of the moment generating function.

3.3.1 MGF for linear combinations of random variables

Suppose that we have a group of independent random variables, X_1, X_2, ... X_n, and that another random variable, Y, is defined as a linear combination of these:

$$Y = a_0 + a_1 X_1 + a_2 X_2 + \cdots + a_n X_n = a_0 + \sum_{i=1}^{n} a_i X_i$$

Each a_i in this definition is just an arbitrary coefficient. Then Y's MGF may be calculated in the following way:

$$m_Y(t) = E\left[e^{tY}\right] = E\left[e^{t\left(a_0 + \sum_{i=1}^{n} a_i X_i\right)}\right]$$

$$= E\left[e^{t(a_0 + a_1 X_1 + a_2 X_2 + \cdots + a_n X_n)}\right]$$

$$= E\left[e^{a_0 t} \times e^{a_1 t X_1} \times e^{a_2 t X_2} \times \cdots \times e^{a_n t X_n}\right]$$

Since $X_1 \ldots X_n$ are independent, we may write:

$$E\left[e^{a_0 t} \times e^{a_1 t X_1} \times e^{a_2 t X_2} \times \cdots \times e^{a_n t X_n}\right]$$

$$= E\left[e^{a_0 t}\right] \times E\left[e^{a_1 t X_1}\right] \times \cdots \times E\left[e^{a_n t X_n}\right]$$

$$= e^{a_0 t} \prod_{i=1}^{n} E\left[e^{a_i t X_i}\right] = e^{a_0 t} \prod_{i=1}^{n} m_{X_i}(a_i t)$$

Note that this is a very general result. An important special case arises when $a_0 = 0$ and $a_1 = a_2 = \ldots = a_n = 1$. Under these circumstances, the MGF of Y is simply the product of the MGFs of each of the random variables that make up the sum that defines Y.

3.3.2 Finding the MGF of the normal distribution

Suppose that a random variable Ψ has normal (μ, σ) distribution. Then by the definition of the moment generating function,

$$m_\Psi(t) = E\left[e^{t\Psi}\right] = \int_{-\infty}^{\infty} e^{t\psi} \frac{1}{\sigma\sqrt{2\pi}} e^{\frac{-(\psi-\mu)^2}{2\sigma^2}} d\psi = \frac{1}{\sigma\sqrt{2\pi}} \int_{-\infty}^{\infty} e^{t\psi - \frac{(\psi-\mu)^2}{2\sigma^2}} d\psi$$

We can rewrite the exponent of the integrand in the following way:

$$t\psi - \frac{(\psi - \mu)^2}{2\sigma^2} = t\psi - (1/2\sigma^2)(\psi^2 - 2\psi\mu + \mu^2)$$

$$= -(1/2\sigma^2)(\psi^2 - 2\psi\mu + \mu^2 - 2\sigma^2 t\psi)$$

$$= -(1/2\sigma^2)[\psi^2 - 2\psi(\mu + \sigma^2 t) + \mu^2]$$

Now the term $\psi^2 - 2\psi(\mu + \sigma^2 t)$ forms the $a^2 - 2ab$ portion of an $(a - b)^2$ factoring. This suggests completing the square by adding and subtracting $(\mu + \sigma^2 t)^2$ to proceed:

$$= -(1/2\sigma^2)[\psi^2 - 2\psi(\mu + \sigma^2 t) + (\mu + \sigma^2 t)^2 - (\mu + \sigma^2 t)^2 + \mu^2]$$

$$= -(1/2\sigma^2)\{[\psi - (\mu + \sigma^2 t)]^2 - (\mu + \sigma^2 t)^2 + \mu^2\}$$

$$= -(1/2\sigma^2)\{[\psi - (\mu + \sigma^2 t)]^2 - \mu^2 - 2\mu\sigma^2 t - \sigma^4 t^2 + \mu^2\}$$

$$= -(1/2\sigma^2)\{[\psi - (\mu + \sigma^2 t)]^2 - 2\mu\sigma^2 t - \sigma^4 t^2\}$$

Substitution of this expression for the original exponent yields:

$$E[e^{t\Psi}] = \frac{1}{\sigma\sqrt{2\pi}} \int_{-\infty}^{\infty} e^{-(1/2\sigma^2)\{[\psi - (\mu + \sigma^2 t)]^2 - 2\mu\sigma^2 t - \sigma^4 t^2\}} d\psi$$

$$= \frac{1}{\sigma\sqrt{2\pi}} \int_{-\infty}^{\infty} e^{\mu t + \frac{\sigma^2 t^2}{2}} e^{-(1/2\sigma^2)[\psi - (\mu + \sigma^2 t)]^2} d\psi$$

$$= \left(e^{\mu t + \frac{\sigma^2 t^2}{2}}\right) \frac{1}{\sigma\sqrt{2\pi}} \int_{-\infty}^{\infty} e^{\frac{-[\psi - (\mu + \sigma^2 t)]^2}{2\sigma^2}} d\psi$$

Notice that the term $\dfrac{1}{\sigma\sqrt{2\pi}} e^{\frac{-[\psi - (\mu + \sigma^2 t)]^2}{2\sigma^2}}$ is the density of a normal distribution with mean $(\mu + \sigma^2 t)$ and variance σ^2, which integrates over the limits $\pm \infty$ to 1. Thus we have the result that if

Ψ has normal (μ, σ) distribution, then its moment generating function is given by:

$$m_\Psi(t) = e^{\frac{\sigma^2 t^2}{2} + \mu t}$$

In the following example, we employ the theorem of Section 3.3.1 along with knowledge of the normal distribution's MGF to make good the promise of Chapter 2 to show that the process of standardization creates a standard normal random variable.

Example 3.3

Prove that if X is a random variable with normal (μ, σ) distribution, then $Z = \dfrac{X - \mu}{\sigma}$ has normal (0, 1) distribution.

The random variable Z can be expressed as a linear combination of X by distributing the factor $1/\sigma$:

$$Z = -\frac{\mu}{\sigma} + \frac{1}{\sigma} X$$

Then from the theorem, Z has the following MGF:

$$m_Z(t) = e^{\frac{-\mu}{\sigma}} m_X\left(\frac{t}{\sigma}\right) = e^{\frac{-\mu}{\sigma}} e^{\frac{\sigma^2 t^2}{2\sigma^2} + \frac{\mu}{\sigma} t} = e^{\frac{-\mu}{\sigma} t + \frac{\sigma^2 t^2}{2\sigma^2} + \frac{\mu}{\sigma} t} = e^{\frac{t^2}{2}}$$

The MGF of a normal (0, 1) distribution is $e^{\frac{1^2 t^2}{2} + 0 \cdot t} = e^{\frac{t^2}{2}}$. As was to be proven, Z has normal (0, 1) distribution.

3.3.3 Linear combinations of normal random variables

Regarding the question of linear combinations of random variables, recall that the most general form is $Y = a_0 + a_1 X_1 + \ldots + a_n X_n$. The familiar $\overline{X}$ can be defined as a particular case of variables of this form, specifically $a_0 = 0$ and $a_1 = a_2 = \ldots = a_n = 1/n$. Suppose that $X_1 \ldots X_n$ each have normal (μ, σ) distribution.

In other words, $\mu_1 = \mu_2 = \ldots = \mu$ and $\sigma_1^2 = \sigma_2^2 = \ldots = \sigma_n^2 = \sigma^2$. From Section 3.3.1 then, we know that the MGF of $\overline{X}$ will be the product of the MGFs of each of the individual random variables:

$$m_{\overline{X}}(t) = \prod_{i=1}^{n} m_{X_i}\left(\frac{t}{n}\right) = \prod_{i=1}^{n} e^{\frac{\sigma^2 t^2}{2n^2} + \frac{\mu t}{n}} = \left(e^{\frac{\sigma^2 t^2}{2n^2} + \frac{\mu t}{n}}\right)^n = e^{\frac{\sigma^2 t^2}{2n} + \mu t}$$

In fact, this is the MGF of a normal distribution with mean μ and variance σ^2/n. This agrees with our earlier calculation of the mean and variance of $\overline{X}$. Finally, however, we can see by the form of its MGF that when a sample is taken from a population that is normally distributed, the mean of the sample itself is normally distributed.

3.3.4 The central limit theorem

Ordinarily, we are not fortunate enough to know the distribution that the observations of interest follow. To show that the distribution of $\overline{X}$ approaches a normal distribution even if X_1, ... , X_n are *not* normally distributed, we introduce a function that is related to the moment generating function.

Definition 3.2 The characteristic function

If a random variable X has the PDF $f(x)$, then the *characteristic function* of X is defined as:

$$\Phi_X(\omega) = E\left[e^{j\omega X}\right] = \int_{-\infty}^{\infty} e^{j\omega x} f(x) \, dx,$$

where $j = \sqrt{-1}$.

Like the MGF, the way to think of the expression $\Phi_X(\omega)$ is, "the characteristic function of the random variable X in terms of the dummy variable ω." Notice that if we replace $j\omega$ with t in the definition above, we have the definition of the moment generating function. The identifying properties of the MGF also hold for the characteristic function, which is to say that if two distributions have the same characteristic function, then they are identically distributed. A natural question that arises when considering them both is whether knowledge of one is preferable to the other. Suffice to say that under some circumstances, calculations with the characteristic function are more convenient than using the MGF. For example, knowledge of a random variable's characteristic function enables one to recover the associated PDF by applying the inverse Fourier transform. Consider the following example, which will be of use to us in proving the central limit theorem:

Example 3.4

If the random variable X is normally distributed with parameters μ and σ, what is its characteristic function?

By the definitions of the characteristic function and the normal distribution,

$$\Phi_X(\omega) = \int_{-\infty}^{\infty} \frac{1}{\sigma\sqrt{2\pi}} e^{-\left[\frac{(x-\mu)^2}{2\sigma^2}\right]} e^{j\omega x} dx$$

$$= \frac{1}{\sigma\sqrt{2\pi}} \int_{-\infty}^{\infty} e^{j\omega x - \frac{(x-\mu)^2}{2\sigma^2}} dx$$

Now if we let $t = x - \mu$, we have $x = t + \mu$ and $dx = dt$. Making these substitutions yields:

$$\frac{1}{\sigma\sqrt{2\pi}} \int_{-\infty}^{\infty} e^{j\omega t + j\omega\mu - \frac{t^2}{2\sigma^2}} dt = \frac{e^{j\omega\mu}}{\sigma\sqrt{2\pi}} \int_{-\infty}^{\infty} e^{j\omega t - \frac{t^2}{2\sigma^2}} dt = \frac{e^{j\omega\mu}}{\sigma\sqrt{2\pi}} \int_{-\infty}^{\infty} e^{\frac{2\sigma^2 j\omega t - t^2}{2\sigma^2}} dt$$

We can complete the square in the numerator of the exponent by adding and subtracting $\sigma^4 j^2 \omega^2$:

$$\frac{e^{j\omega\mu}}{\sigma\sqrt{2\pi}} \int_{-\infty}^{\infty} e^{\frac{-\left(t^2-2\sigma^2 j\omega t\right)+\sigma^4 j^2\omega^2 - \sigma^4 j^2\omega^2}{2\sigma^2}} \, dt$$

$$= \frac{e^{j\omega\mu}}{\sigma\sqrt{2\pi}} \int_{-\infty}^{\infty} e^{\frac{-\left(t^2-2\sigma^2 j\omega t+\sigma^4 j^2\omega^2\right)+\sigma^4 j^2\omega^2}{2\sigma^2}} \, dt$$

$$= \frac{e^{j\omega\mu}}{\sigma\sqrt{2\pi}} \int_{-\infty}^{\infty} e^{\frac{-\left(t-\sigma^2 j\omega\right)^2+\sigma^4 j^2\omega^2}{2\sigma^2}} \, dt$$

And since $j^2 = \left(\sqrt{-1}\right)^2 = -1$,

$$\frac{e^{j\omega\mu}}{\sigma\sqrt{2\pi}} \int_{-\infty}^{\infty} e^{\frac{-\left(t-\sigma^2 j\omega\right)^2+\sigma^4 j^2\omega^2}{2\sigma^2}} \, dt = \frac{e^{j\omega\mu-\frac{\sigma^2\omega^2}{2}}}{\sigma\sqrt{2\pi}} \int_{-\infty}^{\infty} e^{\frac{-\left(t-\sigma^2 j\omega\right)^2}{2\sigma^2}} \, dt$$

Now let $y = t - \sigma^2 j\omega$, which implies that $t = y + \sigma^2 j\omega$ and $dt = dy$:

$$\frac{e^{j\omega\mu-\frac{\sigma^2\omega^2}{2}}}{\sigma\sqrt{2\pi}} \int_{-\infty}^{\infty} e^{\frac{-\left(t-\sigma^2 j\omega\right)^2}{2\sigma^2}} \, dt = \frac{e^{j\omega\mu-\frac{\sigma^2\omega^2}{2}}}{\sigma\sqrt{2\pi}} \int_{-\infty}^{\infty} e^{\frac{-y^2}{2\sigma^2}} \, dy$$

But $\dfrac{1}{\sigma\sqrt{2\pi}} \int_{-\infty}^{\infty} e^{\frac{-y^2}{2\sigma^2}} \, dy$ is a density function for a standard normal random variable, which by the normalization condition must equal 1. Therefore we have the result that when X has $N(\mu, \sigma)$, its characteristic function is

$$\Phi_X(\omega) = e^{j\omega\mu-\frac{\sigma^2\omega^2}{2}}$$

With this result, we may now proceed with an outline of a proof for the central limit theorem. Consider a random variable M, defined as:

$$M = \frac{\overline{X} - \mu}{\sigma/\sqrt{n}},$$

where $\overline{X}$ is the average of the independent random variables X_1, X_2, ... X_n, each one of which has the same distribution, with mean μ and standard deviation σ. Some algebraic manipulations of M's definition yield the following form:

$$M = \frac{\left(\frac{1}{n}\sum_{i=1}^{n} X_i\right) - \mu}{\sigma/\sqrt{n}} = \frac{\frac{1}{n}\left[\left(\sum_{i=1}^{n} X_i\right) - n\mu\right]}{\sigma/\sqrt{n}} = \frac{\frac{1}{n}\left(\sum_{i=1}^{n} X_i - \sum_{i=1}^{n} \mu\right)}{\frac{1}{n}\sigma\sqrt{n}}$$

$$= \frac{\sum_{i=1}^{n}(X_i - \mu)}{\sigma\sqrt{n}}$$

Then the characteristic function for M will be given by:

$$\Phi_M(\omega) = E\left[e^{j\omega M}\right] = E\left[e^{j\omega\left(\frac{1}{\sigma\sqrt{n}}\right)\sum_{i=1}^{n}(X_i - \mu)}\right]$$

If we let X represent any one of the identically distributed random variables X_i, their independence allows us to write:

$$E\left[e^{j\omega\left(\frac{1}{\sigma\sqrt{n}}\right)\sum_{i=1}^{n}(X_i - \mu)}\right] = \prod_{i=1}^{n} E\left[e^{j\omega\left(\frac{1}{\sigma\sqrt{n}}\right)(X - \mu)}\right] = \prod_{i=1}^{n} \Phi_{(X-\mu)}\left(\frac{\omega}{\sigma\sqrt{n}}\right)$$

$$= \left[\Phi_{(X-\mu)}\left(\frac{\omega}{\sigma\sqrt{n}}\right)\right]^n$$

For ease of notation, let $z = \dfrac{\omega}{\sigma\sqrt{n}}$ and $Y = X - \mu$. Now consider the power series expansion of $\Phi_{(X-\mu)}(z)$ about the point $z = 0$. We know from analysis that $e^y = \displaystyle\sum_{k=0}^{\infty} \frac{y^k}{k!}$; therefore, $e^{j\omega y} = \displaystyle\sum_{k=0}^{\infty} \frac{(j\omega y)^k}{k!}$. Then, from the definition of the characteristic function,

$$\Phi_Y(z) = \int_{-\infty}^{\infty} e^{jzy} f(y)\,dy = \int_{-\infty}^{\infty} f(y)\sum_{k=0}^{\infty} \frac{(jzy)^k}{k!}\,dy = \int_{-\infty}^{\infty} f(y)\sum_{k=0}^{\infty} \frac{(jz)^k y^k}{k!}\,dy$$

Expanding the sum and integrating term by term shows the form of the general expression:

$$\Phi_Y(z) = \int_{-\infty}^{\infty} f(y)\,dy + \int_{-\infty}^{\infty} (jz)y\, f(y)\,dy + \int_{-\infty}^{\infty} \frac{(jz)^2}{2} y^2 f(y)\,dy + \cdots + \cdots$$

$$= \int_{-\infty}^{\infty} f(y)\,dy + (jz)\int_{-\infty}^{\infty} y\, f(y)\,dy + \frac{(jz)^2}{2} \int_{-\infty}^{\infty} y^2 f(y)\,dy + \cdots + \cdots$$

$$= \sum_{k=0}^{\infty} \frac{(jz)^k}{k!} E[Y^k]$$

Substitution of this expansion for $\Phi_{(X-\mu)}(z)$, up to a remainder term having order z^3, into the last equation for $\Phi_M(\omega)$ gives:

$$\left[1 + jzE[X - \mu] - \frac{z^2}{2} E[(X - \mu)^2] \right]^n$$

$$= \left[1 + jzE[X] - jzE[\mu] - \frac{z^2\sigma^2}{2} + O(z^3) \right]^n$$

$$= \left[1 - \frac{z^2\sigma^2}{2} + O(z^3) \right]^n$$

Now reversing the substitution of z and rearranging, we have:

$$\left[1 - \frac{\omega^2}{2n} + O\left(\frac{\omega^3}{\sigma^3\sqrt{n^3}} \right) \right]^n = \left[1 + \frac{-\omega^2/2 + O(\omega^3/\sqrt{n})}{n} \right]^n$$

The value of the last manipulation becomes apparent when we consider the fact from the calculus that as n approaches infinity,

$$\lim_{n \to \infty} \left(1 + \frac{x}{n} \right)^n = e^x$$

Applying this result to our situation and observing that the residual term vanishes as n grows large leads to the demonstration of the central limit theorem:

$$\lim_{n \to \infty} \Phi_M(\omega) = \lim_{n \to \infty} \left[1 + \frac{-\omega^2/2 + O(\omega^3/\sqrt{n})}{n} \right]^n = e^{\frac{-\omega^2}{2}}$$

This is the characteristic function of a standard normal random variable, as was proven in the example. The importance of this extraordinary result can hardly be overestimated. It implies that *regardless* of the actual distribution of the variables that we observe (or at least given some very general assumptions concerning it), we can model the distribution as normal with considerable accuracy.

It is natural to wonder at this point about the size of n in practical applications. Proving the central limit theorem depends upon taking the limit as n approaches infinity. Of course, larger samples lead to better approximations. Clearly, though, we will never analyze a sample that "approaches" infinite size. How large must n be, then, before the approximation described by the central limit theorem is reasonable? As might be intuitively clear already, the answer depends on the actual distribution of the random variable being approximated. If the actual distribution is "normal-like" (symmetric, unimodal, and with light tails), then it shouldn't take many observations to use the approximation without stretching the imagination – the distribution is close to normal to begin with. However, if the actual distribution has heavy tails and/or is highly skewed, then it will take many observations before the approximated distribution begins to look normal. Mathematically, this may be accounted for in the proof by [Berry 41] that if the third central moment is finite, then the magnitude of the error for the limiting approximation is bounded by:

$$\left| P\left\{ \frac{\overline{X} - \mu}{\sigma/\sqrt{n}} \leq t \right\} - \phi(t) \right| \leq \frac{2E\left[|X - \mu|^3 \right]}{\sigma^3 \sqrt{n}}$$

The presence of the third moment (which is the skewness of the distribution) and the variance imply the effects that the values of these parameters in the actual distribution can have upon the approximated probabilities. Practically, then, the choice of n is something of an art, since inference of the actual distribution's parameters is usually quite subjective. [Pooch 93] suggests that for reasonably normal-like data, $n = 12$ yields a satisfactory approximation; in cases where the sample appears drastically different from the normal, $n = 100$ or more is appropriate.

Example 3.5

Suppose that in a particular large distributed system, the average load on a single machine is 0.24 (expressed as a percentage of maximum load). The variance is known to be 4 percent. Periodically, a sample of 15 machines is observed and the average load on these machines recorded. If the observed average load is higher than 0.27, then the system needs to be reconfigured. Assuming that machines are chosen at random, what is the probability that, for a given sample, reconfiguration will be indicated?

$$P\left\{ \overline{X} > 0.27 \right\} = 1 - P\left\{ \overline{X} \leq 0.27 \right\} = 1 - P\left\{ \frac{\overline{X} - \mu}{\sigma/\sqrt{n}} \leq \frac{0.27 - \mu}{\sigma/\sqrt{n}} \right\}$$

$$= 1 - \phi\left(\frac{0.27 - 0.24}{\sqrt{0.04}/\sqrt{15}}\right) = 1 - \phi(0.5809) \approx 1 - 0.7193 = 0.2807$$

3.4 Confidence intervals

Suppose that we conduct an experiment, and make several observations of a continuous random variable X. If we observed that $\overline{X} = 20.0$, we would perhaps be tempted to conclude that $\mu = 20.0$; after all, $\overline{X}$ is an unbiased estimator for μ. However, this is almost certainly false, but only because the probability that $\overline{X}$ equals *any* specific real value is zero for continuous data. Instead, we want a conclusion which involves error *bounds*. We can state this interest generally as the answer to the question, "Regardless of μ's actual value, how close will $\overline{X}$ be to it with $(1 - \alpha)\%$ certainty?" Answering this question depends upon the extent of our knowledge regarding X's distribution.

3.4.1 Confidence intervals for the mean of random variables with known variance

Figure 3.3 shows the general scenario that illustrates our interest in a confidence interval:

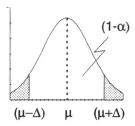

$(1-\alpha)$

$(\mu-\Delta)$ μ $(\mu+\Delta)$

Figure 3.3. A $(1 - \alpha)\%$ confidence interval.

Then what we wish to find may be described as:

$$(1-\alpha) = P\{\mu - \Delta \le \overline{X} \le \mu + \Delta\}$$
$$= P\{\overline{X} \le \mu + \Delta\} - P\{\overline{X} \le \mu - \Delta\}$$

$$= P\left\{\frac{\overline{X}-\mu}{\sigma/\sqrt{n}} \le \frac{\Delta}{\sigma/\sqrt{n}}\right\} - P\left\{\frac{\overline{X}-\mu}{\sigma/\sqrt{n}} \le \frac{-\Delta}{\sigma/\sqrt{n}}\right\}$$

$$= \phi\left(\frac{\Delta}{\sigma/\sqrt{n}}\right) - \phi\left(\frac{-\Delta}{\sigma/\sqrt{n}}\right)$$

The last transformation was accomplished by noting that $(\overline{X}-\mu)/(\sigma/\sqrt{n})$ is a standard normal random variable. Now by the symmetry of the standard normal distribution, $\phi(-\varepsilon) = 1 - \phi(\varepsilon)$, and so:

$$(1-\alpha) = \phi\left(\frac{\Delta}{\sigma/\sqrt{n}}\right) - \left[1-\phi\left(\frac{\Delta}{\sigma/\sqrt{n}}\right)\right] = -1 + 2\phi\left(\frac{\Delta}{\sigma/\sqrt{n}}\right)$$

$$1-\alpha/2 = \phi\left(\frac{\Delta}{\sigma/\sqrt{n}}\right)$$

Let $z_{\alpha/2}$ be the value that satisfies $1 - \alpha/2 = \phi(z_{\alpha/2})$. This leads us to:

$$z_{\alpha/2} = \frac{\Delta}{\sigma/\sqrt{n}} \quad \Rightarrow \quad \Delta = z_{\alpha/2}\left(\frac{\sigma}{\sqrt{n}}\right)$$

Therefore, any particular $\overline{X}$ that is obtained through a process of random sampling will be within $\pm z_{\alpha/2}\left(\sigma/\sqrt{n}\right)$ of μ with probability $(1 - \alpha)$. This gives rise to the concept known as a *confidence interval*.

Definition 3.3 $(1 - \alpha)\%$ confidence interval for the mean (variance known)

If a random sample of n observations is taken of a random variable whose variance is σ^2, then a $(1 - \alpha)\%$ confidence interval of that random variable's mean is given by:

$$\overline{X} \pm z_{\alpha/2}\left(\frac{\sigma}{\sqrt{n}}\right)$$

Notice that this definition says nothing at all about the probability that μ will lie in a particular interval. This subtle difference in meaning arises from the fact that μ is a parameter – *not* a random variable – and as such has no "distribution of probable values." Therefore, either it is in a particular interval or it is not – there is no notion of probability associated with its value. $\overline{X}$, on the other hand, does have a distribution, and so it is meaningful to talk about the idea of using its measured value to make conclusions that concern the probability that we have bounded μ's actual location correctly. The potential for confusion here is great; therefore, we recommend the adoption of a consistent approach to the phrasing of conclusions regarding confidence intervals. One reasonable technique is shown in Example 3.6.

Example 3.6

Suppose that the time between failures (TBF) of a particular machine on a production line is a random variable whose variance is known to be 8.3 hours^2. A random sample of 30 observations of times between failure results in the following dataset:

550.2	555.3	554.1	557.0	550.9	554.8
551.1	557.2	560.0	555.4	557.7	558.2
549.9	558.3	555.9	557.6	554.8	557.3
558.8	551.7	558.1	558.7	553.2	559.1
555.6	560.2	558.7	558.0	554.2	555.7

Using this data, calculate a 95% confidence interval for the mean time between failures (MTBF) associated with this device.

$\overline{X}$ is calculated as the average of the observations, which is approximately 555.9. Our interest is in calculating a 95% confidence interval, which implies that $\alpha = 0.05$, and so $\alpha/2 = 0.025$. Then $z_{.025}$ is the value that satisfies $\phi(z_{.025}) = (1 - \alpha/2) = 0.975$. From the standard normal tables, $z_{.025} = 1.960$. Thus, the desired confidence interval will be:

$$555.9 \pm 1.960 \left(\frac{\sqrt{8.3}}{\sqrt{30}} \right) = 555.9 \pm 1.031$$

One way to state the conclusion that follows from this calculation is:

> "In repeated random sampling, we expect that 95% of all intervals formed in this way would enclose the true mean time between failures."

Since the bounds just calculated form one such interval, it is reasonable to conclude that we are 95% confident that the mean is enclosed by 555.9 ± 1.031.

One should be careful NOT to form a conclusion that states:

> "There is a 95% probability that the true mean time between failures lies in the interval 555.9 ± 1.031."

As was previously discussed, any conclusion of this form is fallacious. Although it is understandable why someone might think that these two conclusions are equivalent, the difference between them is significant enough to make the distinction. More intuitively, the idea of 'confidence' refers to the notion of the probability that existed before sampling that our ultimate conclusion would be a correct one. Thus, it describes our *anticipation* of an error-free conclusion. One other way to interpret the idea of confidence is that if an analyst always used a level of confidence equal to $(1 - \alpha)$ in simulating behaviors or whatever application of the idea might have been required, then over the course of a career, the proportion of conclusions which in fact turned out to be incorrect would approximately equal α.

3.4.2 Confidence intervals for the mean of random variables whose variance is not known

The technique in the preceding section for constructing a confidence interval employed the standardization theorem that was developed in Chapter 2. This theorem, in turn, depends upon knowledge of the random variable's variance. In practice, however, this is not a realistic assumption, since the distribution's variance is a parameter, and as such can *never* be known with certainty. The usual approach to such situations in statistical analysis is to estimate the unknown parameter and compensate for the accepted inaccuracy of the estimate as much as possible. In this case, the logical choice to estimate the variance σ^2 is the sample variance, s^2.

This choice leads to the creation of a new statistic, $(\overline{X} - \mu)/(s/\sqrt{n})$, which is of course a random variable. Intuitively, we would expect that this random variable will have a distribution that resembles the normal, but with longer tails to account for the uncertainty regarding the variance, which arises from our having *estimated* the variance of X, rather than *knowing* it in advance. It can be shown that this new statistic, which we will denote t_γ, follows a distribution which is called *Student's*[†] *t distribution*:

Definition 3.4 Student's t(γ) distribution

A distribution is said to be *t with γ degrees of freedom* if it has a probability density function of the form:

$$f(x) = \frac{\Gamma\left(\dfrac{\gamma+1}{2}\right)}{\sqrt{\gamma\pi}\,\Gamma\left(\dfrac{\gamma}{2}\right)}\left(1 + \frac{x^2}{\gamma}\right)^{-\left(\frac{\gamma+1}{2}\right)}$$

The "degrees of freedom" referred to in the definition should be reminiscent of the chi square distribution discussed in Chapter 2. In fact, if a random variable has Student's t distribution with γ degrees of freedom, then it is the ratio between two independent random variables: the numerator of the ratio is a standard normal random variable and the denominator is the square root of a chi square random variable with γ degrees of freedom divided by γ.

[†] "Student" is the pseudonym that the statistician W. S. Gosset used when he published his discovery of the distribution in 1908.

Thus, any t_γ-distributed random variable may be defined generally in terms of such a ratio:

$$T_\gamma = \frac{Z}{\sqrt{\chi_\gamma^2 / \gamma}}$$

Let us return to the development of the t statistic's distribution. From the definition of the sample variance, we have:

$$t = \frac{\overline{X} - \mu}{s/\sqrt{n}} = \frac{\overline{X} - \mu}{\sqrt{\left(\frac{1}{n-1}\right)\sum_{i=1}^{n}\left(x_i - \overline{X}\right)^2} \Big/ \sqrt{n}}$$

Dividing the numerator and the denominator by σ leads to:

$$t = \frac{\dfrac{\overline{X} - \mu}{\sigma}}{\sqrt{\left(\dfrac{1}{n-1}\right)\sum_{i=1}^{n}\dfrac{\left(x_i - \overline{X}\right)^2}{\sigma^2}} \Big/ \sqrt{n}}$$

(The independence of the components of this ratio may be proven without too much difficulty and is left as an exercise for the reader.) The numerator happens to have a form that was already proven in Example 3.3 to have a standard normal distribution. It can be shown that the term under the radical in the denominator follows a chi square distribution with $(n - 1)$ degrees of freedom. Therefore, the t statistic follows a t distribution with $(n - 1)$ degrees of freedom. Using this distribution in place of the standard normal, we arrive at the definition for a confidence interval when the variance is not known:

Definition 3.5 $(1 - \alpha)\%$ confidence interval for the mean (variance unknown)

If a random sample of n observations is taken of a random variable whose variance is unknown, then a $(1 - \alpha)\%$ confidence interval of that random variable's mean is given by:

$$\overline{X} \pm t_{\alpha/2,n-1}\left(\frac{\sigma}{\sqrt{n}}\right),$$

where $t_{\alpha/2,n-1}$ is the argument which satisfies $P\{T \le t_{\alpha/2,n-1}\} = 1 - \alpha/2$, and T follows a Student's t distribution with $(n-1)$ degrees of freedom.

3.5 Hypothesis testing

The idea that we can bound the probability of incorrectly estimating parameters using observations from a distribution leads to an application of these methods known as *hypothesis testing*. Hypothesis testing is an extension of the idea of a confidence interval to include situations where one is prepared to accept or reject the truth of certain propositions, depending upon the values of statistics obtained through observation.   The process of determining the truth or falsity of propositions in general is known as *inference*; when the determination is made on the basis of a statistical analysis, then the activity is known as *statistical inference*.

Every hypothesis test has five essential components:

- The *null hypothesis*, designated H_0. Often, this is the idea that we are seeking to discredit.

- The *alternative* or *research* hypothesis, H_1. This is the proposition that will be accepted if H_0 is sufficiently discredited by the data.

- The *test statistic*, which is evaluated from the data. Its purpose is to measure the "distance" from the data to the null hypothesis, relative to sampling error.

- The *significance level*, or *p-value*. This value represents the chance that another sample would give results as much in favor of H_1 as does the present sample, if H_0 were true.

- The *rejection criterion*. This is the test that determines if H_0 will be rejected and H_1 accepted. Typically, we reject if the p-value is less than some value α, which will be used to form the confidence interval. Thus we can look upon α as the maximum chance that the null hypothesis will be rejected when in fact it was true.

With the given definitions, the hypothesis testing protocol may be applied by performing these steps:

1) Articulate the null and research hypotheses. In general, we let H_1 assume the role of the hypothesis whose truth or falsity we wish to examine and word its definition in whatever way is most convenient and explanatory. For example, suppose that we are interested in determining whether the average traffic load on a particular network segment is greater than some value. Then one acceptable specification of the null and research hypotheses would be:

H_0: "The average traffic load is greater than 65%."

H_1: "The average traffic load is less than or equal to 65%."

To make sense, H_0 and H_1 must be logical complements of one another.

2) Choose the rejection criterion. Remembering that the p-value indicates the likelihood of seeing another sample which supports H_1 as strongly as does the current sample, even though H_1 is false, it makes sense to word the rejection criterion as, "Reject H_0 if the p-value is less than α." The value α is typically some small amount, as it measures the amount of risk of error in rejecting H_0 that one is willing to accept. Typical values for α are 0.05 and 0.01. Choosing an appropriate rejection criterion must be made based upon the consequences of an incorrect conclusion. If the result of an error is fairly benign, then values for α of 0.10 or higher might be appropriate. For example, if an incorrect conclusion would result in the selection of a sub-optimal, but

nonetheless adequate pizza vendor for a factory refreshment concession, then we might be willing to accept the higher risk corresponding to larger values of α. On the other hand, if the issue at hand is an assessment of air traffic control software performance under certain types of loading, certainly the rejection criterion ought to be very strict indeed.

3) Collect the data required. For our purposes, we assume that each observation is obtained randomly and is therefore independent of every other one.

4) Determine the test statistic. The particular test statistic used, as well as its interpretation, will vary from situation to situation.   Consider the example mentioned in (1).   One reasonable choice would be to calculate the statistic:

$$t_{n-1} = \frac{\overline{X} - 0.65}{s/\sqrt{n}}$$

We know that such a statistic follows a Student's t distribution with $(n - 1)$ degrees of freedom. *In this particular scenario*, larger values of the statistic indicate increased support for H_1, since they tend to confirm the hypothesis that the average traffic load is indeed greater than 65 percent. Be sure that you realize that depending upon how the hypotheses are phrased, this will not always be the case.

5) Calculate the p-value. In this step, one simply calculates the appropriate probability using knowledge of the PDF, or from tables of previously calculated values. Remember, however, that one cannot take a "cookbook" approach to determining the p-value, because the correct probability will differ among the diverse conceivable scenarios, depending upon the semantics of the hypotheses. In general, though, every hypothesis can be categorized according to H_1, and one of two types of tests can be identified as appropriate. If H_1 is of the form $\theta < \theta_0$ or $\theta > \theta_0$, where θ is the parameter of interest and θ_0 is some specified value pertinent to the hypothesis, then we say that the relevant test is a

one-sided test. This is because the probability which describes support for H_1 is the area under the curve of the probability density function on "one side" or the other of the calculated test statistic. In our example, the probability that a statistic that follows a t distribution is *greater* than the observed value of the test statistic forms the p-value. Such a probability would indicate a different sample that would yield a value for $\overline{X}$ supporting the conclusion that network traffic is indeed higher than the hypothetical value. If H_1 is of the form $\theta \neq \theta_0$, the appropriate test is *two-sided*, as one must accommodate the fact that values of the test statistic that are far away from either side of the mean will tend to confirm H_1.

6) Formulate the conclusion. This is accomplished by making the comparison indicated by the rejection criterion and assessing the degree to which H_0 has been discredited by the evidence. When the rejection criterion is met, we reject the null hypothesis and conclude that the alternative hypothesis is true, citing the level of significance (which is α) of the conclusion. If the rejection criteria is not met, we fail to reject H_0. Keep in mind that there is a difference between failing to reject H_0 and concluding that it is true. In either case, the level of significance must always accompany the conclusion, as it is possible (though generally inadvisable) to form a conclusion that accepts a high level of risk of an erroneous conclusion.

Example 3.7

A manufacturer of machine parts claims to employ advanced metallurgical techniques and that, as a result, on average, a particular part can withstand pure axial loads of greater than 157 newtons before yielding. Suppose that a random sample of parts that are ready to be shipped are examined. Out of a sample of 30, the average yield strength of the parts is determined to be 158.9 newtons, with a sample standard deviation equal to 4.722 N. Test the hypothesis that the manufacturer's claim is valid at the 0.05 level of significance.

The hypothesis can be evaluated as follows:

- H_0: Average yield strength ≤ 157.0 N.

- H_1: Average yield strength > 157.0 N.

- Rejection criterion: Reject H_0 if p-value is less than 0.05.

- Test statistic: $t = \dfrac{158.9 - 157.0}{4.722/\sqrt{30}} = 2.204$.

The p-value is calculated by noting that larger values of the test statistic tend to support H_1. Thus, we seek the probability that $T_{29} > 2.204$. From the distribution tables, the probability that $T_{29} > 2.045$ is 0.025. Therefore, the probability that it is greater than 2.204 is something less than 0.025. Since this value is less than the designated $\alpha = 0.05$, the rejection criterion is satisfied. We therefore reject the null hypothesis and conclude that the average yield strength is greater than 157.0 newtons at the 0.05 level of significance.

3.6 Distribution suitability

One often wants to check whether a particular distribution is an adequate model for the data. This may be accomplished in several ways. One straightforward approach is to plot the data's histogram and compare its shape to the shape of the probability density function. Any gross differences between the two forms would be indicative of a distribution which models the data poorly. This procedure has the advantage of being easy to implement, but it lacks power, in that it is mainly useful for detecting particularly bad-fitting models. One technique which adds more precision to the analysis is the method of *quantile plots*. A quantile is simply a generalized comparative point in a distribution, which includes percentiles, quartiles, and deciles as a subset. In general, it is convenient to use percentiles, since it is a familiar metric, but we use the most general term of quantile to indicate that one may plot either set of comparative points.

The motivation for producing a quantile plot is the idea that if the data in fact follow some particular distribution, then the data quantiles should correspond to the distribution's quantiles.

Thus, if we were to plot them against one another on an *x-y* graph, the result should be a straight line through the origin. (Naturally, due to the inherent variability of the data, there will be some deviation from the ideal, even if the data *are* in fact from the distribution of interest.) The general procedure for generating a quantile plot is as follows. Let us define the data set at hand as $X_1, X_2, \cdots, X_n$. Assume that this data came from a $N(\mu, \sigma)$ distribution. Then an appropriate model for the data would be:

$$X_i = \mu + \sigma z_i,$$

where $z \sim N(0, 1)$. We can prove that this model is as good as we can hope for by looking at the expected value:

$$E[X_i] = E[\mu + \sigma z_i] = E[\mu] + E[\sigma z_i] = \mu + \sigma E[z_i] = \mu$$

This is as we would expect: the expected value of the model is the mean of the distribution of the data. Therefore, the model is adequate. Now let r_i represent the *rank* of X_i – the ordinal number indicating where X_i would appear in a sorted sequence of the data values. This implies that $r_i \in [1, n]$.

For the sake of simplicity, we will choose percentiles as the points for each comparison. If we partition the interval between 0 and 1 into *n* evenly spaced subintervals, the points so generated will equally divide the total available percentage, as shown in Figure 3.4.

The sequence $\dfrac{r_i - \frac{1}{2}}{n}$, $r_i \in [1, n]$, will generate the equidistant partitioning shown in Figure 3.4. Now we can define the *i*th quantile as:

$$Q_i = \phi^{-1}\left(\frac{r_i - \frac{1}{2}}{n}\right) = \text{the } 100\left(\frac{r_i - \frac{1}{2}}{n}\right) \text{th percentile of the dataset.}$$

Figure 3.4. Partitioning for equidistant quantiles.

$\phi^{-1}(x)$ is the *inverse cumulative standard normal distribution*. Whereas $\phi(z)$ returns the probability that $Z \le z$, the inverse function maps its argument x to the value z such that $\phi(z) = x$. Having calculated the percentiles of the dataset, we wish to compare them to the percentiles of the distribution of interest, i.e., the $N(\mu, \sigma)$ distribution. These percentiles are simply $\mu + \sigma Q_i$, which implies that if the dataset follows the normal distribution, we would expect to see $X_i \doteq \mu + \sigma Q_i$. This is in fact what we wish to measure in a quantile plot – the degree to which the ranked X_i's correspond with their associated percentiles. Some representative quantile plots are shown in Figure 3.5.

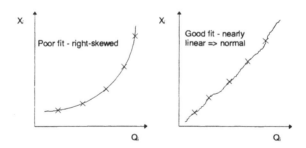

Figure 3.5. Quantile plots.

Note that a certain amount of linearity will always be present, regardless of the actual distribution of the data, as a result of our having ranked the data to begin with to calculate the quantiles. In testing for normality, we are mainly interested in detecting heavy one-tailed skewness, as the departure from symmetry drastically affects the fit.

3.7 Summary

In this chapter, we have presented the fundamental tools used in statistical analysis. In the context of simulation, we use these tools for the purpose of describing processes that contain components which cannot be reproduced deterministically. Since there are a great many activities in the world that lack well-supported analytical models, statistical approaches are almost always employed to some extent in simulation efforts. As well, the techniques described here can be used to explain many aspects of distributed processing, apart from any application to simulation.

3.8 Exercises

3.1   Explain why the notion of random sampling is important to statistical analysis.

3.2   Suppose that a sample of a particular medicine is taken by choosing fifteen bottles of the drug at random from the shelf in a certain retail store. Does this procedure constitute the collection of a random sample? Why or why not?

3.3   Suppose that there exists a database containing 127 employee records. Each record is uniquely identified by a number between 1 and 127. Using the procedure described in Section 3.1, identify 10 record numbers to be used as a random sample.

3.4   The desirability of unbiased estimators was discussed at length in the text. Is it conceivable that use of a *biased* estimator might be worthwhile? Explain your answer.

3.5 X_1, X_2, ... , X_n is a series of independent, random observations of a random variable X. Suppose that from this population, we collect k separate random samples, each of which has a (possibly) different size, n_i. Define the estimator

$$\hat{\theta}_k = \frac{\sum_{i=1}^{k} n_i \overline{X}_i}{\sum_{j=1}^{k} n_j} \ , \quad \text{where } \overline{X}_i \text{ is the mean of the } n_i \text{ observations in}$$

sample i. Assuming that each observation is independent, is $\hat{\theta}_k$ an unbiased estimator for the mean of X?

3.6 Compute the moment generating function of the exponential(β) function and use it to calculate the mean and variance of the exponential distribution.

3.7 Prove that the characteristic function of a random variable X can be represented as a linear combination of the expectations of two sinusoids.

3.8 Is the sample variance an unbiased estimator of the population variance? Justify your answer using the definition of bias.

3.9 A firm specializing in the production of robotic control software has been collecting statistics regarding the percentage of company income from software maintenance alone. In the previous twenty years, the following percentages were recorded:

21.9	22.3	21.8	19.6	19.0
24.0	24.2	17.2	18.9	22.6
22.7	17.2	21.0	20.9	20.8
20.9	21.5	20.2	19.1	17.5

a) Assuming that these observations are independent (which might take some justification, but for the moment we ignore any problem of correlation), form a 95% confidence interval for the mean percentage of annual income due to software maintenance.

b) A company executive claims that on average, company income from software maintenance is in excess of 21%. Test this hypothesis at the 0.05 level of significance.

3.10 Suppose that one knew in advance that for all practical purposes, a population size that was about to be sampled was unbounded in size. It is clear that, in general, the larger the sample size, the smaller the associated confidence interval for the mean. Assuming that the observations are randomly sampled, and that the population variance was known to be 10.56 units^2, how many samples would be necessary to form a 95% confidence interval that was within ±2.0 units of the true mean?

3.11 Given the following independent observations, construct a histogram and a normal quantile plot. Do these suggest that the data are described well by a normal distribution?

1.0	1.2	1.0	2.0	2.3	2.0	2.0
2.7	2.9	2.9	2.9	3.0	3.4	3.0
3.2	3.2	3.4	3.4	3.5	3.6	3.7
3.9	4.0	4.5	4.0	4.1	4.1	4.2
4.3	4.4	4.5	4.6	4.7	4.8	5.0
5.0	5.6	5.0	5.1	5.1	5.1	5.2
5.2	5.6	6.0	6.7	6.0	4.2	

3.9 References

[Berry 41]   A. C. Berry, "The accuracy of the Gaussian approximation to the sum of independent variates," *Transactions of the American Mathematical Society*, Vol. 49, No. 1, pp. 122 – 136, January 1941.

[Blum 72]   J. R. Blum and J. I. Rosenblatt, *Probability and Statistics*, Saunders Press, Philadelphia, PA, 1972.

[Çinlar 75]   E. Çinlar, *Introduction to Stochastic Processes*, Prentice-Hall, Englewood Cliffs, NJ, 1975.

[Helstrom 91]   C. W. Helstrom, *Probability and Stochastic Processes for Engineers*, Macmillan Publishing, New York, NY, 1991.

[Papoulis 91]   A. Papoulis, *Proability, Random Variables, and Stochastic Processes*, McGraw-Hill, New York, NY, 1991.

[Pooch 93]   U. W. Pooch and J. A. Wall, *Discrete Event Simulation*, CRC Press, Boca Raton, FL, 1993.

4

System Modeling

The process of creating a simulation can be very complicated. A fundamental issue is the fact that one is often interested in simulating systems, either real or hypothetical, that have many components. Also, it is not unusual for each of the components to interact with one another in ways that are difficult to quantify. The sheer size of the effort involved with duplicating the behavior of each component makes the simulation activity daunting. These observations suggest that it is advisable to adopt a repeatable methodology for designing, building, and utilizing a simulation.

4.1 Planning

It might seem patently obvious that one ought to have a clear idea of how a simulation is intended to be employed before it is constructed. Experience shows, however, that it is not unusual for the would-be user of a model to begin giving concrete thought to the results being sought only *after* the model is actually built. It seems to be far easier to just jump in right away to the task of programming the simulation with only a vague idea of its expected use and hope that the end product will be able to answer whatever questions are put to it. As might be expected, such a haphazard approach tends to maximize the length of time needed to construct a simulation and form accurate conclusions about the behavior of interest.

Most people would agree that a bit of careful preparation is in order before constructing a simulation. It makes one wonder, then, why simulation design seems to be accomplished with nearly uniform superficiality. The answer probably lies in the fact that most human beings are very poor communicators, and that the extent to which we *are* able to communicate tends to depend upon highly abstract assumptions, rather than rigorous, unambiguous semantic constructs. This unfortunate characteristic of our interaction with one another was mentioned in Chapter 1 as the phenomenon which gives rise to the need for structured modeling tools.

4.2 Modeling

In order to provide a lattice upon which to build the representations of the problem domain which will be used to design the simulation, we must have a way to organize our thoughts about how the system actually functions and about how we intend to model the system. One way of thinking about the problem of modeling is reducing it to the problem of finding an abstract structure that lends itself well to the representation of the knowledge in question, and then defining the allowable methods for manipulating that structure. Notice that these two elements of a representation are dependent and that they must be well matched with one another. For example, a representation which depends upon dynamic allocation and removal of objects cannot be easily manipulated without a structure (such as pointer or access types) which explicitly supports such activities.

The goal of any representation is to simplify the problem to be solved. It does this by imposing *order* and *convention* upon a problem, the result of which is (hopefully) insight. Well-designed representations possess the following characteristics which allow this simplification to take place:

- They make *important* objects and relationships obvious and tend to minimize the contributions of trivial or less significant ones.

- They identify key characteristics of the system that tend to constrain or channel its behavior.

Having selected a technique for representing the knowledge of interest, using that representation to model systems in that domain should be reasonably straightforward.

4.2.1 Modeling protocols

There are certainly hundreds, and perhaps many more, distinct development methodologies in the literature. Each one purports to enjoy an advantage of some sort with respect to the development process. They may be classified according to the techniques employed (such as rapid prototyping or top-down approaches) or by the application domain of the target software (such as real-time systems). Regardless of whether or not any particular design methodology does in fact enhance one's ability to develop a simulation, one thing is clear: there is no definite consensus regarding the desirability of one technique over another. Although an argument could be made in terms of the sheer numbers of results discussed that pertain to a particular class of approaches (e.g., the object-oriented paradigm), it still cannot be said with certainty that one set of ideas is optimal or even generally better than every other.

With that said, we wish to point out that even a brief survey of design methodologies would require more space than would be convenient, given the focus of this book. We therefore settle for a compromise, by describing one specific modeling technique that has found wide application in the simulation development community and has many characteristics in common with other popular modeling protocols.

4.2.2 The IDEF modeling suite

IDEF is the acronym given to a set of modeling methodologies which has come into wide use in the last five years. It stands for "ICAM DEFinition methods," ICAM being yet another abbreviation for "Integrated Computer-Aided Manufacturing." The U.S. Air Force initiated research which led to IDEF in its current form under the ICAM program in the early 1980s. What began as an attempt to streamline communication of product design requirements has grown into a robust methodology for the analysis of dynamic processes and their associated information [Godwin 89].

IDEF is composed of three related sets of modeling protocols. They are defined as:

- IDEF0: Process modeling
- IDEF1X: Data modeling
- IDEF2: Dynamic modeling

Each of these three protocols embodies a set of rules which describe a graphically oriented technique for the representation of aspects of the modeled system. We will briefly discuss IDEF0 and IDEF1X, as they are the methodologies that are most commonly in use.

4.2.2.1 IDEF0: Process modeling

The focus of the IDEF0 protocol is to capture the essence of system *functions* and their associations. A function can represent any activity, action, process, operation, or decision. In an IDEF0 diagram, a system function is represented by a rectangle and an associated textual description of the activity performed.

Functions associate with one another through *Inputs*, *Controls*, *Outputs*, and *Mechanisms* (ICOM). Thus, any meaningful interaction between two processes must be described in terms of one of these four abstractions. The *input* and *output* entities are self-explanatory. A *control* is an entity which acts to constrain the behavior of a function. Depending on the system, a control might represent something tangible, such as a control signal in a digital circuit, or be more abstract, such as the laws that regulate the operation of the airline industry. A *mechanism* is something that enables the defining actions of the process but is not consumed by them.

An ICOM is represented graphically as a vector between function rectangles. The origin of the vector with respect to the function determines which of the four associations it is. Vectors entering a function from the left side are considered inputs; vectors exiting a function from the right are considered outputs. A vector entering from the top of a function is a control, whereas one entering from the bottom is a mechanism. Figure 4.1 shows an example of the IDEF0 approach as applied to a portion of a robotic motion controller.

An IDEF0 diagram is made up of a network of similarly defined functions and associated ICOMs. It is allowable for an output vector with respect to one function to form either an input, control, or mechanism for an adjacent function. Note that this

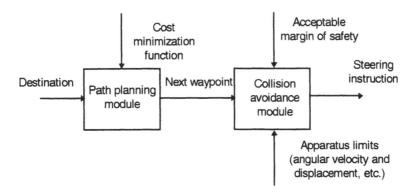

Figure 4.1. An example IDEF0 diagram.

gives rise to a symmetry of the input and output definitions which allows for the representation of a "flow" of entities of some sort. This is a very natural representation for many physical processes such as manufacturing or filtering.

4.2.2.2 IDEF1X: Data modeling

Whereas the IDEF0 protocol is primarily interested in functions, IDEF1X seeks to capture the nature of system *objects* and their relationships. An object can represent any data element, thing, or entity. Every object has a set of defining characteristics called *attributes*. IDEF1X (which, incidentally, is an extension of a previous IDEF1 technique, hence the name) is often used for the purpose of data modeling and database design, but has also been used for the purpose of enterprise integration and information management. Figure 4.2 gives a representative example.

Objects associate with one another through *relationships*. As with objects in a relational database, it is possible for objects to participate in one-to-one, one-to-many, or many-to-many relationships. The graphical representation is simply a line

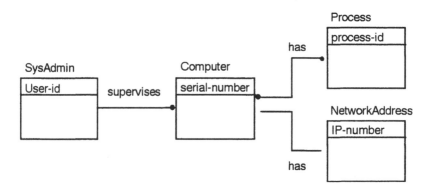

Figure 4.2. An example IDEF1X diagram.

connecting two objects. The meaning of a particular relationship is expressed as a short textual identifier adjacent to the line. The cardinality of the relationship is represented by the presence or absence of dots on the ends of the line. In the supervises relationship shown in Figure 4.2, the dot on the end of the line closest to the Computer object indicates that a single SysAdmin supervises many Computers.

4.3 Validation and verification

Taking steps to ensure that a particular simulation has at least the potential to be used to come to conclusions that have a basis in fact is known collectively as the process of *validation and verification*, or "V&V." To some extent, it may seem reasonable to conclude that the most difficult tasks associated with creating a simulation have been accomplished once the model has been created or designed. It might appear that if one is careful and applies enough attention to the task at hand, then the result of the design step should be a model that is satisfactory. In the earliest days of computing, it seemed as though this might be true; one need only state the model appropriately, present it to the computer, step back, and wait for the results to be generated. As computers grew more widespread in their use, however, it soon became clear that the human capacity for error and oversight made such a viewpoint ill-advised, if not downright dangerous.

Consider the infamous example of the Therac-25, a computer-controlled device used in radiation therapy of cancer patients [Leveson 93]. Several patients were injured or killed by incorrect operation of the system, which tragically was not detected immediately. The ramifications of incidents such as these that are applicable to the development of simulations become clear when one considers most generally how simulation is used to achieve an end. Simulation is used to solve problems, test assumptions, and make predictions about the behavior of the system being modeled. It is essentially used to answer a set of questions that have something to do with the system of interest. Example questions might include:

- How many vehicles may safely pass over a bridge simultaneously and still maintain an acceptable margin of safety?

- What portion of next year's organizational budget should be devoted to marketing, research, and production?

- How is the growth of scar tissue in heart attack patients influenced by varying lipid levels in the bloodstream?

As in the examples given above, it is often the case that an important event will hinge upon the answers gleaned from the application of the simulations.   One is therefore naturally concerned about the accuracy of the conclusions formed through their use.   It would certainly be disastrous, for example, if a simulation predicted that the bridge in the above example could easily sustain traffic of 100 cars at once, but in fact it failed under a load of 76 cars. Thus, a desire to avoid erroneous conclusions, and the possibly dire consequences that might ensue, is one issue which requires one to consider V&V.

A second impetus that forces consideration of the need for V&V concerns the bounded nature of the means required to produce a simulation. In most cases, the creation of a simulation involves the expenditure of a significant amount of organizational resources. Time, money, and computing platforms are needed to design, build, run, and analyze the results of all but the simplest systems. Therefore one would want to have some assurance that the end result of all of this effort would be meaningful.

The two components of V&V are related but subtly distinct. *Validity* is an attribute of models, whereas *verification* is a process applied to an implementation of a model.   More specifically, a valid model has the potential to reproduce the behavior of the actual (or intended) system, but we depend upon the implementation to transform that potential into output which may be verified as having come from the desired model.

4.3.1 Validation

Definition 4.1 Validation

Validation is the process which establishes the extent to which a model does (or does not) acceptably represent the phenomenon of interest.

In the various tasks which comprise the activity of system automation, model validation is one of the most resource-intensive and difficult [Anderson 93]. In fact, the difficulty of validation has made some analysts skeptical about the usefulness of simulation techniques [Fox 89]. Ten years ago, validation often received only a cursory address as a component of the simulation process [Saunders 85], [Finlay 87]. Interestingly, at the same time it was well known that validation was an important aspect of simulation; see [Balci 84] for numerous references to discussions of system validation. At the time, however, there was a lack of well-developed validation methodologies, and as a result most approaches to validation could be applied only to narrowly defined problem domains.

Since validation is such a costly process, one might wonder if it would be feasible to develop automated tools to assist in the effort, such as those that exist for simulation design and implementation. The short answer, as [Deslandres 91] put it, is apparently not. The reason is that the validation process by itself is ambiguous, complex, and difficult. Perhaps the characteristic which contributes most directly to the difficulty of validation is the fact that techniques for validating a conceptual model are difficult to define with rigor. This is because the conceptual model is itself an abstraction. As a result, validation approaches are often subjective. From an engineering perspective, this is highly undesirable.

The problem of describing model validity stems from the difficulty of rank-ordering contenders. The notion of a "better" model depends upon the availability of a metric with which to determine a continuum of models. In order to be useful, this continuum must be well-ordered; it must be possible to say unambiguously that model A is better than, not as good as, or equally as good as model B for all A and B. Immediately one realizes that the nature of such a metric will of necessity be closely tied to the characteristics of the phenomenon of interest. This reinforces Law's observation that a totally general method for validation does not exist [Law 91a].

Any explanatory discussion of validation must include the observation that the "real" model which describes an event *can never be known*. Without becoming embroiled in epistemological issues, we may simply note that, throughout history, some models for the same phenomenon have arisen, enjoyed a period during which they were generally agreed to be useful, re-evaluated in light of new data or theories, and ultimately discarded in favor of a different model. Others have withstood the test of time, which is to say that a better model has not yet been encountered. It would be unwise to conclude that a particular model is optimal, though, purely on the basis of having demonstrated utility over a long period of time. This implies no pessimism regarding the state of existing models. For example, the models that we use to reason about the interaction of mechanical forces seem to allow us to build bridges which exhibit the behavior that their models predict: that is, they do not fall down under the weight of their observed loads (a few notable examples notwithstanding). It merely admits the possibility that a better model may exist.

4.3.1.1 Techniques for validation

Broadly speaking, there are two classes of strategies which may be used to validate a model:

Axiomatic: The existence of a set of assumptions which describe the fundamental truths of the problem domain provides the basis for this approach. The validity of the model follows as a consequence of the application of rules of logical inference to the axioms to prove theorems. Ultimately, the model itself will be proven as a theorem. [Sargent 87] referred to this method as *rationalism*. One advantage of this approach is that it establishes a model which describes causality.

Empirical: The operation of the model is considered to be a filter or a function that maps its inputs to outputs. The performance of the model is compared to our expectation (if the system to be modeled does not exist) or to historical data to determine the model's predictive power. Where historical data exist, we generally infer the adequacy of the model whenever the observed residual values are uncorrelated. If a correlation is observed, this suggests the existence of some additional variable(s) which must be included in the model to make it complete.

These two categorizations of strategies correspond roughly to what Spriet and Vansteenkiste refer to as *theory-driven* and *data-driven* validation, respectively [Spriet 82].

4.3.2 Verification

Definition 4.2 Verification

Verification of a simulation is the process of assessing the degree to which the implementation transforms inputs into outputs *as specified by the model*.

By 'implementation' we include every method that is used to obtain and apply the inputs to the chosen model and to report the outputs. Therefore it includes structures that are peripheral to the model itself, such as the user interface, provisions for permanent storage, etc. The emphasis in the definition statement highlights a point concerning verification that is sometimes confusing. In particular, while it is generally true that the process of verification (assuming that it is successful) increases our confidence that a simulation can be used to produce meaningful results, it must be observed that any notion of a positive effect arising from the process *depends upon the validity of the underlying model*.

Consider the following rather crude analogy. Suppose that a medical researcher has developed a model that maintains that overall health can be predicted by examining only a person's extremities. This is clearly a ludicrous idea, but it suffices for the illustration of a point. This researcher's intention is to "run" the simulation by applying the model to patients that are seen at a clinic and use the results to make a conclusion about the general level of health in some population. In this example, the process of verification would be accomplished by an assessment of how the examinations were performed. So long as there were no inaccuracies in the observations made at the time of each examination, one would have to conclude that the implementation was correct.   Note that this conclusion implies no particular confidence in the power of the model to produce useful results; it merely asserts that the protocol specified by the model was faithfully implemented.

Since most modern simulations are accomplished using a computer (or several computers, in a distributed simulation), it is usually understood that verification amounts to a proof of correctness of the computer program that implements the model. However, accomplishing such a proof for non-trivial simulations is usually prohibitively time-consuming in its fullest generality.

To appreciate this, consider the short program below that purports to sort the values given by the array VALS. N is an integer greater than 2. The lines that are labeled with α_n indicate possible flows of control through the program. Though Ada was used for this example, any declarative language would do equally well. As implied by the syntax rules of the language, the transfer of control at the head of each loop is contingent upon the satisfaction of the loop constraint.   This accounts for the branching character of control flows that emanate from these constructs.

```
procedure SORT is
I, N, COUNTER1, COUNTER2, TEMP : integer;
type ARRAY_TYPE is array (integer range <>) of integer;
;; Initialize N here
VALS : ARRAY_TYPE (1 .. N);
P0: begin
P0:    for I in 2 .. N loop
P1:       COUNTER1 := 1;
P2:       while VALS(COUNTER1) < A(I) loop
P3:          COUNTER1 := COUNTER1 + 1;
P2:       end loop;
P4:       TEMP := VALS(I);
P5:       for COUNTER2 in reverse COUNTER1 .. I-1 loop
P6:          VALS(COUNTER2 + 1) := VALS(COUNTER2);
P5:       end loop;
P7:       VALS(COUNTER1) := TEMP;
P0:    end loop;
P8: end SORT;
```

The numbered P_n labels that precede each statement represent a predicate that is true just prior to each execution of the statement on that line. Note that in the case of loops, the predicate remains true even though the values of the state variables with which it is composed may have changed. Thus, these predicates are often referred to as *loop invariants*, because their truth is invariant over any execution path. The actual predicates are shown below, where the caret symbol (^) is used to indicate the Boolean AND operator:

- P_0: $N > 2$.

- P_1: $[N > 2]$ ^ $[2 \leq I \leq N]$ ^ $[VALS(1) \leq ... \leq VALS(I-1)]$.

- P_2: $[N > 2]$ ^ $[2 \leq I \leq N]$ ^ $[VALS(1) \leq ... \leq VALS(I-1)]$ ^ $[COUNTER1 \geq 1]$.

- P_3: $[N > 2]$ ^ $[2 \leq I \leq N]$ ^ $[VALS(1) \leq ... \leq VALS(I-1)]$ ^ $[COUNTER1 \geq 1]$ ^ $[VALS(COUNTER1) > VALS(I)]$.

- P_4: $[N > 2]$ ^ $[2 \leq I \leq N]$ ^ $[VALS(1) \leq ... \leq VALS(I-1)]$ ^ $[COUNTER1 \geq 1]$ ^ $[VALS(COUNTER1) \geq VALS(I)]$.

- P_5: $[N > 2]$ ^ $[2 \leq I \leq N]$ ^ $[VALS(1) \leq ... \leq VALS(I-1)]$ ^ $[COUNTER1 \geq 1]$ ^ $[VALS(COUNTER1) \geq VALS(I)]$ ^ $[TEMP = VALS(I)]$

- P_6: $[N > 2]$ ^ $[2 \leq I \leq N]$ ^ $[VALS(1) \leq ... \leq VALS(I-1)]$ ^ $[COUNTER1 \geq 1]$ ^ $[VALS(COUNTER1) \geq VALS(I)]$ ^ $[TEMP =VALS(I)]$ ^ $[COUNTER1 \leq COUNTER2 \leq I-1]$.

- P_7: $[N > 2]$ ^ $[2 \leq I \leq N]$ ^ $[VALS(1) \leq ... \leq VALS(I-1)]$ ^ $[COUNTER1 \geq 1]$ ^ $[VALS(COUNTER1) \geq VALS(I)]$ ^ $[TEMP =VALS(I)]$ ^ $[COUNTER1 = COUNTER2]$.

- P_8: $[N > 2]$ ^ $[I > N]$ ^ $[VALS(1) \leq VALS(2) \leq ... \leq VALS(N)]$.

The proof of program correctness proceeds by demonstrating that the truth of an input predicate (P_0 in this case) leads inevitably to the truth of the output predicate (P_8). This can be accomplished by "applying" the predicates to their corresponding statements and noting the effects on the state variables which follow from the syntax of the language. For example, consider α_1. If we accept the truth of the input predicate P_0, then the truth of P_1 follows, for the semantics of Ada cause the state variable I to take on values in the range 2 through N inclusively whenever the path of control follows the α_1 arc. The remaining steps to be proven are left as an exercise.

The preceding proof is known as *proof with respect to a specification*. Alternatively, it is known as a *partial proof* of correctness. The specification in question is formed by making an implication of the input and output predicates: $P_0 \rightarrow P_8$. Figuratively, the proof demonstrates that if P_0 is true when the flow of control enters the program, then P_8 is true when it exits. This notion can be extended to larger programs by decomposing the program into manageable modules and then proving the correctness of each module with respect to some arbitrary sets of inputs. Proof of the program in its entirety would require showing that the outputs of every module satisfy the inputs of the module that follows it in every possible flow of control throughout program execution.

A *complete proof* of correctness is an extension of a partial proof. Such a proof either assumes or demonstrates the correctness with respect to the specification and further establishes that the program halts over every possible input. In this example, a complete proof would require demonstration that the program runs to completion for *all* positive (and non-infinite) integers N greater than 2, in addition to the proof of correctness with respect to the specification. In most cases, it is necessary to proceed by induction to accomplish such a proof, which we will omit here.

The proof described above is quite straightforward, mainly because the functionality of the program is extremely well-defined and there are only a few branches of control. It is therefore easy to discover the forms of the loop invariants. To say that this is rarely the case in non-trivial programs would be to greatly understate the difficulty of proving program correctness in general. However, careful attention to the minimization of coupling during the design phase and highly modular programming can do a great deal to increase the ease with which correctness may be established. While there are other approaches to verification that are less rigorous (such as examination of extreme values and peer review), there have been no results as yet that suggest that these methods can do anything other than eliminate obvious implementation errors. One could not, for example, conclude the absence of errors based upon a satisfactory peer review.

Theoretically, the two facets of V&V could be pursued in an arbitrary order. However, there are some practical concerns which suggest that, in general, one would be well advised to pursue validation of the model prior to implementation and subsequent verification. As was mentioned previously, the fact that there are generally limited amounts of resources that can be devoted to a simulation makes us consider that we would want some assurance of the model's usefulness prior to its employment as the basis of a fully developed system.

4.4 Evaluation of random number generation

As was mentioned in previous chapters, nearly every simulation will require a means of representing the behavior of system components that are stochastic. A few common examples include the interval between arrivals at a manufacturing processing station, the time required to complete a chemical reaction, and the number of malignant organisms per square millimeter in a sample of human blood. To accomplish this, one invariably employs one or more of the numerous known algorithms to cause a computer to generate a stream of pseudorandom numbers having the same distribution as the item of interest. These values are then modified as needed to provide input for the non-deterministic aspects of the system being modeled.

4.4.1 The primal random number generator: $U(0, 1)$

The production of random variates is a vast topic indeed, with entire texts being devoted to the subject. Notable examples are [Devroye 86] and [Yakowitz 77]. For perspective, we note that [Rubinstein 81] describes no fewer than a dozen different techniques for the production of gamma-distributed random variates, and that a bibliography on the subject by [Sowey 72] described more than 300 different approaches to production and testing of random numbers through 1971. At the heart of many of these techniques lies an important observation known as the *inverse transform theorem*.

Definition 4.3 Inverse transform theorem

If $F^{-1}(x)$ is the inverse cumulative distribution function of a random variable X, and U is an independent random variable having $U(0, 1)$ distribution, then $Y = F^{-1}(U)$ and X are identically distributed.

This theorem tells us essentially that *any* distribution may be re-created from a $U(0, 1)$ random variable, given that the inverse CDF of the desired distribution exists. This prerequisite is often easily satisfied, and consequently the creation of $U(0, 1)$ random numbers is considered something of a necessity in special-purpose simulation languages.

Example 4.1

Let the random variable X have the probability density function given by:

$$f(x) = \begin{cases} \dfrac{1 + \alpha x}{2} & -1 \le x \le 1 \\ 0 & \text{otherwise} \end{cases}$$

Describe an algorithm for generating a stream of values having this distribution.

By the inverse transform theorem, the requisite algorithm may be specified in the following way:

1) Generate a value U_1 from a $U(0, 1)$ distribution.

2) Return $F^{-1}(U_1)$ as the value having the desired distribution.

The CDF must be found before obtaining its inverse. Integration of the density function produces:

$$F(x) = \int_{-1}^{x} f(u;\alpha)\, du = \int_{-1}^{x} \frac{1+\alpha u}{2}\, du = \frac{1}{2}\int_{-1}^{x} 1\, du + \frac{\alpha}{2}\int_{-1}^{x} u\, du$$

$$= \frac{1}{2}\left(u\big|_{-1}^{x}\right) + \frac{\alpha}{2}\left(\frac{u^2}{2}\Big|_{-1}^{x}\right) = \frac{1}{2}(x+1) + \frac{\alpha}{2}\left(\frac{x^2}{2} - \frac{1}{2}\right)$$

$$= \frac{2(x+1) + \alpha(x^2 - 1)}{4} = \frac{\alpha x^2 + 2x + 2 - \alpha}{4}$$

To obtain the inverse, we let p represent the value obtained from the range of the CDF. Solving for p in terms of x yields the inverse:

$$p = \frac{\alpha x^2 + 2x + 2 - \alpha}{4} \quad \Rightarrow \quad \alpha x^2 + 2x + 2 - \alpha - 4p = 0$$

$$x = \frac{-2 \pm \sqrt{4 - 4(\alpha)(2 - \alpha - 4p)}}{2\alpha} = \frac{-2 \pm \sqrt{4 - 8\alpha + 4\alpha^2 + 16\alpha p}}{2\alpha}$$

$$= \frac{-2 \pm 2\sqrt{1 - 2\alpha + \alpha^2 + 4\alpha p}}{2\alpha} = \frac{-1 \pm \sqrt{1 - 2\alpha + \alpha^2 + 4\alpha p}}{\alpha}$$

$$= F^{-1}(p)$$

More general conditions than knowledge of the inverse CDF can be described that enable the use of $U(0, 1)$ random numbers as the basis of other distributions. For example, when a random variable's density can be described as a probabilistic combination of other densities, as in:

$$f_X(x) = \sum_{i=1}^{n} \gamma_i f_Y(x), \quad \sum_{i=1}^{n} \gamma_i = 1,$$

and if U_1 and U_2 are independent uniform(0, 1) random variates, then random variates having the same distribution as X may be obtained by calculating $f_k^{-1}(U_2)$, where k is determined by finding the "interval" in which the value of the other uniform random variable is between the sums of the coefficients on either side of the series:

$$\sum_{j=1}^{k} \gamma_j < U_1 \le \sum_{j=k+1}^{n} \gamma_j$$

This is known alternatively as the *composition method* or the *method of mixing*.

Example 4.2

Show that the random variable described in Example 4.1 can be described as a mixture with probability $(1 - \alpha)$ of a random variable that is uniformly distributed on $(-1, 1)$, and with probability α, of a random variable on $(-1, 1)$ whose probability density function is $f(x) = (x + 1)/2$, and provide an algorithm for generating random numbers having this distribution.

Let Y_1 be the random variable having uniform$(-1, 1)$ distribution and Y_2 the other random variable mentioned in the composition of X above. The PDF of Y_1 is $f(y) = 1/2$. Combining the PDFs of these random variables with the coefficients suggested in the question leads to:

$$f_X(x) = (1-\alpha)\frac{1}{2} + \alpha\left(\frac{x+1}{2}\right) = \frac{1-\alpha+\alpha x+\alpha}{2} = \frac{1+\alpha x}{2}$$

This verifies that $X = (1-\alpha)Y_1 + \alpha Y_2$. An algorithm that will produce the desired distribution can be found by applying the inverse transform theorem to the densities given for Y_1 and Y_2 and generating the random variate by means of the assignment:

$$X = \begin{cases} 2\max\{U_1, U_2\} - 1 & U_1 \leq \alpha \\ 2U_1 - 1 & U_1 > \alpha \end{cases}$$

4.4.2 Testing random number generators

Although there may be many candidate techniques for producing random variables having a particular distribution, some methods are decidedly better than others from a variety of perspectives. For example, consider the following bit of Ada code for producing values from a $U(0, 1)$ distribution:

```
package FLOATING_IO is new FLOAT_IO(FLOAT);
for DEX in 1.. integer'large loop
  FLOATING_IO.PUT(DEX/integer'large);
end loop;
```

(For those readers not familiar with the syntax of the Ada programming language, **integer'large** is a compiler-specific attribute which identifies the largest value that variables of integer type may take on.) This routine will print a monotonically increasing sequence of numbers in the range [0, 1]. The sequence obviously meets the most basic test of a uniform distribution, namely, that each one of the values that it may take on is equally likely to occur (within the precision of the increment, at least). It is not the least bit random, however, in the context of the *ordering* of the values. In fact, the order is perfectly deterministic. This characteristic is not a desirable one in random number generators (RNGs), as it represents the injection of bias into the behavior of the stochastic component that is being modeled.

Some might argue that the character of the routine used to generate the numbers in the example above is not inherently random, and therefore it is a red herring to call it a candidate "random number generator." In fact, the same thing is true of *every* so-called random number generator, but to a greater or lesser extent. This is the reason that many purists insist that such computer-based random number generators be referred to as *pseudo-random*. One thing is certain, though: every stream of random numbers that is created using a digital computer must repeat itself at some point. The number of random values which may be generated before this occurs is known as the *period* of the generator. Thus it makes sense to wonder what qualities of a random number generation scheme are considered essential in a simulation setting. As was mentioned in Section 4.4.1, every distribution can be created using a uniform distribution as its base. We therefore confine our remarks concerning desirable properties to $U(0, 1)$ generators.

The minimal requirements for an RNG will vary from simulation to simulation. This is a natural consequence of the differences in variability and range that one encounters in the modeling of various phenomena. Several investigations of the attributes that might be expected to be common across application domains have been conducted to date, for example [Park 88]. So far as the mathematical qualities of the output are concerned, one generally seeks random number generators that have the following characteristics:

- *A long period.* The utility of a given RNG may in some sense be considered to be at least linearly proportional to the period, because the longer period increases the number of domains in which it may be employed.

- *Substantial representation of the interval.* The precision of the values returned by the RNG should include several significant digits. This requirement is often the easiest to satisfy, but may be costly in terms of performance if the numeric representation of the implementation architecture is sparse. In such cases, the precision of numeric representations can be increased in software at the expense of execution speed.

- *No perceivable patterns.* Failure to satisfy this requirement destroys the impression that the modeled component is indeed behaving in a random fashion.

- *Correspondence with the distribution of interest.* Naturally, one must insist that the RNG produce values that are representative of the claimed distribution.

In addition to these desirable statistical qualities, one also hopes for an implementation that is efficient in terms of execution speed and storage space (otherwise known as computational complexity). Concern regarding the RNG complexity is certainly warranted when one considers that it is not unusual to call for a randomly generated value millions of times over the course of a single simulation run.

Several tests have been developed which measure the extent to which a particular RNG possesses each of the qualities discussed above. The discussion by Knuth is quite complete and straightforward [Knuth 69]. Several additional analyses of the issues associated with the evaluation of random number generators are given in the reference section of this chapter. Interestingly, despite the large body of published information that warns of the hazards of using an inadequate RNG, there have been indications that in fairly recent history, many simulation builders did not consider it necessary to independently validate their own random number generation mechanisms or the ones built into the simulation language being used [Park 88]. In consideration of its importance to the simulation effort, one should always validate the RNG. Some of the most commonly used tests to accomplish this are discussed below.

4.4.2.1 The frequency test

The frequency test is a good "first cut" examination of the generator's ability to produce the distribution of interest. It is also extremely simple to implement, because it is essentially just a comparison of a histogram to the corresponding portion of a uniform distribution. To begin, produce a stream of random numbers to be tested. The amount of random numbers should be generous. As will be pointed out in future tests, 5,000 random values is about the smallest amount that one should consider, but much larger amounts should be examined if practical. Next, the range of the RNG is partitioned into a number of intervals. If no other heuristic seems applicable, a good rule of thumb is to use the floor of the square root of the number of random numbers in the data set as the number of partitions. One then simply classifies each of the random numbers as belonging to an appropriate partition depending on its value.

A chi-square statistic is used to compare the observed frequencies of numbers in each partition with the expected frequencies that would be anticipated in the distribution. If O_i indicates the number of values found in the ith partition, and E_i indicates the number of values that we would expect to find in the ith partition, then under the null hypothesis of identical distributions, the following statistic follows a chi-square distribution with $(v - 1)$ degrees of freedom:

$$\chi^2_{v-1} = \sum_{i=1}^{v} \frac{(O_i - E_i)^2}{E_i}$$

Example 4.3

A series of 10,000 random numbers was generated for testing purposes, and the results were classified according to the following partitions:

Partition	Observed	Expected
1	1027	1000
2	963	1000
3	1027	1000
4	1026	1000
5	995	1000
6	1043	1000
7	918	1000
8	1019	1000
9	1000	1000
10	982	1000

Test the hypothesis that the numbers follow a uniform distribution at the 0.05 level of significance.

Notice that for the uniform distribution, $E_1 = E_2 = \ldots = E_n = n/v$. Identifying the parameters of the test, we have:

- H_0: The numbers are uniformly distributed.

- H_1: The numbers are not uniformly distributed.

- Level of significance: $\alpha = 0.05$.

- Computed (observed) test statistic: $\chi_9^2 = 12.786$.

From the tabulated values of the cumulative chi-squared distribution with 9 degrees of freedom, we have the fact that the probability of χ_9^2 being greater than 16.9 is equal to 0.05. Since $12.786 < 16.9$, we fail to reject the null hypothesis and conclude that the evidence does not dispute the assertion that the numbers are uniformly distributed.

4.4.2.2 The Kolmogorov-Smirnov test

The frequency test discussed in the preceding section measures the extent to which the empirical distribution matches the distribution of interest. Using the chi-squared statistic in this way may have a drawback. Since the chi-squared statistic is formed as the sum of the normalized squared deviations between the observed and expected frequencies, it is possible for the effect of a small number of *substantial* deviations to "slip by" in the calculation. This can happen if the counts of most of the other partitions are close to the expected values.

The Kolmogorov-Smirnov (KS) test addresses this vulnerability. Like the frequency test, it measures the degree to which the shape of the empirical distribution matches the desired distribution, with the exception that the KS test makes use of the empirical cumulative distribution $\hat{F}(x)$ instead of the density function. It also differs in that it uses the criteria of *maximal* deviation, as opposed to *average* deviation, to arrive at its assessment of acceptability. Kolmogorov was able to describe the cumulative distribution that can be formed after taking a sample from a particular distribution and, thus, the probability that the difference between the sample distribution and the actual distribution is less than some constant value.

We shall make the discussion more concrete. Suppose that we have a continuous random variable X, with PDF $f_X(x)$ and CDF $F_X(x)$. There exist an infinite number of distinct samples that one could take from the values of X and form the empirical distribution function $\hat{F}(x)$. Because of the variability of X, we would expect that $\hat{F}(x)$ would differ somewhat from sample to sample. Kolmogorov (as modified by Smirnov) showed that the *largest* difference between the empirical and actual distribution functions was a random variable Δ that followed a particular distribution itself, as the size of the sample becomes large. Defining this difference as follows,

$$\Delta = \max_x \left| \hat{F}(x) - F(x) \right|$$

we find that for large n, the following approximate distribution holds:

$$F_\Delta(\delta) = 1 - 2e^{-2n\delta^2}$$

The KS test follows directly from the equation above. Recalling that this CDF can be expressed as "the probability that the largest difference will be smaller than δ," one can stipulate a particular value for this probability and solve for δ. This procedure yields the largest difference for which we would be prepared to accept the hypothesis of identical distributions. For example, if we set our confidence value to be some particular $(1 - \alpha)$, we would have:

$$1 - \alpha = 1 - 2e^{-2n\delta^2}$$

$$\delta_{max} = \sqrt{\frac{-\ln(\alpha/2)}{2n}}$$

Thus if we find that the largest deviation of the empirical distribution from the anticipated distribution is greater than δ_{max}, we will reject the null hypothesis of identical distributions. Although it is common to consult a table of critical values for the KS test, it is clear from the formula above that it may be computed directly without too much difficulty.

Example 4.4

Apply the KS test at the 0.05 level of significance to the data in Example 4.3 to test the null hypothesis that the sample came from a uniform distribution. The partitions are contiguous and the indices are in monotonically increasing order of the observation values.

From the given data, we can create the empirical distribution function and calculate the differences from what we would expect to see in a uniform distribution:

Partition	Observed	$\hat{F}(x)$	$F(x)$	$\left|\hat{F}(x) - F(x)\right|$
1	1027	0.1027	0.1	0.00270
2	963	0.1990	0.2	0.00100
3	1027	0.3017	0.3	0.00170
4	1026	0.4043	0.4	0.00430
5	995	0.5038	0.5	0.00380
6	1043	0.6081	0.6	0.00810
7	918	0.6999	0.7	0.00010
8	1019	0.8018	0.8	0.00180
9	1000	0.9018	0.9	0.00180
10	982	1.000	1.0	0.00000

The largest deviation is in partition number 6, with a value of 0.00810. At the 0.05 level of significance, we calculate the corresponding KS statistic from the formula as 0.013581. Since the largest observed deviation is less than the critical value, we fail to reject the null hypothesis of identical distributions.

4.4.2.3 The permutation test

The preceding two tests mainly address the concern of correspondence of the RNG stream with the distribution of interest. One must also be concerned, however, with the *order* in which those values appear. The permutation test was developed to measure the extent of randomness of ordering present in a sequence of numbers. It is a well-known fact that given n distinct objects, there exist $P(n, k) = n!/(n-k)!$ different orderings of those objects. If we divide a stream of random numbers into partitions of length k, and we assume that no two numbers are equal, then there are $k!$ possible orderings of the values in each partition. Such an ordering is known as a *permutation*, and hence the name of the test. For a uniform distribution with no discernible pattern, we would expect each ordering to be equally likely, and thus we anticipate that any particular ordering will occur with probability $1/k!$. This is the essence of the permutation test. If the RNG exhibits a noticeable tendency to group patterns in a particular order, this will be observed as a significant departure from the expected probability. The test is administered by forming a chi-squared statistic where each of the E_i's $= 1/k!$. To obtain the O_i's, one simply counts the number of times that a particular ordering is observed and divides by the total number of orderings that are examined. Knuth described a clever algorithm in [Knuth 69] which is linear in k, in terms of both storage and execution speed, for identifying a given permutation.

There may be some question concerning an appropriate choice for partition length. There is no universal guidance which suggests that any particular length is especially appropriate under a certain set of circumstances. However, a few rules of thumb can be applied to limit the choices. First, observe that the required storage space and probable analysis speed grows at least as rapidly as the factorial of the partition length (depending on the efficiency of the analytic technique), so one is well advised to keep the partition as small as possible. Second, consider that there may be aspects of the problem domain that suggest a specific length. For example, if we require random numbers to simulate the inter-arrival times for customers to a set of five queues, then we would mainly be concerned about failures of uniformity among the permutations of length five. Larger lengths would not be noticeable, as they would be distributed to different queues. Finally, we note that since the partitions are contiguous, the contribution of a larger partition will be captured by a corresponding smaller one, as one is a subset of the other.

4.4.2.4 The poker test

This is a specialization of the permutation test that is applied to integers in the range of the RNG. When the generator of interest operates over an interval of real numbers, we may proceed by noting that if X is a continuous random variable that is uniformly distributed over $[0, 1]$, then dX is uniformly distributed over $[0, (d - 1)]$. Instead of considering *all* of the different possible orderings, we restrict the analysis to a specific subset, and in particular with respect to a partition of length 5. We seek the frequency of seven "poker hands," two pairs of which are equivalent to one another in the sense that they occur with equal frequency. The combinations of interest are: all different; one pair; two pairs; three of a kind; full house (a triplet and a pair); four of a kind; and five of a kind.

The original paper which described the poker test [Kendall 38] did not seem to emphasize the block size of 5 for any special reasons (although they did use a block size of four to apply the test to a table of purportedly random numbers in the same paper) and so we may consider that another partition length would do just as well. It seems possible that the identification with the permutations of a poker hand was simply an aesthetically pleasing choice. However, given the preceding discussion regarding the choice of partition length, there is probably not much to be gained by using any different size. It is worthwhile to note that this same paper also described the frequency, serial, and gap tests, the latter two of which will be discussed shortly.

To apply the poker test, partition the random number stream into blocks of five, classify each block according to its type, and count the number of times that each type appears. Unlike the permutation test, the task of classifying each block is not too formidable. An algorithm which is implemented in the C++

language to do so is shown below. Suppose that the currently considered "hand" is in an array called `IntegerArray` and that an auxiliary array `Value`, also of size 5, is initialized to all zeros.

```
Result = 0;
for (dex = 0; dex < 5; dex++)
  {
  if (!Value[dex])
    {
    Result++;
    Value[dex] = Result;
    for (chex = dex+1; chex < 5; chex++)
      {
      if (IntegerArray[dex] == IntegerArray[chex] &&
          !Value[chex])
        Value[chex] = Result;
      }
    }
  }
```

Each element in the array `Value` now contains a number whose value identifies the corresponding elements in `IntegerArray` having the same value. `Value[dex]` is one greater than the index of the first incidence in `IntegerArray` of the number in question. For example, if `IntegerArray` had the following values:

7	5	7	3	5

then after the preceding bit of code, `Value` would contain the following elements:

1	2	1	3	2

This has the effect of partitioning each hand into equivalence classes. These classes may map directly to a poker hand. For example, if there are five different numbers in `IntegerArray`, then `Result` will equal five and the corresponding poker hand is "all different." Likewise, if `Result` is four, then the corresponding hand is "one pair." However, if `Result` is three, the corresponding poker hand may be either "two pair," as in the example above, or "three of a kind." Some further processing is needed to fully identify the hand in these cases, which is left as an exercise.

Determining the expected probabilities of each combination, however, is not quite so straightforward. To simplify the calculation, we follow the method of [Knuth 69] and count the number of hands having r distinct values. If we consider the digits in the interval $[0, d]$, the probability of encountering a hand with r different numbers in a block of k is given by:

$$P_r = \frac{d(d-1)\cdots(d-r+1)}{d^k} \left\{ \begin{matrix} k \\ r \end{matrix} \right\},$$

where the notation $\left\{ \begin{matrix} k \\ r \end{matrix} \right\}$ indicates a Stirling number of the second kind for the values k and r. Such numbers may be computed by the formula:

$$\left\{ \begin{matrix} k \\ r \end{matrix} \right\} = r \left\{ \begin{matrix} k-1 \\ r \end{matrix} \right\} + \left\{ \begin{matrix} k-1 \\ r-1 \end{matrix} \right\},$$

$$\left\{ \begin{matrix} x \\ 1 \end{matrix} \right\} = 1 \ \forall \ x > 0, \quad \left\{ \begin{matrix} x \\ 0 \end{matrix} \right\} = 0 \ \forall \ x > 0, \quad \left\{ \begin{matrix} 0 \\ 0 \end{matrix} \right\} = 1$$

As usual, we compare the expected number of observations of a particular type with the actual observations in the stream of random numbers through use of a chi-squared statistic. For the poker test, one begins by considering four degrees of freedom. Because of the exceedingly small probability of obtaining five of a kind, however, it is usually necessary to combine the observations in this category with an the adjacent category (or categories) to obtain at least five observations. This is necessary to form a valid chi-squared statistic and reduces the available degrees of freedom correspondingly.

Example 4.5

Suppose that we generate 10,000 random numbers and observe the following counts:

Five of a Kind	Four of a Kind	Full House	Three of a Kind	Two Pair	One Pair	All Different
1	7	27	153	211	985	616

Apply the poker test to the given data, under the assumption of a uniform distribution.

We must first calculate the expected number of observations in each category. From the formulas given in this section, we have:

	Five of a Kind (one different)	Four of a Kind or Full House (two different)	Three of a Kind or Two Pair (three different)	One Pair (four different)	All Different
Event probability	0.0001	0.0135	0.18	0.504	0.3024
Expected per 10,000	0.2	27	360	1008	604.8

Considering the given data, it is evident that the first two categories will have to be combined, as there is only a single observation in the Five of a Kind category. After combining these two, we calculate the chi-squared statistic with $v = 3$ degrees of freedom:

$$\chi_3^2 = \frac{(35-27.2)^2}{27.2} + \frac{(364-360)^2}{360} + \frac{(985-1008)^2}{1008} +$$

$$\frac{(616-604.8)^2}{604.8}$$

$$= 3.0134$$

The tabulated value for this chi-squared statistic at the 0.05 level of significance is 7.81. Thus, we fail to reject the null hypothesis of uniform distribution.

4.4.2.5 The serial test

Like the poker test, the serial test is also applied to integral values. It is applied by considering each pair of integers as they are produced. If the stream is in fact uniform on $[0, d]$, then we would expect that each one of the $(d + 1)^2$ ordered pairs would appear with probability $1/(d + 1)^2$. The usual chi-squared statistic is calculated, with $(d + 1)^2 - 1$ degrees of freedom. Note that for the chi-squared statistic to be valid, we must discard each pair as it is counted. Failure to do so violates the implied independence of each observation and invalidates the calculation of the statistic.

One usually thinks of conducting the paired test in terms of a matrix of entries, the row index of which indicates the first element of a pair, and the column index indicating the subsequent value. Suppose that the following stream of random numbers is observed:

$$7, 6, 1, 1, 0, 9, 7, 2, 3, 0, 8, 1, 3, 0, 9, \ldots$$

If every entry of the matrix is initialized to zero, one simply increments the appropriate matrix entry as each pair is examined. Using the sequence of numbers above, the counting would proceed by incrementing the $(7, 6)$ entry, then the $(1, 1)$ entry, followed by the $(0, 9)$ entry, and so on. As most modern computer programming languages have some built-in support for the use of multidimensional arrays, the counting is often very easy to implement. Although we discuss the paired serial test here, it is a straightforward task to extend the approach to triplets, quadruples, and beyond. The fact that the storage required grows exponentially as a function of the block size would tend to discourage very large dimensions, however.

4.4.2.6 The gap test

The gap test is related to the serial test and is the last of the four empirical examinations suggested by Kendall and Babington-Smith's paper. It looks at the probabilities associated with the length (in terms of numbers) of intervals between the repetition of any particular random number. For example, consider the sequence of digits on [0, 9] discussed in the preceding section. The first time that the number 7 appears, we have some expectation that it may be immediately followed by another 7. In fact, we anticipate that this will be the case roughly 1/10th of the time, since every number is as likely to appear as any other. This would be an example of a "gap of length zero." Similarly, of the one hundred different ways that two digits can follow the original numeral seven, there are nine different ways that a gap of length one may occur, namely: 7-0-7, 7-1-7, ... 7-6-7, 7-8-7, 7-9-7. Thus we expect that the probability of a gap of length one is 0.09. Note that these probabilities are related to the notion of the number of trials until a success is observed, which was discussed in Chapter 2. The test is applied by counting the number of gaps of a particular length and comparing the observed amounts with the expected amounts using a chi-squared statistic.

4.5 Experimentation

Having constructed a model and obtained an implementation, the stage is set for actual use of the simulation. Even at this point, however, it does not suffice simply to apply the inputs and collect whatever output follows. Lest we come to erroneous conclusions about the meaning of a particular simulated result, it is necessary to remember that every simulation run is an experiment. The inputs that we provide are the controlled parameters for the experiment, and the simulation itself governs the outcomes that are observed. As with all experiments, it is necessary to take precautions that ensure that the combined influence of factors which are exogenous to the system of interest is minimized.

4.5.1 The choice of run length

Assuming an adequate model, the validity of conclusions may be dependent upon dynamic characteristics that are inherent in the system. Under such circumstances, output from identical inputs to the model may vary considerably as a function of the time that the simulation is allowed to run. An example of such behavior from a simulation of disk queueing in a client-server system is shown in Figure 4.3.

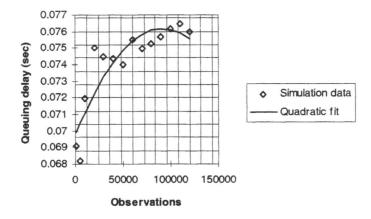

Figure 4.3. Identification of steady-state.

The phenomenon observed here is a familiar one in dynamic systems such as networks of queues. In such systems, a relatively short period of transient behavior is observed at system start-up, during which the state variables which describe the system tend to change quickly with small increments of simulated time. This stage is followed by a resolution of the system at equilibrium, where system outputs are essentially stable. As this steady-state condition dominates the behavior of the system over time, it is often the case that the primary interest of the investigation concerns the response of the system once equilibrium is achieved. It is therefore necessary to consider the dynamic characteristics of the model before measurements are taken.

When the presence of a significant transient period is suspected, it becomes necessary to estimate its length. Examination of the system output in a graphical form over time is a useful technique, but because the interpretation of the magnitude of a state variable's change is largely scale-dependent, it may not be obvious when the system's steady-state condition has been achieved. By elongating the horizontal axis in Figure 4.3, for example, the rate of change in delay may be made to appear visually quite small. In order to estimate the approach of steady-state, some knowledge of the global behavior of the system over time is needed.

4.5.2 The number of simulation runs

Typically one must make several runs of a simulation in order to obtain confidence intervals for the statistic of interest. Choosing the exact number of runs may be straightforward, if it is known that a single run produces a single independent observation of the desired behavior. For example, if we are estimating the mean of a normally distributed random variable, we simply specify a desired precision Δ and confidence α and solve the equations given in Chapter 3 for the width of the confidence interval as:

$$n \geq \left(\frac{\sigma z_{\alpha/2}}{\Delta} \right)^2$$

If each run produces more than one independent observation, then the choice of the number of runs becomes more philosophical. If one agrees that the random number generator is well validated, then we would have no reason to believe that any particular run is not representative, assuming a large number of observations. Therefore a single run of some length essentially equates to as many individual runs of length one. Most people that work with simulations would feel uncomfortable with this approach, though, because the random number generator tests that are employed are generally empirical. As such, they do not offer *proof* that the RNG is satisfactory over all intervals. Thus, most investigators would want to examine the performance of a simulation over the course of several independent runs, using different seeds, even if it would be feasible to collect enough observations to form an acceptable confidence interval in a single run.

4.6 Summary

The creation of a simulation that accurately portrays the relevant characteristics of the system of interest can be very challenging. While many aspects of the process are mechanical, there are many issues which must be resolved through observation and experience. As such, the production of a successful simulation incorporates a certain amount of artistry in addition to hard science. In the process of designing and using a simulation, one must always guard against the tendency to assume that every result that we observe has a basis in fact. Thus, a healthy measure of good sense, coupled with knowledge of the application domain, must be employed when analyzing the output.

4.7 Exercises

4.1   The IDEF0 methodology is a hierarchically structured technique, in the sense that a single function may be decomposed into any number of subfunctions, which in turn may be themselves decomposed, and so on. Show how a process of your own choosing may be represented using the IDEF0 conventions, and show a decomposition of at least one function. For more details concerning IDEF0 syntax, the interested reader should consult [NIST 93a], which was available electronically from ncsl.nist.gov at the time of this writing.

4.2   Explain the differences between the processes of validation and verification.

4.3   It was stated that the "real" model governing the behavior of a system can never be known with certainty. If this is true, then why do we concern ourselves with validation at all?

4.4   Complete the proof of program correctness that was begun in Section 4.3.2.

4.5   Discuss the importance of random number generator validation in the context of the simulation of arrival processes, e.g., vehicles at an intersection, packets in a network, etc.

4.6   Derive an algorithm that will generate random numbers having an exponential distribution with parameter 3.0. Use your algorithm to generate a sequence of 5,000 random numbers, and show that these numbers fit the required distribution using the frequency and KS tests.

4.7   Given a stream of random digits in the interval [0, 9], calculate the expected probabilities of the occurrence of gaps of lengths 3, 4, 5, and 6.

4.8 References

[Anderson 93] R. H. Anderson, S. C. Banks, P. K. Davis, H. E. Hall, and N. Z. Shapiro, *Toward a Comprehensive Environment for Computer Modeling, Simulation, and Analysis*, RAND Corporation, Santa Monica, CA, 1993.

[Balci 84] O. Balci and R. G. Sargent, "A bibliography on the credibility assessment and validation of simulation and mathematical models," *Simuletter*, Vol. 15, No. 3, pp. 15 – 27, July 1984.

[Balci 88]   O. Balci, "How to assess the acceptability and credibility of simulation results," *Proceedings of the 1988 Winter Simulation Conference*, pp. 62 – 71, 1988.

[Clark 88]   G. M. Clark, "Analysis of simulation output to compare alternatives," *Proceedings of the 1988 Winter Simulation Conference*, pp. 19 – 24, 1988.

[Deslandres 91]   V. Deslandres and H. Pierreval, "An expert system prototype assisting the statistical validation of simulation models," *Simulation*, Vol. 56, No. 2, pp. 79 – 89, February 1991.

[Devroye 86]   L. Devroye, *Non-Uniform Random Variate Generation*, Springer-Verlag, New York, NY, 1986.

[Finlay 87] P. N. Finlay and J. M. Wilson, "The paucity of model validation in operational research projects," *Journal of the Operational Research Society*, Vol. 38, No. 4, pp. 303 – 308, April 1987.

[Fishman 73] G. S. Fishman, *Concepts and Methods in Discrete Event Digital Simulation*, Wiley & Sons, New York, NY, 1973.

[Fox 89]   M. S. Fox, N. Husain, M. McRoberts, and Y. V. Reddy, "Knowledge-based simulation: An artificial intelligence approach to system modeling and automating the simulation life cycle," in *Artificial Intelligence, Simulation, and Modeling*, Widman, Loparo, and Nielsen, eds., Wiley & Sons, New York, NY, 1989.

[Godwin 89] A. N. Godwin, J. W. Gleeson, and D. Gwillian, "An assessment of the IDEF notations as descriptive tools," *Information Systems*, Vol. 14, No. 1, pp. 3 – 28, January 1989.

[Hjorth 94]   J. S. Hjorth, *Computer-intensive Statistical Methods: Validation and Model Selection*, Chapman & Hall, London, 1994.

[Hodges 92] J. S. Hodges and J. A. Dewar, *Is It You or Your Model Talking?: A Framework for Model Validation*, RAND Corporation, Santa Monica, CA, 1992.

[Kendall 38]   M. G. Kendall and B. Babington-Smith, "Randomness and random sampling numbers," *Journal of the Royal Statistical Society*, Vol. 101, pp. 147–166, 1938.

[Kneppel 93] P. L. Kneppel and D. C. Arango, *Simulation Validation: A Confidence Assessment Methodology*, IEEE Computer Society Press, Los Alamitos, CA, 1993.

[Knuth 69] D. E. Knuth, *The Art of Computer Programming, Vol. 2: Seminumerical Algorithms*, Addison-Wesley, Reading, MA, 1969.

[Law 91a]   A. M. Law and M. G. McComas, "Secrets of successful simulation studies," *Proceedings of the 1991 Winter Simulation Conference*, New York, NY, pp. 21 – 27, 1991.

[Law 91b] A. M. Law and W. D. Kelton, *Simulation Modeling & Analysis*, McGraw-Hill, New York, NY, 1991.

[Leveson 93] N. G. Leveson and C. S. Turner, "An investigation of the Therac-25 accidents," *IEEE Computer*, Vol. 26, No. 7, pp. 18 – 41, July 1993.

[Manna 74] Z. Manna, *Mathematical Theory of Computation*, McGraw-Hill, New York, NY, 1974.

[McLeod 82] J. McLeod, *Computer Modeling and Simulation: Principles of Good Practice*, Society for Computer Simulation, La Jolla, CA, 1982.

[NIST 93a]   National Institute of Standards and Technology, *Federal Information Processing Standards Publication 183: Integration Definition for Function Modeling (IDEF0)*, National Technical Information Service, 1993.

[NIST 93b]   National Institute of Standards and Technology, *Federal Information Processing Standards Publication 184: Integration Definition for Information Modeling (IDEF1X)*, National Technical Information Service, 1993.

[Park 88] S. J. Park and K. W. Miller, "Random number generators: Good ones are hard to find," *Communications of the ACM*, Vol. 31, No. 10, pp. 1192 – 1201, 1988.

[Pooch 93] U. W. Pooch and J. A. Wall, *Discrete Event Simulation: A Practical Approach*, CRC Press, Boca Raton, FL, 1993.

[Rubinstein 81] R. Y. Rubinstein, *Simulation and the Monte Carlo Method*, John Wiley & Sons, New York, NY, 1981.

[Sargent 87] R. G. Sargent, "An overview of verification and validation of simulation models," *Proceedings of the 1987 Winter Simulation Conference*, pp. 33 – 39, 1987.

[Sargent 91] R. G. Sargent, "Simulation model verification and validation," *Proceedings of the 1991 Winter Simulation Conference*, pp. 37 – 47, 1991.

[Saunders 85] C. Saunders, "Model validation: The missing process," *Journal of Systems Management*, Vol. 36, No. 8, pp. 26 – 29, August 1985.

[Seila 91] A. F. Seila, "Output analysis for simulation," *Proceedings of the 1991 Winter Simulation Conference*, pp. 28 – 36, 1991.

[Sowey 72] E. R. Sowey, "A chronological and classified bibliography on random number generation and testing," *International Statistical Review*, Vol. 40, No. 3, pp. 355 –371, December 1972.

[Spriet 82] J. A. Spriet and G. C. Vansteenkiste, *Computer-aided Modeling and Simulation*, Academic Press, London, 1982.

[Tsang 91] C. Tsang, "The modeling process and model validation," *Ground Water*, Vol. 29, No. 6, pp. 825 – 831, December 1991.

[Yakowitz 77] S. J. Yakowitz, *Computational Probability and Simulation*, Addison-Wesley, Reading, MA, 1977.

[Yourdon 89]   E. Yourdon, *Modern Structured Analysis*, Prentice-Hall, Englewood Cliffs, NJ, 1989.

5

Distributed Systems

The ability to simultaneously apply multiple computer processors to a problem has dramatically increased the scale of problems that may be addressed through simulation. However, the use of multiple processors brings additional complexity to the software engineering effort. As we will discuss in detail, there is overhead associated with using multiple processors. Intrinsically serial operations will not benefit from the use of multiple processors. The von Neumann bottleneck occurs when a single processor issues sequential instructions that can be executed only one instruction at a time.

Multiple processor systems may be divided into two general categories: parallel processors (multiprocessors) and distributed systems (multicomputers). We characterize parallel processors as tightly coupled homogeneous processors which share the same main memory space. A distributed system is a loosely coupled collection of often heterogeneous processors which communicate through message passing.

In this book we are primarily concerned with distributed simulations, that is, simulations implemented over distributed systems. When designing a distributed simulation, it is common to consider the use of parallel machines as an alternative. Therefore, we will briefly discuss parallel architectures and observe that implementing a parallel simulation on a multiprocessor has many of the same issues associated with implementing a distributed simulation. It is not unreasonable to expect shared memory multiprocessors to be a component of a larger, message passing, distributed system.

5.1 Overview of parallel and distributed systems

The primary frame of reference for uniprocessor computers is the von Neumann architecture, named for the brilliant Princeton scientist, John von Neumann.   Figure 5.1 illustrates a von Neumann machine using architectural abstractions to represent the physical devices of a computer.   The lines with black arrowheads represent instructions and the lines with white arrowheads represent control information.

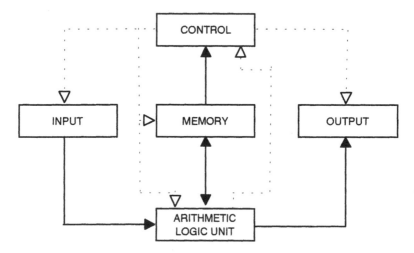

Figure 5.1. Diagram of a von Neumann architecture.

The characteristics of the von Neumann architecture are summarized by [Baer 80].

- The input transmits data and instructions from the user/operator to the memory.

- The memory stores instructions, data, and intermediate and final results.

- Control interprets the instructions and causes them to be executed.

- Output provides results and messages to the user/operator.

This architecture limits the execution of instructions to one per clock cycle. For many applications, this architecture is not only adequate, but optimal. There are many cases where a very fast single processor can outperform a multiprocessor. These cases most often occur when significant parts of the computation must be executed one instruction after another or when the length of the computation is not long enough to justify the overhead imposed by distributing the computation across multiple processors.

Data dependencies can impose a sequential execution regardless of the hardware available. When instructions are dependent upon results determined by previous instructions, then there is no opportunity for speed up by adding processors. Consider the following statements:

```
001:   x := 5;

002:   y := 9 + x;
```

Statement 2 is dependent upon statement 1. Statement 2 cannot complete correctly as written prior to the completion of statement 1. This is an example of the von Neumann bottleneck. However, there are many applications that can benefit from multiple processors. Many linear algebra problems have a great deal of inherent parallelism. In the following matrix addition:

$$\begin{bmatrix} a_{11} & a_{12} \\ a_{21} & a_{22} \end{bmatrix} + \begin{bmatrix} b_{11} & b_{12} \\ b_{21} & b_{22} \end{bmatrix} = \begin{bmatrix} c_{11} & c_{12} \\ c_{21} & c_{22} \end{bmatrix}$$ each element in matrix $\mathbf{C}$

can be computed independently. Therefore additional processors could theoretically speed up the computation. Unfortunately, there is overhead associated with distributing this computation across several processors. For trivial computations, the overhead is likely to exceed the performance improvement of additional processors.

When distributing an application, two essential design considerations are the *degree of parallelism* of the application and the *overhead costs* associated with moving parts of the application to different processors. The degree of parallelism measures how much of the application can be executed on different processors. As noted earlier, matrix addition is an example of an application with a high degree of parallelism. Applications which can be partitioned in a manner that limits the amount of communication across partitions often have a high degree of parallelism. Overhead costs tend to be dominated by the communications costs between nodes.

We exploit parallelism by adding processors. There are two general strategies for applying additional processors to a problem. The first is to build a parallel computer composed of multiple processors. The second is to physically connect independent computers and build a distributed system based on the sharing of software resources through message passing.

5.1.1 Parallel processors

More than twenty years ago, Flynn classified parallel computers based upon their instruction streams and their data streams [Hwang 93]. Although it should be noted that advances in architecture design have considerably blurred the distinctions between machine classes, Flynn's taxonomy remains useful. The four classifications are:

1. Single Instruction, Single Data (SISD).

2. Multiple Instruction, Single Data (MISD).

3. Single Instruction, Multiple Data (SIMD).

4. Multiple Instruction, Multiple Data (MIMD).

SISD systems are physical implementations of the von Neumann machine. SISD systems have one CPU capable of processing a single stream of instructions. [Maccabe 93] defines MISD architectures as pipeline machines where multiple instructions are performed simultaneously on different parts of a single data stream.

SIMD machines perform the same operation on different (multiple) data. SIMD machines are generally implemented on shared memory architectures (Figure 5.2) or on distributed memory architectures with static interconnection networks that allow synchronized data exchange.

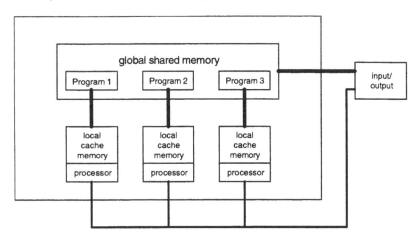

Figure 5.2. Parallel processor with shared memory.

Shared memory systems allow all processors access to the global memory space, but generally they do not scale well. As more processors are added to a SIMD machine, contention for memory access will limit the number of processors able to run concurrently. Cache memory, which is local memory private to each processor, can overcome this bottleneck to a certain extent. However, the introduction of local caches also introduces the difficulty of keeping all the cache memories updated. This is known as the cache coherence problem.

Shared memory multiprocessors may be further classified as having a unified memory access (UMA), a non-uniform memory access (NUMA), or a cache-only memory access (COMA). UMA systems allow all processors access to the shared main memory. The Sequent Symmetry S-81 uses UMA. NUMA systems, such as the BBN TC-2000 Butterfly, do not allow uniform access. COMA systems use only cache memory. The KSR-1 is a COMA machine. All the caches form a global address space. For a detailed discussion on shared memory architectures, we refer the reader to [Hwang 93].

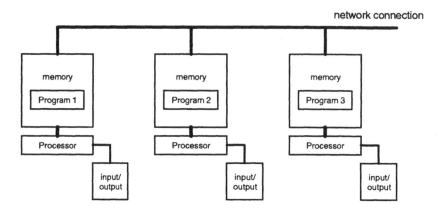

Figure 5.3. Parallel processor with distributed memory.

In Figure 5.3 we show a MIMD system in which each processor has its own private memory. All communication between processors is done by message passing. The processors in a MIMD architecture can operate asynchronously. A traditional MIMD machine is typically composed of integrated, and largely homogeneous, interconnected processors.

Parallel processors are much more tightly coupled than distributed systems. Parallel processors are well suited for particular applications with high degrees of parallelism. Distributed systems are more general purpose systems and are suitable for enterprise-wide operations.

5.1.2 Distributed systems

Distributed systems are more often described than defined. Often the term distributed system is used synonymously (and erroneously) with networked systems. Distributed systems are based upon cooperative computing while networked systems simply share resources. Most interpretations of a distributed system involve processing at remote sites. Remote processing is commonly organized on geographical, functional, or mission-related attributes. This categorization is intuitive if one considers how to reasonably partition a system.

One of the first attempts at a distributed system taxonomy, proposed by Enslow in 1978, focused on technology and geography [Enslow 78]. A general definition for distributed systems was given at the New Advances in Distributed Computer Systems conference held at the NATO Advanced Study Institute in 1981. There, a distributed system was defined as a system where processing is distributed among several computers which are independent of their geographic location [Beauchamp 82].

In the early 1970s, distributed processing meant processing of data at remote locations with communication networks linking multiple computers [Breslin 78]. In a more up-to-date definition provided by Casavant and Singhal, a distributed system consists of autonomous computers which do not share memory and are connected by a communication network [Casavant 91].

Although distributed systems have many of the attributes of MIMD-based parallel processors, distributed systems are more akin to a local area network (LAN) than a parallel processor. What differentiates a local area network from a distributed system is primarily the degree of integration between stations. Our definition of a distributed system is based upon an integration spectrum bounded on one end by unconnected, standalone, uniprocessors and bounded on the other end by highly connected, highly integrated distributed systems. Distributed systems may be defined as:

> Applications using servers to deliver services over a communications network through user interfaces to end users, managed as a single set of cooperating entities.

Figure 5.4 shows the integration hierarchy of uniprocessor-based computers. Stand alone systems are, as the name implies, completely non-integrated. LANs allow the sharing of software applications across platforms. A software package stored on one machine may be executed on another machine on the same network. A distributed application is able to integrate multiple processors to work on the same problem either synchronously or, more typically, asynchronously.

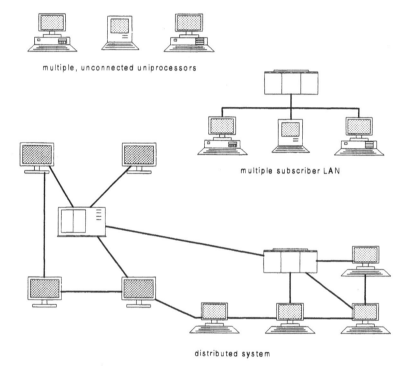

Figure 5.4. Spectrum of distributed multiprocessing.

Having given our definition of a distributed system, it is worthwhile to summarize some of the more important distributed computing terms as defined in [Sochats 92].

- **Distributed Operating System**: An operating system wherein functionality is allocated to multiple processors connected by high-speed network facilities.

- **Distributed Processing System**: A network-based computing system wherein similar transactions are processed at many locations or a single transaction is processed at multiple locations.

- **Distributed Application**: A configuration of processors and other information processing and network processing devices that allocates control and processing functions to each device in an independent manner.

- **Distributed Database**: A database that is stored at multiple locations within a network either by partitioning the database or replicating the database.

- **Distributed File System**: A file system wherein files are distributed across the network nodes but are made available as though they were stored on a local processor secondary storage device.

The individual computers of a distributed system are often geographically separated, though this is not a requirement. Unlike a parallel processing computer, which has all of its processors in the same box, distributed systems have their CPUs housed separately.

In any message passing system, a global state cannot be assumed. Message passing must be used to create a coherent global state. Thus, a fundamental problem in distributed computing is to ensure that a global state constructed in this manner is meaningful [Babaoglu 93].

Partitioning is a defining characteristic of a distributed system. A partition is a logical or physical boundary between groups of machines, processes, information, or users. The purpose of a partition is to assign responsibility for some aspect of the system to a specific processor. The overall objective of a particular partitioning scheme is to implement the distribution of effort in order to maximize the efficiency of the system.

Usually we think of efficiency in terms of process execution speed. In order to improve efficiency, it is desirable to minimize the overhead associated with interprocess communication costs. This is the basis for any partitioning strategy. In some cases we might want to partition a system based on physical locations, or we might want to partition on the basis of functionality, e.g., personnel systems, accounting systems, etc.

The relative merits of a partitioning scheme are dependent upon the operational behavior and physical implementation of the distributed system. Figure 5.5 is an example of a distributed system for a corporation headquartered in the United States and a sales division based in Australia. Intuitively, it might make sense to attempt to partition this system along geographic boundaries. One way to achieve this is making the client processes which require access to a database run on hosts which are on the same local area network as the database being accessed.

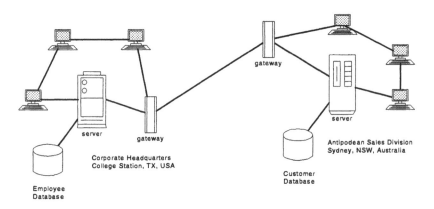

Figure 5.5. Example of a distributed system.

Local data distribution is highly desirable for applications which frequently access that data. A client in Sydney which frequently accesses the employee database in College Station is going to experience significant latency establishing trans-Pacific terminal sessions. Moving the employee database to Australia is unlikely to improve this situation if corporate headquarters in College Station also frequently accesses the employee database.

Replication of the database in both locations will require some means of ensuring that both databases remain consistent with each other. Partitioning and distributing the database is one solution and will be discussed in more detail in Section 5.3.

Partitioning according to the data characteristics is only one way to assign processor responsibility for portions of a computation. It is common to make these assignments dynamically based on processor loading or other factors, which can change rapidly. A processor may be designated as the default site to host sessions of a particular type. If enough is known about a type of session to classify it, then a reasonable estimate may be made in advance of the maximum number of sessions required. This estimate provides a basis for establishing an upper bound on loading.

5.2 Models for distributed systems and services

Large organizations often operate in geographically dispersed areas. Distributed systems provide the means to support computing needs across an organization. Science is no longer the dominant domain for distributed systems. Distributed systems are now well established in business, government, and a variety of other fields of endeavor.

Typical enterprise-wide computing activities are engineering systems, administrative systems, communications systems, and production systems. In Figure 5.6, Umar illustrates a distributed computer hierarchy. Distributed applications are implemented on what Umar calls a distributed computing platform [Umar 93]. Distributed applications are system implementations across the enterprise such as databases, personnel systems, requisitioning systems, etc. Because of its typically complex nature, considerable effort is necessary to provide users with access to a distributed system which hides most of the technical implementation issues.

5.2.1 Operating system support for distributed systems

An essential element of any distributed system is operating system support. Operating system support may come either from network operating systems or from distributed operating systems. In the reference model in Figure 5.9, operating system support is mapped to the servers. Figure 5.7 illustrates the difference between a network operating system and a distributed operating system [Goscinski 91].

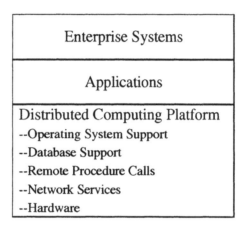

Figure 5.6. Distributed computing hierarchy [Umar 93].

Network operating systems are characterized as running on top of existing local operating systems. Each computer connected via a networked operating system has its own private operating system, instead of running as part of a global, system-wide distributed operating system.

5.2.2 Network services support for distributed systems

Network services are provided by packet-based data communications through a layered architecture. A layered architecture is a useful abstraction where functionality is divided into separate layers, with no sharing of functionality between layers. Each layer uses the services of the layer immediately below it and provides services to the layer immediately above it. Layers that are not adjacent do not communicate.

Networks are often linked using equipment from different vendors and based on differing network standards [Coulouris 94]. Connecting networks with different architectures is a standard feature of a distributed system. Distributed systems are generally not built from scratch. Rather, existing hardware is connected and existing networks are interconnected. This ability to interconnect disparate systems is what makes distributed systems extensible.

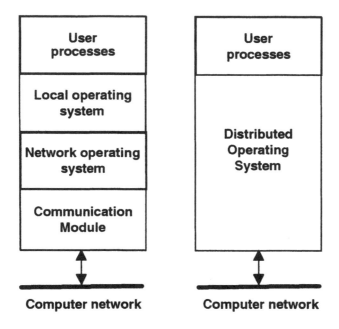

Figure 5.7. Network operating system vs. distributed operating system.

In order to interconnect different network architectures, data must be translated and reformatted appropriately. The International Organization for Standardization (ISO) Open System Interconnection (OSI) Reference Model provides a useful abstract model to guide interconnection efforts through a generic mapping of network functionality. The reference model should not be confused with a specific protocol. The OSI model is a very popular reference for interconnecting differing network architectures.

[Tanenbaum 96] merges the OSI and TCP/IP models to create a hybrid model. Tanenbaum's hybrid model is an attempt to benefit from both the clean design structure of the OSI Reference Model and the widespread practical experience using TCP/IP. There are many specific mappings from one protocol to another protocol that predate or otherwise ignore the OSI model. The major contribution of the OSI is its very generality, which allows an abstract functional decomposition of a network protocol. The seven layers of the OSI model are shown in Figure 5.8.

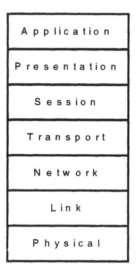

Figure 5.8. Open System Interconnection Reference Model.

Communication protocols are designed to operate between corresponding layers in different nodes. For example, in the OSI model, the Transport layer at one node uses the services of the Network layer at its node in order to pass protocol data units (packets) to the Transport layer at another node. Each peer layer is logically connected between nodes, although the real (physical) connection is at the physical layer.

The functionality of the OSI model can be seen in the implementation of parts of the Internet Protocol Suite. The protocols used in providing distributed file service or remote file service match well with the OSI reference model, as shown in Table 5.1. However, it must be stressed that the upper protocol stack layers that are not adjacent in some cases do communicate and that some services may overlap. The Internet protocols and applications listed in Table 5.1 are described below.

- **NFS** The Network File System is a distributed file service that transparently delivers (serves) remote files to client users. NFS was implemented using RPCs developed by Sun Microsystems.

Table 5.1 Internet NFS matched against the OSI model.

OSI Reference Model	Protocol or Application
Application Layer	NFS
Presentation Layer	XDR
Session Layer	RPC
Transport Layer	UDP/TCP
Network Layer	IP
Link Layer	IEEE Standard 802.2
Physical Layer	IEEE Standard 802.3

- **XDR** External Data Representation is the standard used to encode the values in the RPC call and reply messages [Stevens 94].

- **RPC** Remote Procedure Calls are a network programming tool.

- **UDP** User Datagram Protocol is an unreliable, simple, efficient transport service.

- **TCP** Transmission Control Protocol is a reliable, sequenced stream of bytes which uses buffered transfer

across a virtual circuit.   It is an alternative transport
service to UDP.

- **IP**   Internet Protocol is a network layer service which
  provides packet routing and connectionless delivery of
  packets.

- **802.2** IEEE data link layer standard used in the TCP/IP
  protocols.

- **802.3** IEEE Ethernet standard which is one of the
  physical connection means popularly used by TCP/IP.

The Internet Protocol Suite is one of the most popularly
used network protocol stacks. We will discuss two components
of the suite, NFS and RPC, later in this chapter.

The network support provided to a distributed system is of
vital importance.   When working properly, the communication
network should be transparent to the user. Should the underlying
network perform poorly, or not at all, the illusion of transparency
quickly breaks down.   Network services provide more than just
high-speed connections.   Performance can be hampered by the
cumulative effect of translating data between software layers.
Communication overhead is strongly affected by the efficiency of
the interfaces between the underlying layered protocols.

Figure 5.9 shows our view of a distributed system reference
model. This view emphasizes two critical points: the separation
of users and resources and the connecting communications

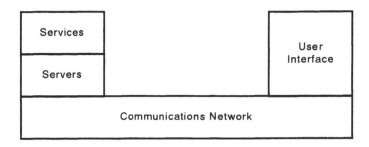

Figure 5.9. Distributed system reference model.

network. This view is consistent with the client/server model of distributed computing.

5.2.3 The client/server model for distributed systems

[Baker 94] points out that definitions of client/server computing vary. In Figure 5.10 we see an illustration of a client/server system. A distributed file system has files distributed across the network nodes. The files are made available as though they were stored on a local processor secondary storage device. In some respects a distributed file system appears similar to a distributed database. [Satyanarayanan 93] cites four major differences between distributed file systems and distributed databases:

- *Encapsulation* – A file system views the data as an uninterpreted byte sequence; a database encapsulates information about the data items and relationships stored within it.

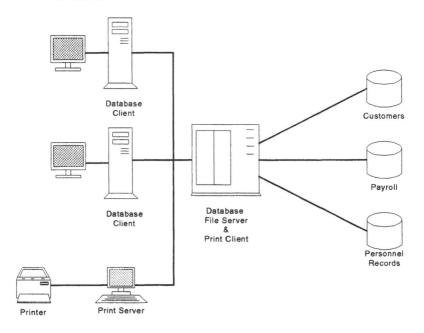

Figure 5.10. A client/server application.

- *Naming* – A file system is accessed by file name; a database allows associative access.

- *Ratio of search time to usage time* – When the ratio is low, access by a file system is adequate. When the ratio is high, then the additional effort to create a database is appropriate.

- *Shipping strategies* — Distributed file systems ship data to the point of use; distributed databases ship computation to the site of data storage.

The distributed file system is a significant element in implementing what Date calls "Rule Zero" for distributed systems. Rule Zero states that, to the user, a distributed system should look exactly like a non-distributed system [Date 92]. An excellent and widely used distributed file system is the Network File System. NFS is implemented as a set of Remote Procedure Calls to pass arguments between clients and servers. NFS is transparent to the user, thus obeying "Rule Zero." [Stern 91] observes that NFS has two levels of transparency:

1. The file system *appears* resident on a disk attached to the local system. Both files and directories are viewed the same way whether they are local or remote. NFS hides the location of the file on the network.

2. NFS-mounted file systems contain no information about the file servers from which they are mounted. The NFS file server may be of a different architecture or running an entirely different operating system with a radically different file system structure. NFS hides differences in the underlying remote file system structure and makes the remote file system appear to be of the exact same structure as that of the client.

The very popular X Window System which runs on top of the UNIX operating system is an implementation of the client/server model.   In X-Windows, client applications communicate with a local display server. [Bloomer 91] observes that the terms "client" and "server" are used differently in X-Windows than in RPCs. Interestingly, both clients and servers may exist on the same machine, as shown in Figure 5.10 [Rosenberry 92].

5.2.4 Remote procedure calls

Remote procedure calls keep the details of network services hidden from the distributed application. RPCs manage the communications requirements between servers and clients. In Figure 5.10 we differentiate between local procedure calls and remote procedure calls in the same manner as [Bloomer 91].

Figure 5.11 shows why it is possible to have clients and servers on the same machine as well as on different machines. If a server is not local, then a remote procedure call is implemented. While these requirements may vary, [Rosenberry 92] observes that there are two fundamental functions every distributed application must perform:

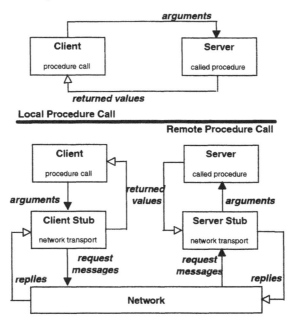

Figure 5.11. Remote and local procedure calls [Bloomer 91].

1. **Open a connection and transmit data.** This task poses several problems for programmers. The communications tasks form a completely new programming model which usually has nothing to do with the application at hand. Communication is always transport-specific to some extent and introduces new system errors that the program has to check for and recover from, making it hard to port to other environments.

2. **Organize data into a stream of messages suitable for transmission.** This stream is quite different from a function's argument list, which simply states the order and data types of arguments. Furthermore, programmers might need to convert the data into another machine's data format, an extremely complicated task that must be redone each time an application is ported to a different machine.

Figure 5.11 illustrates the layered nature of RPCs. The client process and the server process execute separately, usually on different machines. The two processes communicate through stubs which map the calling procedure into remote calls. All of this is transparent to the client, who only sees his request and the results of his request.

In this section we have attempted to show the differences between distributed systems and networked systems and to illustrate the primary characteristics of distributed systems.

5.3 Distributed databases

The need to access and manipulate large databases across multiple remote sites has been a prime motivator in the development of distributed systems. A *distributed* database is one in which the data is physically stored in different locations [Lans 88]. Distributed database systems have four distinct advantages over centralized processing schemes:

1. **Data integrity.** If a database is partitioned and stored on different machines, the threat to data integrity is limited to the data on a particular segment.

2. **Compartmentalization.** Access to one component of users' data need not imply access to the database in its entirety.

3. **High granularity.** Manipulating large amounts of data requires significant computing power to achieve any acceptable level of performance. The distribution of data across multiple sites allows users to more efficiently access and manipulate the data.

4. **Damage limitation.** Catastrophic events such as flood, fire, or nuclear attack do not preclude access to data stored elsewhere.

In our example illustrated in Figure 5.5, the system is distributed but the databases are not. Users in Sydney may access the employee database in College Station, but the employee database itself is not distributed – it is stored entirely in College Station.

We could distribute the employee database by partitioning it based on country of origin. Files for Australian and New Zealand employees would be stored in a database in Sydney and files for North American employees would be stored in College Station.

Two general methodologies exist for distributing databases. One uses a master database and the other uses no intermediaries. When a master database is used, the central database manager receives all input and directs all output. When a query calls for information from another location, the master database locates and retrieves it. [Baker 94] outlines the steps:

1. A distributed query first goes to a database that maintains records of the links.

2. If the query includes a reference to the database link, the first database will generate a query to the second database, asking it for the relevant data.

3. When the second database responds with the data, the first database then does any necessary processing and sends the result to the client system.

The client doesn't have to know that there is a second database, or how to gain access to it. The first server also acts as a client, submitting a request for data to the second server.

When an intermediate or centralized database management system (DBMS) is not used then the query or update goes directly to the designated database. This is often viewed as the "truly" distributed database model. In this model a single statement should allow data retrieval and make simultaneous updates on multivendor databases running on different computers. Non-trivial distributed commit protocols are required to maintain database consistency. In Example 5.1, we give an example of a distributed commit protocol.

Example 5.1

Let T_1 and T_2 be independent, asynchronous tasks which both want to modify A. The execution steps for T_1 and T_2 are shown in Figure 5.12. To ensure consistency we must prevent both from writing to A at the same time. Therefore, transactions are not allowed to write into a database until its commit point is reached. The commit protocol works to ensure:

*   A transaction cannot write into the database until it has reached its commit point.

*   A transaction cannot release any locks until it has finished writing into the database; therefore locks are not released until after the commit point.

In Example 5.1, if T_1 terminates while executing the steps in Figure 5.12:

1. T_1's lock on B must be removed.

2. The update A in step 3 must be revoked.

3. The value of A in step 7 is "dirty" and T_2 must be returned to its previous state or "rolled back."

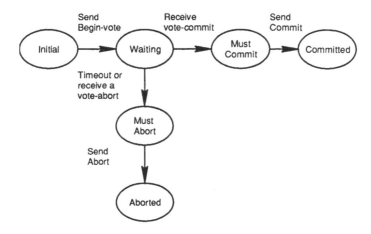

Figure 5.12. Illustration of the two-phase commit protocol.

This leads to cascading rollbacks. That is, as a step is rolled back to its previous state, this may require other steps in other transactions to be rolled back. This is clearly undesirable. In Figure 5.13, consider transaction **T** with distributed subtransactions $T_1 \ldots T_n$.

Step	T_1	T_2
(1)	Lock A	
(2)	Read A	
(3)	A:=A-1	
(4)	Write A	
(5)	Lock B	
(6)	Unlock A	
(7)		Lock A
(8)		Read A
(9)		A:=A*2
(10)	Read B	
(11)		Write A
(12)		Commit
(13)		Unlock A
(14)	B:=B/A	

Figure 5.13. Strict two-phase locking.

Ensuring atomicity is a critical consideration. All stations must agree on the final outcome, that is, vote for either a commit or an abort. **T** must commit at all stations or abort at all stations. A transaction coordinator is required to send the begin-vote requests to all stations. At each remote station a local transaction manager determines whether **T**'s request can be accommodated and either a vote-abort or a vote-commit is sent to the central transaction coordinator, ending phase I.   In phase II, the transaction coordinator receives the responses from the remote sites.   If there is a unanimous vote-commit, **T** is allowed to proceed; otherwise it is aborted.

The two-phase commit is a comparatively simple protocol. (Very few aspects of distributed systems are actually simple!) One shortcoming of the two-phase commit is that it does not prevent blocking. If a remote station fails during the transaction, then some recovery is possible. If the remote station fails before voting, the transaction coordinator can interpret a time-out as a vote-abort.   If the station fails after voting, the transaction coordinator may ascertain the current status by sending query-status messages to all stations and then aborting or rolling back actions based on the information received from the queries. Unfortunately, there is no recovery if the transaction coordinator fails. Thus blocking may occur until the transaction coordinator recovers.

[Korth 91] observes that a three-phase commit protocol may be used to prevent blocking. The extra phase is used to make a preliminary decision about **T**. This information is distributed to all participating stations. Thus if the transaction coordinator fails, the remote stations have enough information to make a commit or abort decision.

5.4 Fault tolerance in distributed systems

Fault tolerance is becoming more important in many areas of computer science. A fundamental attribute of distributed systems is the capacity to implement fault tolerance. We consider systems to be fault-tolerant if the system exhibits:

- The ability to accommodate noisy, incomplete, or erroneous inputs.

- A graceful degradation of outputs when a failure occurs.

- Resistance to errors caused by external sources.

- A capacity for responding to errors in the system's own design.

5.4.1 Definitions and terminology

[Johnson 89] provides a very useful introduction by defining the fault-error-failure hierarchy, as shown in Figure 5.14 and described below:

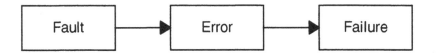

Figure 5.14. Relationship of faults, errors, and failures.

- **Fault**. A fault is a physical defect or flaw that occurs in either hardware or software. An example of a hardware fault is a short in the electrical circuitry. An example of a software fault is an infinite loop which cannot be terminated.

- **Error**. An error occurs when the fault becomes apparent. A software fault which initiates an infinite loop will not manifest itself as an error until the loop is entered.

- **Failure**. If the error results in the system performing one of its functions incorrectly then a system failure has occurred.

The importance of this hierarchy is that it implies the latency between each step. Considerable time may elapse before a fault becomes an error and an error becomes a failure. Fault latency is the time between the occurrence of a fault and an error. Error latency is the time between the appearance of an error and system failure. Again, consider the case of a non-exiting infinite loop fault embedded in the software code. If the code segment that contains the loop is never invoked, the fault will never appear as an error. When the loop is invoked, considerable time may elapse before the system fails or the error may be non-fatal and merely continue wasting system resources before it is terminated.

5.4.2 Error detection

The first step for any fault tolerant system is error detection. No recovery is possible if the system does not detect the error. Faults may be either hardware originated or software originated. Hardware faults may occur due to variances in manufacturing control tolerances, exceeding an environmental design parameter (such as maximum ambient air temperature), or acts of nature such as lightning strikes which generate a power surge. The errors produced by these faults may generate messages such as "device not available" or "parity error."

Hardware faults are more predictable than software faults. Many hardware devices have well-measured mean times between failure (MTBF). Such information provides the capability to increase monitoring when a MTBF expires.

Software faults are more subtle and more difficult to detect. Unlike hardware faults, they are generally unpredictable. Software faults, euphemistically called "bugs," occur because of some flaw(s) in the software engineering process.

5.4.3 Coping with errors

There are three strategies to defend against faults: fault avoidance, fault masking, and fault tolerance [Johnson 89]. Figure 15.15 illustrates their relationship with each other.

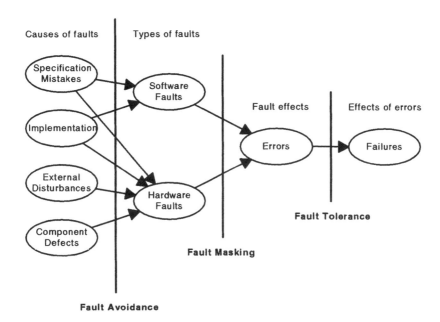

Figure 5.15. Fault avoidance, masking, and tolerance [Johnson 89].

- *Fault avoidance* attempts to prevent the occurrence of faults. The use of surge is one means of fault avoidance. Formally proving the correctness of a critical part of software is another example of fault avoidance.

- *Fault masking* prevents faults from introducing errors into the system. Voting among redundant modules allows a majority "vote" to mask the decision of a faulty module. An example of this is illustrated in Figure 5.16.

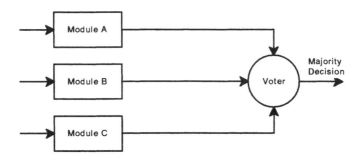

Figure 5.16. Redundant module voting.

- *Fault tolerance* allows a system to operate correctly after the occurrence of errors. Reconfiguration removes the faulty component and allows the system to continue to operate correctly, although possibly in a degraded mode. A successful reconfiguration requires the ability to detect, locate, and contain the faulty entity.

Fault avoidance, fault masking, and fault tolerance are not mutually exclusive, but rather, lend themselves to an integrated design strategy to increase reliability.

5.4.4 Implementing fault tolerance

In order for a system to continue correctly executing after the manifestation of errors it must have the capability to recognize the error and then identify and purge itself of the results of that error. A simple example of recovery is a parity error. Resetting the offending bit would be sufficient to correct the error. In a database system, an error may result in numerous erroneous transactions, all of which must be rolled back to return the system to an acceptable state. In some cases, the effects cannot be reversed, as in the case of hardware damage.

An error which destroys the key integrity of a database removes any ability to synchronize entries. Transactions following the manifestation of the fault cannot be reliably tracked. Barring the use of a secondary key (such as a time-stamp), the entire database must be considered unreliable without a complete rollback.

In order to implement fault tolerance, we must first locate the error and either remove it or make arrangements to operate correctly in spite of the error. Determining that a fault exists and determining the locus of the fault are distinct tasks with their own difficulties. Most fault tolerant systems employ mechanisms which record the pertinent system state variables, as well as the transactions which result in changes to these states. Back-tracking through system states to find the first state where the error occurred is often viable if the system's states were correctly specified beforehand. The transaction which caused the transition from the most recent error-free state to the subsequent states in which the error exists should provide insight as to the cause of the fault and thus contribute a necessary ingredient to its removal. If the error corrupts the state recording mechanism, the effectiveness of this strategy is diminished. Replicating the storage of state information often provides reasonable protection against loss.

Distributed systems are sufficiently complex that the causes of every fault cannot always be located and dispatched. In this case, and when it is impossible to shut down the system, some accommodation of the system in its erroneous state must be made. In general, this is accomplished through isolation of the module containing the fault, so that its effects will not further damage the system. In Figure 5.16, if one module is determined to be faulty, then the faulty module might be physically disconnected or logically disconnected.

5.5 Implementing distributed systems

Successfully implementing a distributed system requires expertise in many computer science disciplines. Good distributed systems require work in computer-human interaction, software engineering, networking, algorithm design, as well as an understanding of the mission and the organization to be supported.

5.5.1 Naming

Distributed systems are based on the sharing of resources. The names assigned to resources or objects must have global meanings that are independent of the locations of the object, and they must be supported by an interpretation system that can translate names in order to enable programs to access named resources. An issue is to design naming schemes that will scale adequately with respect to anticipated system size, and in which names are translated efficiently to meet appropriate goals for performance [Coulouris 94].

5.5.2 Load balancing

Load balancing is key to achieving efficient performance. Workloads may change dynamically. An overloaded processor may become a system bottleneck. In centralized systems, all processor and memory resources are readily available for allocation. The absence of readily accessible global state information makes load balancing difficult in a distributed system.

The first issue to be addressed in load balancing is whether the overhead cost of migrating processes is worth the gain in performance from distributing the workload. Overhead costs include both the movement of the process as well as the cost of gathering the data to make migration decisions. Particularly in a system with processors of varying capability, care must be taken to ensure that a less capable processor is not overloaded through a load balancing effort. It is difficult to compare workloads of different processors. Any load balancing scheme must select processes for migration and determine when and where to migrate them.

The formulation and application of metrics in a distributed system is a major research topic in its own right [Marti 95]. In order to successfully apply metrics, it is necessary to understand the purposes of the system. Load balancing should facilitate:

- *Acceptable performance* of the system under overloaded conditions.

- *Fairness of service* where acceptable performance is provided to all stations. (Based on the mission of the system, acceptable performance may vary considerably from station to station.)

- *Flexibility*, that is, the ability to continue to effectively balance loads in the face of dynamically reconfigured systems. Such reconfigured systems may be the result of recovery from a subsystem fault or simply a change in operations.

* *Minimal idle time*, maximizing processing while avoiding unacceptable delays.

5.6 Summary

Despite formidable challenges, multiprocessing and multicomputing systems are rapidly growing in capability and popularity. Hardware devices are approaching bounds imposed on them by physical laws. It is becoming increasingly difficult to increase the speed of a single processor. Therefore, parallel or distributed processing is advocated as a promising approach for building high-performance computing systems [Bhuyan 89].

As we have established in this chapter, the potential benefits of a distributed system outweigh the costs associated with increased complexity. Distributed systems can expand the availability of resources to more users. Resources can be shared among different users and different sites. Geographic distribution is an essential aspect of disaster recovery and limits the scope of the disaster. For most existing and proposed applications, it is practically impossible to predict future demands for the system. A major strength of distributed systems is their ability to accommodate additional disparate hardware resources. The attributes which make distributed systems attractive for enterprise networking also make them an attractive platform for simulation.

5.7 Exercises

5.1 Why might a computer architecture built on single data streams be unsuitable as a host for a distributed simulation?

5.2 What are the pros and cons of using a distributed operating system instead of a network operating system to support an enterprise-wide distributed system?

5.3   Why would a client/server model be preferable to simply distributing the appropriate resources to the client's local machine? When might this not be the case?

5.4   Can client/server models be implemented over systems that are not distributed? Why or why not?

5.5   Why are distributed databases more difficult to implement than a distributed file system?

5.6   Transactions may be ordered by time-stamping. Would ordering distributed database requests in time-stamp order obviate the need for commit protocols? Would it be useful to incorporate time-stamping into a commit protocol? Why or why not?

5.7   How serious are faults which do not manifest themselves as errors?

5.8   In this chapter we discussed hardware redundancy. Is software redundancy feasible? How could this be implemented?

5.8 References

[Babaoglu 93] O. Babaoglu and K. Marzullo, "Consistent global states of distributed systems: Fundamental concepts and mechanisms," in *Distributed Systems, 2e,* S. Mullender, ed., Addison-Wesley, Reading, MA, 1993.

[Baer 80] J. L. Baer, *Computer Systems Architecture*, Computer Science Press, Rockville, MD, 1980.

[Baker 94] R. H. Baker, *Networking the Enterprise*, McGraw-Hill, New York, NY, 1994.

[Beauchamp 82]   K. G. Beauchamp, *New Advances in Distributed Computer Systems*, D. Reidel Publishing, Boston, MA, 1982.

[Bhuyan 89]   L. N. Bhuyan, Q. Yang, and D. P. Agrawal, "Performance of multiprocessor interconnection networks," *IEEE Computer*, Vol. 22, No. 2, pp. 25 – 37, February 1989.

[Bloomer 91]   J. Bloomer, *Power Programming with RPC*, O'Reilly & Associates, Inc., Sebastopol, CA, 1991.

[Breslin 78]   J. Breslin and C. B. Tashenberg, *Distributed Processing System: End of the Mainframe Era*, Amacom, New York, NY, 1978.

[Casavant 91]   T. L. Casavant and M. Singhal, "Distributed computing systems," *IEEE Computer*, Vol. 24, No. 8, pp. 12 – 27, August 1991.

[Coulouris 94]   G. Coulouris, J. Dollimore, and T. Kindberg, *Distributed Systems, 2e*, Addison-Wesley, Reading, MA, 1994.

[Date 92]   C. J. Date and H. Darwin, *Relational Database Writings, 1989-1991*, Addison-Wesley, Reading, MA, 1992.

[Enslow 78]   P. H. Enslow, "What is a distributed system?," *IEEE Computer*, Vol. 11, No. 1, pp. 13 – 21, January 1978.

[Goscinski 91]   A. Goscinski, *Distributed Operating Systems*, Addison-Wesley, Sydney, Australia, 1991.

[Hwang 93]   K. Hwang, *Advanced Computer Architecture*, McGraw-Hill, New York, NY, 1993.

[Johnson 89]   B. W. Johnson, *Design and Analysis of Fault Tolerant Digital Systems*, Addison-Wesley, Reading, MA, 1989.

[Korth 91]   H. F. Korth and A. Silberschatz, *Database System Concepts, 2e*, McGraw-Hill, New York, NY, 1991.

[Lans 88]   R. F. van der Lans, *Introduction to SQL*, Addison-Wesley, Reading, MA, 1988.

[Maccabe 93] B. Maccabe, *Computer Systems*, Richard D. Irwin, Homewood, IL, 1993.

[Marti 95]   W. F. Marti, *Distributed System Performance Management and Metrics*, Ph.D. dissertation proposal, Texas A&M University, 1995.

[Rosenberry 92] W. Rosenberry, D. Kenney, and G. Fisher, *Understanding DCE*, O'Reilly & Associates, Inc., Sebastopol, CA, 1992.

[Satyanarayanan 93]   M. Satyanarayanan, "Distributed file systems," *Distributed Systems, 2e*, S. Mullender, ed., Addison-Wesley, Reading, MA, 1993.

[Smith 88] P. D. Smith and G. M. Barnes, *Files and Databases*, Addison-Wesley, Reading, MA, 1988.

[Sochats 92] K. Sochats and J. Williams, *The Networking and Communications Desk Reference*, Prentice-Hall, Carmel, IN, 1992.

[Stern 91]   H. Stern, *Managing NFS and NIS*, O'Reilly & Associates, Inc., Sebastopol, CA, 1991.

[Stevens 94]   W. R. Stevens, *TCP/IP Illustrated, Vol. 1*, Addison-Wesley, Reading, MA, 1994.

[Tanenbaum 90]   A. S. Tanenbaum, *Structured Computer Organization, 3e*, Prentice-Hall, Englewood Cliffs, NJ, 1990.

[Tanenbaum 96] A. S. Tanenbaum, *Computer Networks, 3d ed.*, Prentice-Hall, Englewood Cliffs, NJ, 1996.

[Taylor 95] S. J. E. Taylor, F. Fatin, and T. Deltaire, "Estimating the benefit of the parallelisation of discrete event simulation," *Proceedings of the 1995 Winter Simulation Conference*, Washington, DC, pp. 13 – 21, December 3 – 6, 1995.

[Umar 93]   A. Umar, *Distributed Computing*, Prentice-Hall, Englewood Cliffs, NJ, 1993.

6

The Object-Oriented Paradigm

Object-oriented methodologies are part of a paradigm shift that has been percolating in the software engineering community for many years. The long-term nature of software development and the extensive experience required to successfully develop software makes it difficult for any paradigm shift to occur suddenly. Nonetheless, object-oriented methodologies continue to gain momentum. Object design can support atomic actions and better recovery. A software product can be characterized as a model of the real world, a world that is constantly changing [Schach 93]. A strong case can be made that effective object-oriented modeling and implementation can greatly facilitate software maintenance. This is an enabling technology that allows software changes to keep pace with system changes.

Distributed computing is an area that offers significantly new and powerful capabilities at the cost of additional complexity. Now large distributed computing systems are becoming commonplace [Stankovic 94]. Object decomposition and modeling seem naturally suited for distributed computer systems. In the previous chapter, the importance of interfaces in a distributed system was discussed. The object-oriented paradigm fully supports the design of common interfaces for heterogeneous objects. Message passing and other interobject communication methods are fully supported.

In this chapter we will provide an overview of the object-oriented paradigm, common methodologies, how it is an outgrowth of discrete-event simulation, and then its applicability to distributed systems.

6.1 Fiction and fact almanac

The term "paradigm shift" is a consultant's best friend. The hype associated with object-oriented methods has exceeded the hype of structured techniques. The "software crisis," the inability of software development to keep pace with demand, has been well documented. Software products continue to be late, over budget, and deficient in meeting stated requirements. Modeling systems has been difficult because real-world systems do not directly map to current functional decomposition strategies. In a distributed system this is even more bothersome since functional decompositions do not easily lend themselves to implementation on a distributed system. Even in a distributed problem domain such as a neural net, a functional decomposition is unlikely to produce an easy mapping to a distributed design.

Software engineering is a discipline which overlaps and is intertwined with simulation. Implementing a simulation model on a computer is a specialized application of software engineering. Figure 6.1 shows a simple relationship between simulation and software engineering. The iterative nature of the process is noted by the bi-directional arrows.

System modeling is the key to simulation design. Modeling is directly related to the software engineering design phase. Hence, object-oriented analysis and design techniques are of interest to both the simulation designer and the software engineer.

Compared to the more traditional functional decomposition methods, object-oriented methodologies make it easier to decompose a problem in which the design and the implementation more closely resemble the real-world problem domain. An implementation in which the computer-oriented structures are closely tied to real-world-oriented structures is inherently easier to maintain. Any worthwhile system will be changed – both during development and after deployment. If the implementation resembles the real-world system, many of the changes can be anticipated or at least made in a manner consistent with the real-world change. Conveniently, not only does the object-oriented paradigm support real world modeling, it also supports partitioning and allocation across multiple processors.

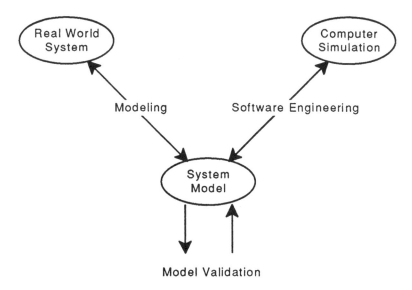

Figure 6.1. Relationship between modeling and implementation.

No one can deny the continued impact that the object-oriented paradigm is having across the broad spectrum of computer science. Support for object-oriented programming (OOP) is becoming an absolute requirement for many programming languages. Interestingly, some projects specifically require the use of an OOP but then do not bother to use an object-oriented methodology. Other projects have used object-oriented analysis (OOA) and object-oriented design (OOD) methods and then implemented the design in a language with only limited object-oriented support. Despite some fitful starts, however, the object-oriented paradigm has continued to gather momentum. Enough major software projects have been built using object-oriented methodologies to ensure that object-oriented methods continue to be a major part of 21st-century software engineering.

6.2 Definition of terms

The term "object-oriented" is used in many contexts. System life-cycle activities of interest are:

- object-oriented analysis (OOA)

- object-oriented design (OOD)

- object-oriented programming (OOP)

Increasingly, OOA and OOD are seamlessly integrated and are often referred to as object-oriented analysis and design (OOAD). There exists an entire alphabet soup associated with the object-oriented paradigm. Object-oriented environments, object-oriented graphical user interfaces, object-oriented databases, and a seemingly never ending list of applications and techniques which can have "object-oriented" added as a prefix. Some OO labels have been applied more correctly than others [Lawlis 92]. We will confine ourselves to defining the software life-cycle and development aspects of the object-oriented paradigm.

Basic Terms:

Class – description of a collection of like "things" (objects), including their structure and behavior; description of a set of objects that share a common structure and a common behavior [Booch 91]. Classes provide a template which includes a set of attributes and a set of services (*methods* or *operations*).

There are two general types of classes: classes of instances and classes of classes (sometimes called *meta-classes*). Meta-classes have members which also must be classes. A class of computer workstations could be composed of subclasses of workstations such as DEC Alpha, RS6000, or Sun SPARC types (class of classes). A class of Sun SPARCs would have instances of individual workstations named Luke, Yoda, and Lando (class of instances).

Instance — description of a particular member of a class (object). The term object is sometimes used with the same meaning, but some authors extend the definition of object. We prefer using *instance* because it is less ambiguous. An instance assumes all characteristics of the class unless specifically overridden and has a "state" defined by the information known about it (specific values of its attributes). Instance example: A Macintosh IIcx is not an instance of a class of computers (it's a subclass). A specific Mac named Deathstar is an instance of a Macintosh IIcx model computer. Each instance has a unique identity. An instance (object) has identity, state (determined by the values of its attributes), and behavior. The structure and behavior of similar objects are defined in their common class. Any number of Mac IIcxs may be instantiated. In such a case each instance will have its own unique state information. It is possible for a class or subclass to have only one instance.

Attributes — definition of the structure of the data in a class or instance; some data or state information for which each instance of a class has its own value. This is similar in nature to the attributes of a database entity. Usually fields of a record define the structure of the class (a data structure definition). Attribute example:

```
type printer is
    record
        Speed               :pages_per_minute;
        Resolution          :dots_per_inch;
        Memory              :megabytes;
        Paper               :boolean;
    end record;
```

Behavior – description of the actions and reactions of classes and instances. Behavior is how an object acts and reacts, in terms of its state changes and message passing. Behaviors are often implemented by procedure or function calls. An object sends a message to a service (its own service or that of another object) to trigger an action. The service which responds to the message may take one or more of the following actions:

Examine the state of the object to which it belongs (one or more attributes).

Change the state of the object to which it belongs (one or more attributes).

Trigger another message to another service.

Behavior example: A procedure call is made to the service, which prepares a file for printing and dispatches that file to the printer. That is, a message is sent from some other object and received by the printer object. A check is made to ensure that the printer has paper. The state of the object is examined via a call to a service of the object (call to a boolean function.) The file is printed. The printer's paper count is decremented, changing the state of the object.

Relationships – description of organization or structure among classes and instances (including *inheritance*). Relationships describe how classes and objects relate to one another. They demonstrate that an object is an instance of a particular class. Relationships can show that a class or object depends on another class or object in order to accomplish its behavior. Two relationships of particular importance are the whole-part relationship and the generalization-specialization relationship. We will discuss each of these in more detail later in this chapter.

Programming languages such as Ada 95 and Smalltalk are referred to as "object-oriented programming languages." To be considered an object-oriented language, the language needs to support abstraction, encapsulation, inheritance, and polymorphism.

Abstraction is the ability to separate objects and operations on those objects. Abstraction is a key concept in any modeling or design effort. The system designer concentrates on the essential aspects of an entity and is not concerned with unimportant properties. A high-fidelity simulation of automobile traffic is not likely to model an automobile's cigarette lighter because it is unlikely to have a major impact upon traffic patterns. Hence the model automobile is an abstraction that includes only the characteristics necessary to ensure fidelity with the real-world system.

Encapsulation is the process of hiding an object's internal implementation details while providing an external interface which is accessible to other objects. One way to look at encapsulation is in terms of *coupling* and *cohesion*. Cohesion refers to the degree of interaction within an object. Coupling is the degree of interaction between objects. Encapsulation keeps related content together; it minimizes traffic between different parts of the work; and it separates certain specified requirements from other parts of the specification that may use those requirements [Coad 91a].

Inheritance allows new abstractions to acquire properties from existing abstractions. Inheritance is a generalization-specialization relationship. Inheritance is a relationship among classes wherein one class shares the structure and/or behavior defined in one (single inheritance) or more (multiple inheritance) other classes. In an inheritance relationship, the specialized classes have many of the same attributes and services as their superclasses (parent classes), but they can also extend these attributes and/or extend the services.

Figure 6.2 illustrates a general class of passenger vehicles. We can specialize the general class into classes of specific models such as minivans, pickup trucks, and sedans. These models can

be further specialized into specific makes such as a Dodge
Caravan or Ford Aerostar which can inherit attributes from the
minivans class. An example of multiple inheritance, where the
class of Caravans inherits from both the trucks class and the
minivans class, is shown in Figure 6.3.

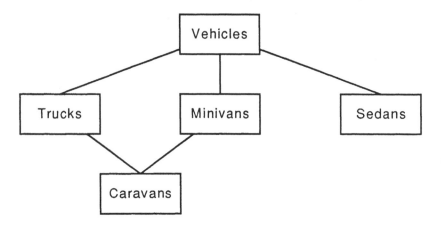

Figure 6.2. Multiple inheritance example.

Polymorphism means to have many forms. In terms of
object-oriented programming languages, it refers to the ability for
a language construct to assume differing types or to interface with
objects assuming different types. *Parametric polymorphism* uses
types as parameters in generic type definitions [Khosh 90].

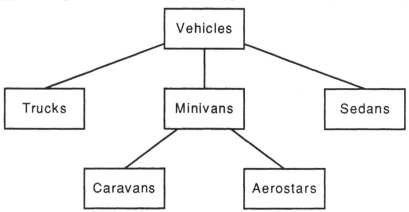

Figure 6.3. Single inheritance example.

Overloading is another form of polymorphism. An overloaded operator can be applied to a different type. For example, an overloaded "+" operator may be applied to integers and then applied to floating point numbers.

6.3 Classic object-oriented methodologies

We have chosen four of the representative methods to consider in some detail. The first three methods, authored by Booch, Coad and Yourdon, and Rumbaugh *et al*, are currently among the most popular used and cover analysis, design, and implementation. The Rubin and Goldberg method takes a significantly different approach. It is important to note that we are providing only a very brief overview of each author's method.

6.3.1 Booch

Grady Booch, a distinguished graduate of and later faculty member at the Air Force Academy, is a leading object-oriented expert and author. His earlier works used Ada83 as an exemplar implementation language [Booch 87]. By all accounts, Ada83 is at best an object-based language which supports abstract data type design but lacks support for inheritance and polymorphism [Ada 95]. However, as Booch noted in his address to the 1995

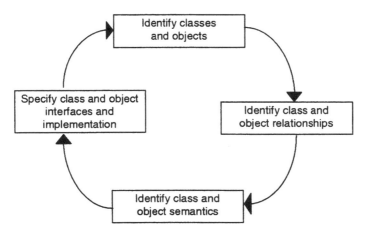

Figure 6.4. Booch's micro-development process.

Software Technology Conference, Ada95 provides full support for object-oriented methodologies.

Booch has been improving his process and method since 1980. He observes that two traits are present in virtually all successful object-oriented systems. First, is the existence of a strong architectural vision. Second is the application of a well-managed iterative and incremental development life cycle [Booch 94]. The guidance given for the micro-development process is:

- Identify the classes and objects at a given level of abstraction.

- Identify the semantics of these classes and objects.

- Identify the relationships among these classes and objects.

- Implement these classes and objects.

Step 1: Identify Classes and Objects

Discover the key abstractions in the problem space through a domain analysis. This is done by:

- Learning the vocabulary of the problem domain.

- Determining the tangible things in the problem domain.

- Determining the roles they play.

- Determining the events that may occur.

Booch advocates the use of CRC (class, responsibility, collaboration) cards throughout the process. CRC cards are simply index cards listing a class, the responsibilities of the class, and the collaborators of the class. CRC cards can support the abstraction process as candidate classes and objects are identified.

The primary product from this step is a data dictionary which Booch describes as a "central repository for the abstractions relevant to the system."

Step 2: Identify the Semantics

The purpose of this step is to establish the meaning of the classes and objects identified from the previous step. This is done to determine the behavior and attributes of the classes and objects. Interfaces become a critical concern. If Ada is the implementation language, it is at this stage that the package specifications are developed.

One useful technique is to write a script for each object, identifying its life cycle from creation to termination, including its characteristic behaviors. The ubiquitous CRC cards can be used for informal story boarding. More formal scripting may use object diagrams or interaction diagrams. In this step the emphasis is on behavior, not structure.

Step 3: Identify the Relationships

Once behavior is identified, the next step is to determine the relationships among classes and objects. This is done by establishing exactly how things interact within the system. Patterns among classes which permit re-organization and simplification of the class structure are sought. Visibility decisions are made at this time. The end result of this step is the production of class diagrams, object diagrams, and module diagrams.

Step 4: Implementing Classes and Objects

This is an iterative process. As classes and objects are refined, other classes and objects may be identified. This will provide additional new inputs for the micro-development process. Classes and objects are allocated to modules, and programs to processors. At this point the design process is often repeated, this time focusing on a lower level of abstraction. At any level of design, a leap is often required to lower level key abstractions and mechanisms upon which higher level classes and objects are composed.

It should be noted that Booch has published a detailed notation to create the class diagrams, object diagrams, state transition diagrams, and module diagrams needed to support the above methods.

6.3.2 Coad and Yourdon

Peter Coad and Ed Yourdon are distinguished computer scientists who have made many contributions to the field both separately and together. Coad and Yourdon have published *Object-Oriented Analysis* [Coad 91b] and *Object-Oriented Design* [Coad 91a]. Although defined separately, their method is consistent to include notation between OOA and OOD.

6.3.2.1 Coad and Yourdon's object-oriented analysis

Their OOA strategies consist of the following steps:

- Find classes-&-objects.

- Identify structures.

- Identify subjects.

- Define attributes.

- Define services.

1. Find Classes-&-Objects

Naming conventions are important. It is best to use a singular noun or adjective and noun. Adhere to the standard vocabulary for the problem domain. This can only lessen confusion when striving for a high-fidelity representation and ease of later maintenance.

Classes and objects are derived by observing firsthand the system to be modeled and actively listening to the system operators. Secondary sources include previous OOA results, related systems, manuals, regulations, procedures, after action, reports and organizational charts. Prototyping can be used to move to more detailed levels of abstraction, discover additional required classes and objects, and then return to a higher level of abstraction.

2. Identify Structures

Recall the earlier discussion of generalization-specialization structures (inheritance). Whole-part relationships occur when a set of classes or objects are a part of another class or object. For example, as shown in Figure 6.5, we can define a vehicle class. Engine, wheels, and body are the parts of the whole vehicle. Similarly, wheels can also be a whole structure made up of rims and tires as parts.

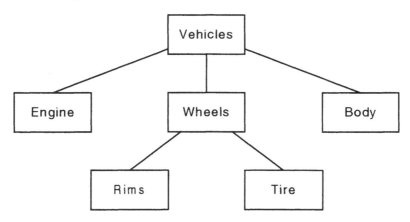

Figure 6.5. Whole-part hierarchy example.

3. Identify Subjects

A subject is a mechanism for guiding a reader (analyst, problem domain expert, manager, client) through a large, complex model. The root class in a structured hierarchy is selected as a subject. Problem subdomains, minimal interdependencies, and minimal interactions are used to refine the subjects. Subjects may be collapsed, partially expanded, and fully expanded. In Figure 6.6 is an example of expanded subject notation showing one layer. The Class symbol is used to represent a generalization class from the public domain whose corresponding objects are portrayed by its specializations, Class-&-Object symbols [Coad 91a]. The Class-&-Object symbol represents a class and its object.

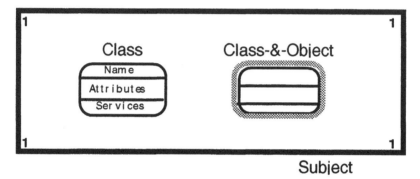

Figure 6.6. Subject notation example.

4. Define Attributes

An attribute is some data for which each object in a class has its own value. Ideally, attributes capture an atomic concept. Each attribute requires a name, description, and constraints. That captured atomic concept is either a single value or a tightly related grouping of values. Each attribute should have a defined range and be assigned to the class-&-object it best describes.

5. Define Services

A service is a specific behavior of an object. Typical services might include: create, connect, access, release, calculate, monitor.

6.3.2.2 Coad and Yourdon's object-oriented design

Coad and Yourdon describe four elements to their OOD strategy:

- Designing the problem domain component.

- Designing the human interaction component.

- Designing the task management component.

- Designing the data management component.

1. Designing the problem domain component

The problem domain design starts with the results of the OOA process. Coad and Yourdon recommend the following strategy to design the problem domain [Coad 91a].

- Apply OOA.

- Use OOA results – and improve them during OOD.

- Use OOA results – and add to them during OOD.

It should be noted that this does not mark the end of the analysis. Iteration is necessary since analysis is an ongoing process.

2. Designing the human interaction component

Software writers do not always interact with their products in the same manner as the projected users. During OOA, the following steps are taken:

- Classify the humans.

- Describe the humans and their task scenarios.

- Design the command hierarchy.

- Continue to prototype.

- Design the human interaction component.

• Design, accounting for graphical user interfaces (GUIs) (when applicable).

The purpose of this design step is to build on the lessons learned during OOA and to design the interaction specifics which support positive user reaction.

3. Designing the task management component

Task is another name for process. As Coad and Yourdon state, separate tasks separate behaviors that must take place concurrently. The recommended strategy for selecting and justifying tasks is:

• Identify event-driven tasks.

• Identify clock-driven tasks.

• Identify priority tasks and critical tasks.

• Identify a coordinator.

• Challenge each task.

• Define each task.

Task definition consists of naming and describing the task; determining whether it is clock-driven or event-driven; and determining how it communicates.

4. Designing the data management component

Coad and Yourdon cover the three major data management schemes:

• Flat file: with basic sorting and file handling capabilities.

- Relational: a table-driven system with atomic values represented in its cells.

- Object-oriented: generally one of two emerging strategies. Either a relational database extended to support inheritance, abstract data types and some services to handle objects or classes, or object-oriented programming languages augmented with database capabilities.

Coad and Yourdon also have developed a thorough notation to support their methodology. Component notations may be expanded or collapsed as necessary to represent the appropriate level of abstraction. Templates are included for class-&-object specification. State transition diagrams are used within the templates to show behavior. Flow chart style notation is used to chart services.

6.3.3 Rumbaugh, Blaha, Premerlani, Eddy, and Lorensen

The authors developed their method at the General Electric Research and Development Center in Schenectady, New York [Rumbaugh 91]. This is a combinative approach, using three different familiar models and then defining a method for integration. The three models used in this approach are:

- Object model – a variation of entity-relationship diagrams.

- Dynamic model – a variation of state transition diagrams.

- Functional model – a variation of data flow diagrams.

This has intuitive appeal for those who have learned to use the models in other contexts. However, the trade-off is that there is a tendency to proceed with the previous models without bothering to make a paradigm shift.

The object modeling technique has three primary phases: analysis, system design, and object design. As with the previous models, this is an iterative process in which more details are added to the model at successively lower levels of abstraction. Subsystems can be designed independently and concurrently at lower levels of abstraction.

Analysis Phase

The goal of analysis is to build a correct and comprehensible model of the real world. Needs of users, developers, and managers provide the information needed to develop the initial problem statement. User interviews, domain knowledge, and experience are used to build models in terms of objects and relationships, dynamic control flow, and functional transformations. Once the initial problem is defined, then the following steps are taken:

- Build an object model to include object model diagrams and a data dictionary.

- Develop a dynamic model to include state diagrams and global event flow diagrams.

- Construct a functional model to include data flow diagrams and constraints.

- Verify, iterate, and refine the three models.

As noted in other methodologies, there is no absolute dividing line between analysis and design. The desired goal of analysis is to specify the problem and application domains without bias.

System Design Phase

During the analysis phase emphasis is on identifying what needs to be done. Design concentrates on how to get things done. In general, the following steps need to occur in any system design:

- Organize the system into subsystems.

- Identify concurrency inherent in the problem.

- Allocate subsystems to processors and tasks.

- Choose the basic strategy for implementing data stores.

- Handle access to global resources.

- Choose an approach to implementing software control.

- Consider boundary conditions.

- Establish trade-off priorities.

- The resulting architecture forms the high-level structure of the system.

Object Design Phase

The object design phase defines the classes, interfaces, and associations used in the implementation. In Rumbaugh's methodology, the following steps are part of the object design.

- Obtain operations for the object model from the other models.

- Design algorithms to implement operations.

- Optimize access paths to data.

- Implement software control for external interactions.

- Adjust class structure to increase inheritance.

- Design implementation of associations.

- Determine the exact representation of object attributes.

- Package classes and associations into modules.

As might be expected, this is also an iterative process. Operations from the functional and dynamic models must be transferred to the object model. The object design provides the detailed basis for the implementation.

There are three notations, one for each model:

1. Object model notation: A variation of entity-relationship diagrams. It includes generalization (inheritance), aggregation, associations, and ordering. The object modeling notation is designed to represent large complex systems. It is an inherent part of the object modeling technique. Naturally the notation provides full support for the methodology

2. Dynamic model notation: Based on Harel's state charts [Harel 87].

It is a special form of state transition diagrams which avoids the problems of flat diagrams. Rumbaugh *et al* give the following example: an automated teller machine may want to split control and then re-synchronize control. After dispensing cash, the machine does not want to reset until the customer has retrieved both his cash and his card. The order in which the customer accomplishes these actions is unpredictable. In more complex applications, control may be split into multiple threads of control. Each thread of control may have more than one intervening substate, as illustrated in Figure 6.7.

3. Functional model notation: Based on data flow diagrams. *Data flow diagrams*, or DFDs, are a standard method to represent the functional relationships of the values computed by a system. A DFD typically includes transactions or processes, the data stores, the actors that produce and utilize data, and the data flows themselves.

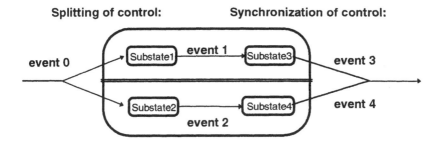

Figure 6.7. Sample dynamic model notation [Rumbaugh 91].

6.3.4 Rubin and Goldberg

Adele Goldberg was an early pioneer of the object-oriented paradigm, noted for her work with Smalltalk among other things. Rubin and Goldberg published their "Object behavior analysis" (OBA) in 1992 [Rubin 92].

Rubin and Goldberg note several truisms about OOA. In large systems you cannot assume a formal and correct requirements specification exists. Conceptual objects can be just as important as tangible objects, but much harder to capture. Some tangible objects may not require separate representation in a computer-based system.

As the name indicates, OBA is a behavioral approach to OOA. Rather than first defining the objects, the analyst first understands the system behaviors. Traceability across all steps is a major objective of this process. OBA is a 5-step process.

Step 0: Set the analysis context

As would be expected, this initial step provides the basis for the entire analysis. Goals and objectives, as well as appropriate resources, for analysis are identified. The major parts of the system, the core activity areas, which require analysis are identified. Completing the previous substeps allows for the generation of a preliminary analysis plan.

Step 1: Understand the problem

This is the mission analysis step of the process. The objective is to determine what the system is supposed to do and for whom and with whom it is supposed to do it. The first substep, scenario planning, consists of choosing the major scenarios. Mapping the scenarios to core activity areas is next. Scripting of the scenarios is accomplished next. Scripts are designed to capture the information needed to define a sequence of service requests in order to accomplish some overall task. Terminology defined in the scripting process is used to build glossaries to support traceability. The final substep is deriving attributes for each party in the scripts. This is done by examining scripts for initiator and participant attributes. Attribute glossaries are then generated.

Step 2: Define objects

In this step, the data that has been collected is organized. Object modeling cards are generated. Object modeling cards are adapted CRC cards with expanded information content. The following actions lead to the development of the object modeling cards (Figure 6.8):

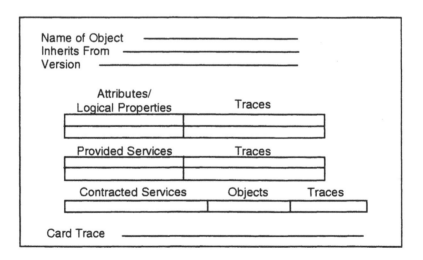

Figure 6.8. Object modeling card example.

- Determine different types of objects.

- Accumulate attributes.

- Accumulate provided services.

- Accumulate contracted services.

Step 3: Classify objects and identify relationships

This step allows the completion of the object modeling cards. Contracted services are described in order to derive relationships between objects and to ensure that responsibility for services is assigned. Objects are organized into hierarchies by choosing organizing principles, determining abstractions and specializations, and generating/updating a reorganization table.

Step 4: Model system dynamics

This step of the OBA is concerned with modeling those parts of a system which change over time. The steps include:

- Generating state definition glossaries, which determine states associated with each object, and defining those states.

- Determining object life cycles by identifying events and organizing them into a life cycle.

- Determining the sequencing of operations.

Specific notation tools are:

- Object modeling cards (see Figure 6.8).

- Object relationship diagrams: Essentially a hierarchical organization chart.

- System and object life cycle diagrams: Harel's [Harel 87].

Rubin and Goldberg attempt to define what happens and what terminology is used in table form. A script captures each action, what initiates it, what participates in it, and what service must be provided to accomplish it. In addition to a definition, a glossary captures such information as traces (for traceability), roles, and participants.

6.3.5 Classifying object-oriented methods

Many object-oriented methodologies have been developed. Monarchi and Puhr listed twenty-three methods in their study of object-oriented research typology [Monarchi 92]. Booch, Coad and Yourdon, and Rumbaugh *et al.* were selected because their methods are among the most complete. Some methods, such as the highly respected work by Shlaer and Mellor, concentrate on particular aspects such as OOA [Shlaer 92]. Rubin and Goldberg was selected because it is a very different approach [Lawlis 92]. Methods tend to be tightly coupled with software tools. The quality of the tools can affect the perceived quality of the method. Additionally, all of the major methods continue to undergo improvements and refinements. It would be inappropriate and misleading to attempt to rank order the various methods. However, it should be noted that Booch, Coad and Yourdon, and Rumbaugh *et al.* all cover the four critical components of an object-oriented methodology: OOA process, OOD process, representations, and complexity management [Lawlis 92].

Table 6.1 Critical component summary.

	Booch	**Coad & Yourdon**	**Rumbaugh** *et al*	**Rubin & Goldberg**
OOA Process	X	X	X	X
OOD Process	X	X	X	
Representations	X	X	X	X
Complexity management	some	some	some	

Monarchi and Puhr detail the specific aspects of each critical component [Monarchi 92]. [Lawlis 92] adds Rubin and Goldberg. All of the above methods provide good OOA coverage. Booch, Rumbaugh *et al.,* and Rubin and Goldberg are noted for their handling of dynamic behaviors and their placement of behaviors. Coad and Yourdon as well as Rubin and Goldberg cover the placement of classes and attributes.

All four methods provide good coverage of representation issues. Using Monarchi and Puhr's typology, Booch covers all representation issues. Coad and Yourdon do not fully cover dynamic behavior. Rubin and Goldberg do not cover aggregation. Booch, Coad and Yourdon, and Rumbaugh *et al.* address the structural component of complexity management, but do not address behavioral complexity.

Time and space constraints do not permit us to address the many other important methods. Comparison and contrast of these methods is difficult. As object-oriented methodologies mature, it is becoming clear that integrating these methodologies into the software development process is the next challenge. Whether using a "pure" object-oriented strategy or an adaptive strategy, the important question is not what method but rather how do we integrate the method.

6.4 Applying O-O designs to distributed systems

A distributed system can be modeled in terms of objects and threads [Martin 94]. In this context we view an object as a set of defined states, a current state, and a set of operations.

Two approaches to concurrency in object-based languages are defined in [Kramer 94]:

- The *thread model of concurrency* (multiple threads of execution within an object).

- The *active object model of concurrency* (the objects themselves are considered active but sequential).

The active object model of concurrency restricts the grain of concurrency to coincide with an object. The thread model of concurrency permits objects to create new threads of execution by invoking commands such as cobegin .. coend. Kramer, Magee, Sloman, and Dulay [Kramer 94] note that "Each thread can in turn send messages to invoke methods on other server objects, which could themselves introduce further concurrency − thereby forming a 'tree' of execution threads through objects."

Modularity is a fundamental principle of software engineering. The object-oriented paradigm provides major support for modular design. In order to define object interfaces, it is important that object behavior is defined as services required and services provided. In a distributed system, object interfaces can be defined as the set of typed ports representing the methods that the object provides and the set of typed remote port references representing the methods required from other objects.

In Martin, Pedersen, and Bedford-Roberts' taxonomy [Martin 94], threads of control are defined to impose a partial ordering of events in the distributed computing system. Objects in and of themselves have no inherent notion of time. The top level decomposition is made in three parts: threads, object properties, and separation. A thread of control is an execution series predefined by the programmer. When more than one thread is executing at the same time, we call these *concurrent* threads.

Object properties are defined for objects in isolation. Martin, Pedersen, and Bedford-Roberts define the following object properties:

Persistent − A persistent object does not depend on a thread for its existence.

Restorable – A restorable object can have prior states restored under programmer control.

Replicated – A replicated object has multiple copies in the system that a client object can identify as a single object.

Partitioned – An object is partitioned if the object's state and methods are on different nodes in the system.

Protected – Services that allow owners to selectively protect their objects from other users.

Existent – Creation and destruction of objects.

Separation is the trade-off between optimal integration of interacting objects and the flexibility achieved through non-integration. Separation encompasses identification, communication, partial failures, migration, and heterogeneity.

OOA and OOD techniques seem intuitively natural for modeling a distributed system. However, it must be noted that few programming languages provide natural support for both the object-oriented paradigm and the specific requirements of a distributed system. Object-oriented language design does not address failure transparency nor such techniques as replication and migration transparency [Wegner 92]. Future language designers need to be aware of both the transparency concerns of distributed systems as well as the abstraction needs of OOA and OOD software design methods.

Few vendors will admit to selling anything but an "open" system. However, the phrase "open system" is almost as abused and overused as "object-oriented." An accepted definition for an open system is a system with behavior that can be easily modified and extended. Openness can be achieved dynamically through reactiveness or statically through modularity [Wegner 92]. A reactive (interactive) system can react to stimuli by modifying its state and emitting a response. A modular (encapsulated) system is one in which the number of components and/or functionality can be statically extended by an external agent. Most flexible open systems are both reactive and modular. Since object-oriented systems are both reactive and modular, they are considered strongly open.

6.5 Summary

The object-oriented paradigm is not really new. Many of these concepts were being discussed by the Simula community nearly thirty years ago. Object-oriented modeling concepts make it possible for software developers to communicate better with the customer. Timothy Budd of Oregon State University observes that in an object-oriented program, the various entities in the universe are described, as well as how they will interact with one another, and then set in motion. This is similar to the methodology long used in discrete-event simulation.

Budd writes, [Budd 91]

> In brief, in a discrete event simulation, the user creates computer models of the various elements of the simulation, describes how they will interact with one another, and sets them moving. This is almost identical to the average object-oriented program, in which the user describes what the various entities in the universe for the program are, and how they will interact with one another and finally sets them in motion. Thus in object-oriented programming we have the view that computation is simulation.

In this chapter we have defined the basic terminology of the object-oriented paradigm. We have surveyed four of the major mainstream object-oriented methodologies. Finally we have shown that the object-oriented paradigm is directly related to discrete event simulation and the natural analysis and design method for modeling distributed computing systems.

6.6 Exercises

6.1   Consider the O-O methodologies of Coad and Yourdon, Booch, and Rumbaugh *et al.* Which one if any is more suited for developing a distributed application and why?

6.2   What are the pros and cons of allowing multiple inheritance in a distributed system?

6.3   Why are software methodologies important in the design and implementation of a distributed simulation?

6.4   In Chapter 4 the importance of interface design in a distributed system was discussed. Discuss interface design in the context of the object-oriented paradigm.

6.5   Compare and contrast multilevel generalization-specialization structures with multilevel single inheritance structures.

6.6   What criteria would you establish to determine when to transition from analysis to design?

6.7   When and why is polymorphism desirable?

6.7 References

[Ada 95] *Ada 95 Rationale*, Intermetrics, Cambridge, MA, 1995.

[Booch 87]   G. Booch, *Software Components with Ada*, Benjamin/ Cummings, Menlo Park, CA, 1987.

[Booch 91]   G. Booch, *Object-Oriented Design*, Benjamin/Cummings, Menlo Park, CA, 1991.

[Booch 94] G. Booch, *Object-Oriented Analysis and Design*, Benjamin/ Cummings, Menlo Park, CA, 1994.

[Budd 91]   T. Budd, *Object-Oriented Programming*, Addison-Wesley, Reading, MA, 1991.

[Coad 91a] P. Coad and E. Yourdon, *Object-Oriented Design*, Prentice-Hall, Englewood Cliffs, NJ, 1991.

[Coad 91b] P. Coad and E. Yourdon, *Object-Oriented Analysis*, Prentice-Hall, Englewood Cliffs, NJ, 1991.

[Harel 87]   D. Harel, "Statecharts: A visual formation for complex systems," *Science of Computer Programming*, Vol. 8, No. 3, pp. 231–274, June 1987.

[Khosh 90] S. Khoshafian and R. Abnous, *Object Orientation*, John Wiley & Sons, New York, NY, 1990.

[Kramer 94] J. Kramer, J. Magee, M. Sloman, and N. Dulay, "Configuring object-based distributed programs in Rex," in *Readings in Distributed Computing Systems*, IEEE Computer Society Press, Los Alamitos, CA, 1994.

[Lawlis 92]   P. K. Lawlis and J. A. Hamilton, Jr., *Object-Oriented Concepts Tutorial*, presented at the US Army Computer Science School, Fort Gordon, GA, November 1992.

[Martin 94]   B. E. Martin, C. H. Pedersen, and J. Bedford-Roberts, "An object-based taxonomy for distributed computing systems," in *Readings in Distributed Computing Systems*, IEEE Computer Society Press, Los Alamitos, CA, 1994.

[Monarchi 92] D. Monarchi and G. Puhr, "A research typology for object-oriented analysis and design," *Communications of the ACM*, Vol. 35, No. 9, pp. 35 – 47, September 1992.

[Rubin 92]   K. S. Rubin and A. Goldberg, "Object behavior analysis," *Communications of the ACM*, Vol. 35, No. 9, pp. 48 – 57, September 1992.

[Rumbaugh 91] J. Rumbaugh, M. Blaha, W. Premerlani, F. Eddy, and W. Lorensen, *Object-Oriented Modeling and Design*, Prentice-Hall, Englewood Cliffs, NJ, 1991.

[Schach 93] S. R. Schach, *Software Engineering, 2nd ed.*, Aksen Associates, Homewood, IL, 1993.

[Shlaer 92] S. Shlaer and S. Mellor, *Object Life Cycles – Modeling the World in States*, Prentice-Hall, Englewood Cliffs, NJ, 1992.

[Stankovic 94] J. A. Stankovic, "Distributed computing," in *Distributing Computing Systems*, IEEE Computer Society Press, Los Alamitos, CA, 1994.

[Wegner 92] P. Wegner, "Dimensions of object-oriented modeling," *IEEE Computer*, Vol. 25, No. 10, pp. 15 – 18, October 1992.

7

Resolution in Simulation

Resolution in simulation is a question of *detail* and is closely related to *fidelity*. Fidelity is a measure of how closely the simulation approximates the real world [Bailey 92]. We can bound our notion of fidelity by defining perfect fidelity as a simulation that is indistinguishable from reality. Advances in virtual reality demonstrate that perfect fidelity may be achieved for some systems. A generalized means for achieving perfect fidelity in non-trivial simulations is still in the realm of science fiction.

On the other end of the spectrum, the Ptolemaic model of the solar system bears little relation to the actual solar system. Models with zero fidelity may occasionally and incidentally appear useful, but generally are not. A weather prediction model that predicts "it will either rain or not rain in College Station on November 28th" is of little use. We would consider such a model to be of low resolution although it can be determined that this prediction perfectly approximates the real world. The information may be accurate, but insufficiently detailed to be useful. A more typical weather forecast, "there is a 90% chance of rain in College Station on November 28th," is certainly useful for a bicycle commuter. An aviator (or aviatrix) would want a considerably more detailed forecast before flying. Artillerymen will often launch their own weather balloons because they need detailed information about winds.

This brings us to the major component of resolution, the level of detail that the simulation can input and output. If a combat model could input, process, and output information concerning individual soldiers, the resolution could be substantially increased. Whether the fidelity of such a model would be increased is dependent upon the validity of the additional detail and the ability of the simulation to process the additional detail.

We increase fidelity when we increase the resolution of a *valid* model. Adding invalid detail does not increase the fidelity of the model and may seriously degrade fidelity. Generally, the simulation builder strives to minimize resolution and maximize fidelity. Resolution which does not increase fidelity merely adds computational complexity. In this chapter we will explore several different views of resolution and fidelity.

7.1 Resolution, fidelity, and model simplification

Simplifying a model without loss of fidelity is a desirable objective. Simpler models are computationally less expensive, are easier to validate, and their implementations easier to verify. As noted in Chapter 5, validation is a difficult problem and some simulations defy mathematically rigorous validation. Often users will want to substitute resolution for validation. Face validity is hard to apply to a large complex simulation. Therefore it is natural for the users to want increased detail in order to see if small parts of the simulation are working correctly. Col. Archie D. Andrews (ret.), who produced theater-level combat models at the Army War College, made the following observations:

> When I was building Theater War Game models I was often asked for the capability to "zoom in" and examine a small section of the battle. Since I was using a Lanchester model that was, of course, impossible. I also felt the only reason the commander might want to do that was to gain confidence that the model was representing the truth. Since my models were representing the probability of a happening, the absolute truth was hard to find and impossible to display [Andrews 93].

The proper objective for the simulation designer is to eliminate details that do not enhance fidelity. Further, the simulation designer must be cognizant of the requirement for resolution. Unwanted detail merely adds expense at every step of the process.

7.1.1 Simplification

It is a common modeling strategy to hold some factors constant while studying the interactions and reactions of other factors. Exact models of non-trivial systems would be too complex to comprehend and are computationally infeasible. The simplification strategy chosen is dependent upon the view of the problem at hand. [Innis 83] classifies model simplification in terms of brevity, clarity, and efficiency. Figure 7.1 shows the design of a high-resolution International Organization for Standardization (ISO) open systems interconnection (OSI)-based model of a computer network. Although all computer networks have essentially the same functionality specified in the OSI model, implementations vary considerably. Let us examine an example of each in terms of Figure 7.1.

Brevity: A shorter model is a simpler model. If we determine that we are strictly interested in traffic and connectivity and not in the user interface software or other applications, we can limit our model to the network layer and below. This shortens and simplifies the model considerably.

Clarity: An easier model to understand is a simpler model. Instead of mapping the network architecture to the OSI model, we can simply incorporate the specific network architecture into the simulation. For example, if we are working with an Ethernet network, we could directly represent the Ethernet layers instead of mapping them to the OSI model. This loss of generality will be compensated by simplifying the implementation of the Ethernet model. Of course a network model of heterogeneous network protocols may not be able to accommodate such a loss of generality in the design.

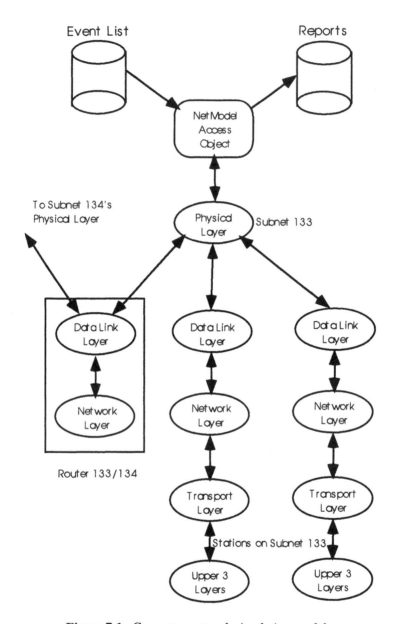

Figure 7.1. Computer network simulation model.

Efficient: A more efficient model's implementation runs faster. If the model is driven by an event list (or a table or some other means) and we can replace that with a Poisson distribution, then we can increase the efficiency of the model. There are many aspects of network modeling poorly represented by the Poisson distribution [Paxson 95]. This may or may not be significant depending on the fidelity requirements of the simulation.

These three views of simplification are not mutually exclusive. In the next section we will present a mini-case study in which model simplification is accomplished in a manner that increases brevity, clarity and efficiency with only a nominal loss of fidelity.

7.1.2 Resolution in the point-mass equation

The U.S. Department of Defense has been a technological world leader in the area of distributed simulation. The Naval Postgraduate School's NPSNET is a real-time graphical distributed simulation which focuses on the interaction of ground and air vehicles in a combat environment [Zyda 92]. The role of indirect fire (field artillery) is decisive but was not originally modeled in NPSNET. A significant majority of U.S. casualties in the four major wars of the 20th century were caused by artillery/mortar shell fragments [Dupuy 90]. Between the world wars, the U.S. Army developed the greatest enhancement of artillery firepower since Gustavus Adolphus. Precision fire direction allowed for the massing of fires from many firing units into a demoralizing crescendo of destruction onto a single target [Dupuy 84]. Therefore, there was considerable interest in adding an indirect fire representation in NPSNET to allow modeling of artillery systems and their effects.

[Nash 92] surveyed ballistic weapons models within the context of a real-time graphical simulation. The desired model was a high-fidelity representation of a projectile moving through space that was computationally efficient. There are several factors besides gravity which affect spin-stabilized projectiles in flight. The modified point mass model [Lieske 66] provides an equation of motion for a free-flight projectile that applies factors such as air drag, yaw, lift, and the Coriolis effect. The equation of motion given by Lieske's point-mass model is shown here.

$$\frac{d\bar{u}_i}{dt} = -\left\{\frac{\rho\pi m_r v_{i-1}\left[C_D + C_{D_{\alpha^2}} + \left(Q\alpha_e\right)^2\right]}{8Cm}\right\}\bar{v}_{i-1} + \left(\frac{\rho\pi d^2 Lv^2_{i-1}}{8m}\right)\times$$

$$\left(C_{L_\alpha} + C_{L_{\alpha^3}} \alpha_e^2\right)\bar{\alpha}_e + \bar{g} + \bar{\Lambda} + \left(\frac{-\rho\pi d^3 pQ C_{N_{P\alpha}}}{8m}\right)\left(\bar{\alpha}_e \times \bar{v}_{i-1}\right)$$

[Nash 92] determined that the following simplifying assumptions could be made without seriously compromising model fidelity:

- Mass of the bullet is constant $\left(m_r = m\right)$.

- Coriolis effect is negligible $\left(\bar{\Lambda} = (0,0,0)\right)$.

- The force of gravity acts only along an axis that is perpendicular to the trajectory.

- No winds are present $\left(\bar{u} = \bar{v}\right)$.

These assumptions resulted in the simplified model shown below.

$$\frac{d\bar{v}_i}{dt} = -\left\{\frac{\rho\pi v_{i-1}\left[C_{D_0} + C_{D_{\alpha^2}} + \left(Q\alpha_e\right)^2\right]}{8C}\right\}\bar{v}_{i-1} + \left(\frac{\rho\pi d^2 Lv^2_{i-1}}{8m}\right)\times$$

$$\left(C_{L_\alpha} + C_{L_{\alpha^3}} \alpha_e^2\right)\bar{\alpha}_e + \bar{g} + \left(\frac{-\rho\pi d^3 pQ C_{N_{P\alpha}}}{8m}\right)\left(\bar{\alpha}_e \times \bar{v}_{i-1}\right)$$

The simplified point-mass model is computationally more efficient than Lieske's original model. The U.S. Army has rigorously established standards and methods for determining field artillery firing data. The simplification of the model did result in a loss of fidelity, but this loss was quantified, compared with the established standards, and determined acceptable [Nash 92].

Some may look at the above equation and question whether it has really been simplified. In fact, we can see each of the three views of model simplification. The elimination of even a few variables contributes to the clarity of a complex model. The simplification is shorter and more efficient. A simple visual comparison of the two previous equations confirms that the simpler model is shorter. Additionally, the definition of the gravitational acceleration of the Earth as $\vec{g} = \begin{bmatrix} 0 & g & 0 \end{bmatrix}^\mathsf{T}$ reduces the complexity of the vector addition since two of the components are zero. Since the simplified model has fewer multiplications and additions and no additional factors, it is clearly more efficient computationally.

7.2 Decomposition

Decomposition is a technique used in the study of nearly all large systems. Sometimes simplification is not a viable strategy. An alternative and sometimes complimentary strategy is to break down the system and model the component part. Unfortunately, not all large systems are easily decomposed. [Courtois 85] details some of the pitfalls in decomposing complex systems under the following circumstances:

- When the different time or size scales are not far apart.

- When the interesting behavioral properties to be analyzed are related to rare events caused by weak interactions in the system.

- When events at many scales of time or size from each other nevertheless have a non-negligible influence on each other (multiscale relations).

In the next section we illustrate these same pitfalls in modeling computer networks. Then we will explore the concept of nearly decomposable systems. We will see that, in any system, there is a certain amount of interaction between subsystems. Simon and Ando demonstrated the consequences of disregarding weak interactions between subsystems [Simon 61]. However, the relationship between degree of subsystem coupling and model fidelity is not yet precisely defined [Courtois 85].

7.2.1 Decomposition of a computer network

The challenges defined by Courtois can be experienced modeling computer networks. Let us return to the network simulation example in Figure 7.1. We see the network protocols are layered with different functionalities per layer. It is not immediately obvious which layers need to be explicitly modeled. There are interactions between the model layers and these interactions often influence the interactions within a layer.

Time scales. A further complication is that activity on a network typically takes place in a very compressed time scale. Figures 7.2 and 7.3 show approximately sixty seconds of simulated Ethernet traffic on a twenty-five node subnetwork. Whole-second resolution, as shown in Figure 7.2, is coarse, particularly when sixty seconds produces more than 9,000 data points. This is an insufficient time scale for many items of interest, which typically occur at resolutions of a small fraction of a second. Figure 7.3 shows a finer grain millisecond resolution

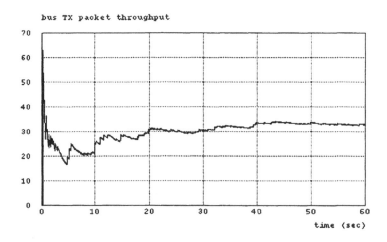

Figure 7.2. Simulated Ethernet traffic at whole-second resolution.

where the individual discrete measurements are shown.

Rare events. If we are interested in dropped packets in a normally reliable Ethernet network, we might have to wait weeks before we see a dropped packet. What network elements can we safely discard from our simulation without compromising our ability to see a dropped packet? Weak interactions may be the cause of the rare event. If we eliminate the weak interactions, the rare event may never occur in the simulation.

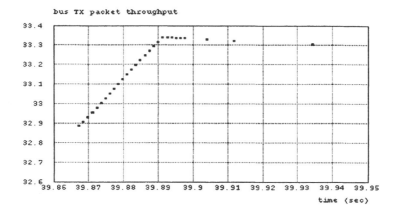

Figure 7.3. Simulated Ethernet traffic, millisecond resolution.

Hidden thresholds. Some systems experience major changes when a certain threshold is crossed. [Courtois 85] cites the example of thrashing in operating systems. A computer may be executing concurrent programs efficiently, requesting additional main memory as it is needed. If the sum of these requests crosses a certain threshold, system performance will drastically drop. This occurs because the memory space allocated to the programs already executing shrinks. This means that those programs occupy their memory space longer, which in turn causes an increase in the number of programs needing system resources.

This concept can be applied to networking. Ethernet is a carrier sense, multiple access, collision detection (CSMA/CD) protocol. [Nemzow 92] outlines how CSMA/CD operates, as shown in Table 7.1.   When a significant number of collisions begins to occur, the throughput on that network rapidly drops off. Where this performance threshold occurs is very difficult to pinpoint.   Traffic loads just under this threshold will have reasonable throughput, but once this threshold is reached, throughput deteriorates precipitously.

Finally, we know that users engage in stochastic activities which determine the activity that occurs on the wire.   This stochastic activity is often difficult to predict.

Table 7.1 Ethernet characteristics.

CSMA/CD	Characteristics
Carrier Sense:	Listen before transmitting
Multiple Access:	Transmit when channel is free
Collision Detection:	Transit delays allow collisions
	Detect collision and retry
	Delays a random length of time
	Algorithm generates delay
Advantages:	Efficient with load less than 40 percent capacity
Disadvantages:	Nondeterministic; throughput drops off sharply under heavy loads

7.2.2 Nearly decomposable systems

Subsystems which operate with limited and clearly defined interactions with the system are clearly a target for decomposition.   Such decomposition facilitates a distributed design and implementation. Additional interactions increase the difficulty of isolating a subsystem from the rest of the system. If the interactions are unknown, then decomposition can lead to an unpredictable loss of fidelity. [Courtois 75] provides the following observations:

- Interactions *within* groups can be studied as if interactions *among* groups did not exist.

- Interactions *among* groups can be analyzed without referring to the interactions *within* groups.

Clearly any group which depends only upon the variables of that group is *completely* decomposable because such a group executes in a completely independent manner. Then, as Courtois observes, any system may be decomposed into as many subsystems as there are completely decomposable groups. Unfortunately, most systems have interactions between groups as well as interactions within groups. However, if the interactions between groups are weak, we can still use this technique to yield a reasonably approximate model.

Matrix algebra provides a rigorous concept for decomposition. [Hadley 61] defines an nth-order matrix as decomposable if by interchanging some rows and their corresponding columns it is possible to obtain a null matrix in the lower left-hand corner so that A can be written as (A_{11}, A_{22} square), as shown in Figure 7.4.

$$A = \begin{bmatrix} A_{11} & A_{12} \\ 0 & A_{22} \end{bmatrix}$$

Figure 7.4. The canonical form of a decomposable matrix.

If rows i and j are interchanged, then columns i and j must also be interchanged. A_{11} and A_{22} may also be decomposable. Hadley further notes that A is indecomposable if it is not possible to obtain the single zero element in the lower left position. Consider matrix A:

$$A = \begin{bmatrix} 1 & 0 & 0 & 0 & 0 \\ 1 & 1 & 1 & 1 & 1 \\ 1 & 0 & 1 & 1 & 0 \\ 1 & 0 & 0 & 1 & 0 \\ 1 & 1 & 1 & 1 & 0 \end{bmatrix}$$

If A is decomposable, the resulting block matrices that appear on the diagonal show the subsystem partitioning which will reduce communications overhead. To realize this reduction requires a distributed system configuration that allows the components of the block matrices to be hosted locally. This reduction occurs when communication takes place in the same partition, thus reducing the global communications costs between partitions.

If the subsystems and their interactions are represented as a graph, then the block matrices in the main diagonal correspond to the *strongly connected components* of the graph. We transform A into the canonical form shown in Figure 7.4 by interchanging rows and then interchanging the corresponding columns. We determine the appropriate transitions by following a seven-step process.

Step 1: If necessary, exchange rows so that diagonal entries are non-zero. This requires moving row 5; so we exchange rows 2 and 5, resulting in:

$$A = \begin{bmatrix} 1 & 0 & 0 & 0 & 0 \\ 1 & 1 & 1 & 1 & 0 \\ 1 & 0 & 1 & 1 & 0 \\ 1 & 0 & 0 & 1 & 0 \\ 1 & 1 & 1 & 1 & 1 \end{bmatrix}$$

Step 2: Construct a digraph corresponding to the matrix. Reflexive transitions are not shown.

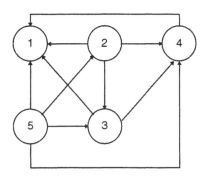

Step 3: Create and negotiate a stack to identify transitions. Start at an arbitrary node and move to a new node along a transition. Record the start node on the stack. When no untraversed transitions exist from a node, we close it out and move to another node. Starting at node 1 we see no transitions so we record 1, then remove it from the stack, and move to another node. We put node 2 on the stack and have a choice of moving to nodes 1, 3, or 4. One is closed out so we choose 3 and place 3 on the stack. From 3 the only node we can transition to that is not closed out is 4, so we move to 4. The only transition from 4 is 1, which is closed out so 4 is closed out and removed from the stack. This returns us to 3, which also has no transitions to an open node and is therefore closed out and removed from the stack. Node 2 is similarly closed out and removed from the stack. Since there are no other open nodes, node 5 is recorded and closed out.

		4*			
	3	3	3*		
1*	2	2	2	2*	5*
Step 1	Step 2	Step 3	Step 4	Step 5	Step 6
Index 5		Index 4	Index 3	Index 2	Index 1

*indicates node is closed out

We identify candidate row-column exchanges by creating an index corresponding to the closed-out nodes on the stack. Start with an index equal to the number of nodes in the system (which is the order of the original matrix). Create pairs of candidate exchanges by assigning the most recently closed-out node to the current index. After each assignment, decrement the index by one.

Step 4: We identify potential transitions by pairing the point where the node closes out with the corresponding index number. This produces the following candidate transitions:

$$1 \leftrightarrow 5, \ 4 \leftrightarrow 4, \ 3 \leftrightarrow 3, \ 2 \leftrightarrow 2, \ 5 \leftrightarrow 1$$

Step 5: We determine the row/column permutations by discarding any of the candidates in step 4 of the form $\alpha \leftrightarrow \alpha$. Applying this rule to the transitions above we are left with $1 \leftrightarrow 5, 5 \leftrightarrow 1$.

Step 6. Depending upon the order in which the transitions are applied, the indices of the intended transition may change. Therefore we decide on an arbitrary ordering and apply the following procedure to account for the possible relocation of the indices. If either of the indices indicated in a transition has been previously interchanged, it is necessary to determine that index's present location. This is accomplished by scanning the list of transitions in the intended order of application and determining if an index in the current transition appears earlier in the list. If it does not, no action is needed. If it does, then we determine the current label of the index by tracing its participation in previous transitions. Note that there may be several previous transitions, and that both indices in the current transition must be evaluated for previous appearances in the list. In this example, we scan the list and determine that both indices in the second transition appeared previously. By relabeling the indices, the list of candidate transitions is now $1 \leftrightarrow 5, 1 \leftrightarrow 5$.

Step 7. We search the list for duplicate transitions and eliminate one from any pair that appears. The transitions that remain are the ones that will permute the original matrix into canonical form.

Therefore, we interchange row 1 with row 5 and column 1 with column 5, resulting in:

$$A = \begin{bmatrix} 1 & 0 & 0 & 0 & 0 \\ 1 & 1 & 1 & 1 & 0 \\ 1 & 0 & 1 & 1 & 0 \\ 1 & 0 & 0 & 1 & 0 \\ 1 & 1 & 1 & 1 & 1 \end{bmatrix} \Rightarrow \begin{bmatrix} 1 & 1 & 1 & 1 & 1 \\ 1 & 1 & 1 & 1 & 0 \\ 1 & 0 & 1 & 1 & 0 \\ 1 & 0 & 0 & 1 & 0 \\ 1 & 0 & 0 & 0 & 0 \end{bmatrix} \Rightarrow \begin{bmatrix} 1 & 1 & 1 & 1 & 1 \\ 0 & 1 & 1 & 1 & 1 \\ 0 & 0 & 1 & 1 & 1 \\ 0 & 0 & 0 & 1 & 1 \\ 0 & 0 & 0 & 0 & 1 \end{bmatrix}$$

row interchange   *column interchange*

In this example, the result is a triangular matrix and no further decomposition is possible. Decomposition to the triangular case indicates a system that cannot be partitioned to minimize communications overhead in any distributed sense. Every diagonal element in a triangular matrix is a one-element block matrix.

Figure 7.5 shows a digraph representing the interactions between elements of a distributed system. The reflexive

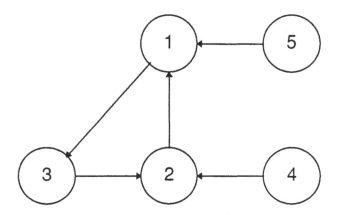

Figure 7.5. A graph of system interactions.

interactions are not shown and assigned a non-zero constant value.   We can construct the following matrix of system interactions from Figure 7.5:

$$\begin{bmatrix} 1 & 0 & 1 & 0 & 0 \\ 1 & 1 & 0 & 0 & 0 \\ 0 & 1 & 1 & 0 & 0 \\ 0 & 1 & 0 & 1 & 0 \\ 1 & 0 & 0 & 0 & 1 \end{bmatrix}$$

Applying the algorithm to produce the stack creates the candidate transitions $\{2\leftrightarrow5, 3\leftrightarrow4, 1\leftrightarrow3, 4\leftrightarrow2, 5\leftrightarrow1\}$. None of the transitions are of the form $\alpha\leftrightarrow\alpha$, so we proceed with step 6. We may apply the transitions in any order, so choosing the sequence that was used to enumerate them above will suffice. Scanning from left to right, we note that an index in the transition $1\leftrightarrow3$ appears in the transition that precedes it. Index number 3 was exchanged with number 4, and thus the third transition is changed to $1\leftrightarrow4$. Continuing in this fashion, we notice that both of the indices in the fourth transition have been modified in the ones that precede it. Therefore, this transition becomes $3\leftrightarrow5$. The last transition must also be adjusted, since both of its indices appear previously as well. The final list of transitions which must be applied is $\{2\leftrightarrow5, 3\leftrightarrow4, 1\leftrightarrow4, 3\leftrightarrow5, 2\leftrightarrow4\}$.

By applying the seven steps described in the previous example we determine we can decompose this matrix into the following form by applying the set of transitions listed above.

$$\begin{bmatrix} \begin{bmatrix} 1 & 0 & 1 \\ 1 & 1 & 0 \\ 0 & 1 & 1 \end{bmatrix} & \begin{matrix} 0 & 0 \\ 0 & 0 \\ 0 & 0 \end{matrix} \\ \begin{matrix} 0 & 1 & 0 \\ 0 & 0 & 1 \end{matrix} & \begin{matrix} [1] & 0 \\ 0 & [1] \end{matrix} \end{bmatrix}$$

Transposing this matrix completes the permutation to canonical form. In this matrix three block matrices appear on the diagonal. By keeping track of where the elements of the original matrix have moved, we can determine a partitioning scheme.

$$
\begin{bmatrix}
\begin{bmatrix} (3,3) & 0 & (3,2) \\ (1,3) & (1,1) & 0 \\ 0 & (2,1) & (2,2) \end{bmatrix} & 0 & 0 \\
\begin{matrix} 0 & (5,1) & 0 \\ 0 & 0 & (4,2) \end{matrix} & \begin{matrix} [(5,5)] \\ 0 \end{matrix} & \begin{matrix} 0 \\ [(4,4)] \end{matrix}
\end{bmatrix}
$$

In this case we recognize that elements 1, 2, and 3 are strongly connected and should be placed on the same partition if possible. There is no identifiable advantage in a particular placement of elements 4 or 5.

Identifying the interactions between subsystems greatly eases the distributed implementation. Consider a computer network in a university. It is entirely possible some stations and subnets cannot or simply do not interact with each other. In such a case, it would be reasonable to partition the system so that the independent subsystems execute on separate processors.

Simon and Ando defined nearly decomposable systems in [Simon 61]. The following physical illustration of this concept is given in [Courtois 85] and [Simon 61]. Let Figure 7.6 illustrate a building divided into rooms and offices. The thermal equilibrium of the building is the system of interest. We assume that the outer walls of the building are perfect thermal insulators. The building is subdivided into eight rooms, shown in Figure 7.6 as lines with narrow gaps. Each room is further subdivided into four offices, shown in Figure 7.6 as lines with wide gaps. Each room has walls that are good, but not perfect, thermal insulators. The rooms are divided into offices by partitions that are very poor thermal insulators.

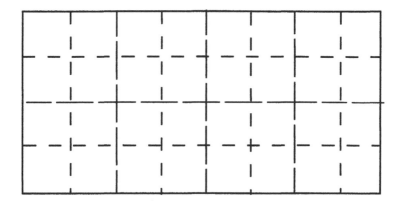

Figure 7.6. A building subdivided into rooms and offices.

Assume the building is initially in a state of thermal disequilibrium; that is, there are wide temperature variances between rooms and between offices. A thermometer is in each office. After several hours, the temperature variance between offices will approach zero, though the temperature variance between rooms may still be significant. Eventually, since we have a closed system, temperature differences between rooms will be virtually non-existent.

It is possible to construct a matrix of temperature differences between offices. Let matrix R be a matrix whose element r_{ij} represents the rate of heat transfer between office i and office j per degree of temperature difference. Simon and Ando observe that if r_{ij}'s are large when the offices are in the same room and are close to zero when i and j are in different rooms, then the resulting matrix is nearly decomposable. An analyst could conclude that thermometers were unnecessary in every office and that thermal equilibrium could be monitored by placing a thermometer in each room. In the building in Figure 7.6, that would result in a need for only eight thermometers instead of forty-eight thermometers. More important, the model can be decomposed because it was determined that the significant interactions occur between rooms and not between offices in the same room.

7.3 Adjusting resolution dynamically

A major limitation of both decomposition and simplification is that neither method provides a means to dynamically change resolution. Conventional simulation design methods fix the level of resolution in the design. Thus, changing the resolution of the model requires restarting the simulation, at a minimum, and possibly a redesign/reimplementation of the model.

[Davis 92] outlines some methods of varying simulation resolution:

- Using high resolution to provide a *picture* when the lower-resolution depiction seems too abstract.

- Invoking high resolution for *special processes* within the course of an otherwise low-resolution simulation (e.g., in a combat simulation, when one force's artillery has a qualitative advantage such as weapons range and that is of particular interest).

- Using high resolution to *establish bounds* for parametric analyses using lower-resolution models (e.g., the number of retries to deliver a packet).

- Using high resolution to *calibrate* lower resolution (or vice versa), recognizing that our knowledge of the world comes at all levels of detail.

- Using low resolution for *decision support*, including rapid analysis of alternative courses of action.

- Using low resolution to *generate adaptive scenarios,* as when attempting to provide and maintain context for high-resolution decision-making in which objectives depend on higher level considerations and coordination requirements.

Varying resolution provides flexibility in modeling and analysis and can improve the computational efficiency of the simulation. Simulating large systems forces simulation designers to make efficiency trade-offs. Let us return to our example of simulating computer networks. A simple 25-station network may have up to 600 possible source–destination pairs of senders and receivers. If we are studying network traffic between source–destination pairs, then we cannot assume symmetric behavior between stations. As stations are added, the complexity of the network *traffic between pairs* grows rapidly on the order of $n^2 - n$, where n is the number of stations.

Simulating a non-trivial network with a high measure of resolution is computationally expensive. So much data may be provided that the analyst may be overwhelmed. A more practical strategy is one in which some parts of the network can be studied in detail while other parts of the network run at a lower level of resolution in the background. [Wall 93] demonstrated mixed resolution with his traffic simulation model implementation using the SimBuilder environment developed by [Vidlak 93].

7.3.1   SimBuilder

In traditional simulation environments, access to parameters and variables is limited to model construction and experiment evaluation. Vidlak observed that the increased sophistication of graphical user interfaces allows the development of interactive simulations that challenge these limitations. This led to the development of SimBuilder [Vidlak 93].

SimBuilder features generic objects which may be interactively modified by the user. This flexibility allows the analyst to change resolution during the execution of the simulation. The original research motivation for SimBuilder was experimentation with object-oriented user interfaces.

SimBuilder is a framework of simulation tools to support building of domain-specific simulations such as the traffic simulation model (TSM). SimBuilder provides four major class structures: *system, draw item, simulation,* and *miscellaneous.* System classes are primarily means to manipulate the Macintosh environment. Prograph, the programming language used to implement SimBuilder, provides this basic support, which ensures that SimBuilder applications have the standard Macintosh features.

The value editor class is an example of a system class. Figure 7.7 shows an instantiation of a value editor as a source-sink editor. The source-sink editor allows the analyst to choose the distributions to model the arrivals. The draw item classes consist of the methods and attributes that allow the user to physically build the simulation and manipulate the drawn objects within a window on the screen. The simulation classes are the methods and attributes for actually running the simulation.

Figure 7.7. Source-sink editor.

A high-level view of the simulation engine is shown in Figure 7.8. The graphs shown in Figure 7.8 are the typical graphs that comprise the source code for the Prograph programming language. The SimBuilder program cycles through the local methods shown and advances the simulation clock to the time of the event that was executed [Wall 93]. To begin an event cycle, the get current event local method checks the simulation class event list and each of the intersection and source-sinks event list. The earliest occurring event is chosen as the current event

and is passed to the process current event local method.
The simulation engine updates the progress window and
continuously monitors for the Stop button on the progress
window (Handle Event) or the expiration of the designated
run time. The compact-memory primitive is used during each
cycle to compensate for memory-hungry Macintosh methods.

[Wall 93] notes that other types of events are generated and
handled by SimBuilder. The general form for an event is the time
for execution, the name of the event itself, and any additional
information needed by the method processing the event.

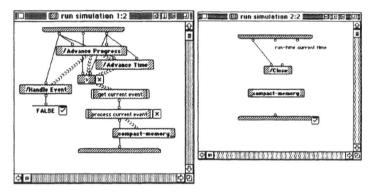

Figure 7.8. The simulation engine [Wall 93][Vidlak 93].

Additional information may include items such as the traffic
object requesting the event or the traffic object being impacted by
the event.

[Vidlak 93] observes that SimBuilder allows the analyst to
interactively modify the model as the experiment is running, after
the model is built and all parameters specified. Arrival rates,
queue utilization, and simulation time are presented through
various means. The analyst can save "snapshots" of the current
state of the simulation at will for further analysis later. Vidlak
claims that the interactive capabilities of SimBuilder make it
possible to obtain performance measures of the system design by
dynamically changing design parameters at run time.

7.3.2 The Traffic Simulation Model

[Wall 93] describes the traffic simulation model, (TSM). This model was based on the control system that the city of College Station, Texas, previously used to sequence traffic lights and control traffic flow. Wall found the model satisfactory for investigating an object-oriented simulation environment that permits interaction at multiple levels of abstraction.

Increasing capacity for vehicular traffic primarily involves the configuration and control measures used at intersections and the physical layouts of the roads leading from one intersection to another. Physical constraints such as the number of lanes dedicated to turning traffic, restrictions on turn direction, and the traffic signal timing mechanism are among the more important variables associated with intersections.

The traffic signal timing mechanism is a complex aspect of TSM. The first variable is the *cycle* – the amount of time allotted for a traffic signal to completely cycle once through all desired configurations. If a red light stopping traffic in an easterly direction was just observed to change to green, the cycle time is the amount of time (usually expressed in seconds) required to pass before the light will turn green again and permit movement to the east. Light signal changes are dictated by the configuration of the intersection, traffic lights, and the permitted turns.

The ordered list of desired light changes, called the *sequence*, must be established for each light. In most cases (and depending upon the configuration of the intersection), movement in at least two directions is allowed with each light change. The time allotments for light changes, called *splits*, are expressed as a percentage of the cycle time.

Figure 7.9 shows a hypothetical four-way intersection with dedicated left-turn lanes. It can be seen from the figure that left turns are permitted and controlled by the traffic light. A given trafffic coordination sequence may pair the following lanes of traffic: (② and ⑥), (① and ⑥), (③ and ⑦), (④ and ⑧), and (② and

⑤). This means that each pair will receive the same instruction from the traffic light at the same relative time. For example, traffic in lanes ② and ⑥ have the option of moving straight ahead or turning right during the same time allotment. A typical split may be denoted as 16/16/16/28/24. If the cycle was 180 seconds, the respective times for the duration of the green light for each of the above pairs would be 28.8, 28.8, 28.8, 50.4, and 43.2 seconds.

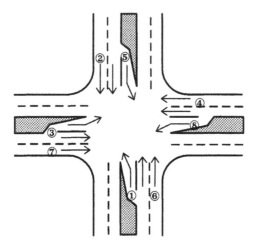

Figure 7.9. Traffic intersection in TSM [Wall 93].

As Wall notes, this is the basis for the design of TSM. As we will see in the next section, the SimBuilder environment provides an easy-to-use interactive environment that allows the analyst to build his own traffic models and then dynamically model them.

7.3.3 TSM implemented in SimBuilder

The tool palette depicted in Figure 7.10 is built into the TSM implemented in SimBuilder. The palette in Figure 7.10 is used to build the desired traffic network. The function of each item on the palette is described below:

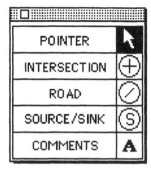

Figure 7.10. Tool palette [Wall 93].

- The Pointer tool is used to place traffic objects in the simulation window or to select and deselect these objects for movement, editing, or deletion.

- The Intersection tool places intersection objects at desired locations in the window.

- The Source/Sink tool places objects in the simulation window that may represent a source, a sink, or both.

- The Road tool connects Source/Sinks and Intersections to each other. A Source/Sink may have only one connection. An intersection must have either a Source/Sink or another intersection connected to each point of the crossed lines in the center of the icon. If a proper connection is not made, the road snaps back to the point where it began. For a successful completion of a connection, a dialog window appears for inputting the name of the road.

- The Comment tool provides a means to add comments anywhere in the simulation window.

Another instantiation of SimBuilder's value editor class is shown in Figure 7.11. The intersection values for the light cycles and the splits as well as the type of intersection are entered here.

Note in the upper right hand corner, the analyst is able to choose between two levels of resolution.

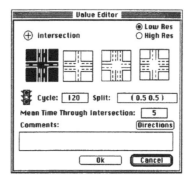

Figure 7.11. Intersection value editor.

Using the tool palette shown in Figure 7.10, the traffic network in Figure 7.12 was created. The source/sinks (the circumscribed S) were defined using the source-sink editor (Figure 7.7). The intersections were defined using the intersection value editor (Figure 7.11). The queue lengths at each intersection may be directly observed during run-time.

SimBuilder allows each intersection in the traffic simulation to be run at either high resolution or low resolution. In high-resolution intersections, cars are accounted for individually and the moves of each car are subject to a series of events. Even though Wall uses event-jumping to improve performance, the price of high resolution is slower execution. Information about individual cars in an intersection cannot be captured if the intersection is set to low-resolution mode.

In low-resolution mode, the simulation class generates an event that is to occur at the current simulation time plus the time increment. The event message itself is composed of only two elements: the time the event is to be executed and the name of the event. These events are maintained in a list called "event list" that is an attribute of the simulation class. Each intersection operating in the low-resolution mode is processed to determine the most probable outcomes of all car activity occurring during the time

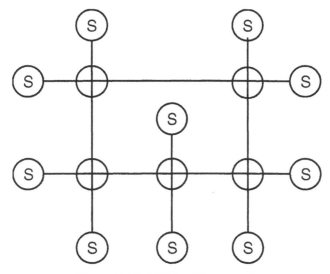

Figure 7.12. TSM traffic network.

increment. The outcomes are derived from stochastic processes reflecting input parameters, which are based on collected data.

Figures 7.13 and 7.14 show intersection meters running in low resolution and high resolution. In TSM, low resolution is essentially probability distribution-based simulation and high-resolution is event-driven simulation. The analyst may switch resolution dynamically. It should be noted that when an intersection is switched from high-resolution to low-resolution mode, the ability to track individual cars is lost.

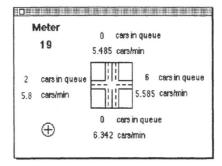

Figure 7.13. Intersection meter at low resolution.

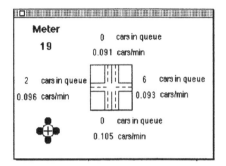

Figure 7.14. Intersection meter at high resolution.

7.4 Summary

Model resolution is a critical component in determining the usefulness of a simulation. Model fidelity is a closely related concept, but one does not imply the other. Higher resolution does not necessarily increase fidelity. Simplification and decomposition are two strategies to reduce the computational expense of resolution while limiting the loss of fidelity. Simulation models are under development which allow the analyst to dynamically alter the resolution of the various components. This capability will add considerable flexibility and increase the scope of problem domains which may be studied through simulation.

7.5 Exercises

7.1   What is the difference between abstraction and resolution?

7.2   In mixing the use of event lists and PDFs, how would you characterize the resolution of models using both?

7.3   What validation method would you use to validate the traffic simulation model (TSM)?

7.4   Describe the differences between simplification and decomposition.

7.5 Why does higher resolution not guarantee higher fidelity in a simulation model?

7.6 Describe a problem domain which could be modeled with varying resolution. Discuss the trade-offs involved.

7.7 In section 7.2.2 we stated that the following matrix could be decomposed as follows:

$$
A = \begin{bmatrix} 1 & 0 & 1 & 0 & 0 \\ 1 & 1 & 0 & 0 & 0 \\ 0 & 1 & 1 & 0 & 0 \\ 0 & 1 & 0 & 1 & 0 \\ 1 & 0 & 0 & 0 & 1 \end{bmatrix} \Rightarrow \begin{bmatrix} \begin{bmatrix} 1 & 0 & 1 \\ 1 & 1 & 0 \\ 0 & 1 & 1 \end{bmatrix} \begin{matrix} 0 & 0 \\ 0 & 0 \\ 0 & 0 \end{matrix} \\ \begin{matrix} 0 & 1 & 0 \\ 0 & 0 & 1 \end{matrix} \begin{matrix} [1] & 0 \\ 0 & [1] \end{matrix} \end{bmatrix}
$$

Explicitly show the creation and negotiation of the stack and the resulting candidate permutations.

7.6 References

[Andrews 93] A. D. Andrews, Electronic mail correspondence, Software Engineering Institute, Carnegie-Mellon University, August 1993.

[Bailey 92] M. P. Bailey and W. G. Kemple, "The scientific method of choosing model fidelity," *Proceedings of the 1992 Winter Simulation Conference*, Society for Computer Simulation, pp. 791 – 797, December 1992.

[Courtois 75] P. J. Courtois, "Decomposibility instabilities, and saturation in multiprogramming systems," *Communications of the ACM*, Vol. 18, No. 7, pp. 371 – 377, July 1975.

[Courtois 85] P. J. Courtois, "On time and space decomposition of complex structures," *Communications of the ACM*, Vol. 26, No. 6, pp. 590 – 603, June 1985.

[Davis 92] P. K. Davis, *An Introduction to Variable-Resolution Modeling and Cross-Resolution Model Connection*, RAND Report R-4252-DARPA, 1992.

[Dupuy 84] T. N. Dupuy, *The Evolution of Weapons and Warfare*, Da Capo Press, New York, NY, 1984.

[Dupuy 90] T. N. Dupuy, *Attrition: Forecasting Battle Casualties and Equipment Losses in Modern War*, Hero Books, Fairfax, VA, 1990.

[Hadley 61] G. Hadley, *Linear Algebra*, Addison-Wesley, Reading, MA, 1961.

[Hamilton 95] J. A. Hamilton, Jr., G. R. Ratterree, and U. W. Pooch, "A toolkit for monitoring the utilization and performance of computer networks," *Simulation*, Vol. 64, No. 5, pp. 297 – 301, May 1995.

[Innis 83] G. S. Innis and E. A. Rexstad, "Simulation model simplification techniques," *Simulation*, Vol. 41, No. 1, pp. 7 – 15, July 1983.

[Lieske 66] R. F. Lieske and M. L. Reiter, *Equations of Motion for a Modified Point Mass Trajectory*, Ballistics Research Laboratories Report No. 1314, March 1966.

[Nash 92] D. A. Nash, *NPSNET: Modeling the In-flight and Terminal Properties of Ballistic Munitions*, M.S. thesis, Naval Postgraduate School, Monterey, CA, September 1992.

[Nemzow 92] M. A. W. Nemzow, *The Ethernet Management Guide*, McGraw-Hill, New York, NY, 1992.

[Paxson 95] V. Paxson and S. Floyd, "Wide area traffic: The failure of Poisson modeling," *IEEE/ACM Transactions on Networking*, Vol. 3, No. 3, pp. 226 – 244, June 1995.

[Pooch 93]   U. W. Pooch and J. A. Wall, *Discrete Event Simulation*, CRC Press, Boca Raton, FL, 1993.

[Simon 61]   H. A. Simon and A. Ando, "Aggregation of variables in dynamic systems," *Econometrica*, Vol. 29, No. 2, pp. 111 – 138, April 1961.

[Vidlak 93]   M. D. Vidlak, *User-Object Interfaces in an Object-Oriented Discrete Event Simulation Environment*, Ph.D. dissertation, Texas A&M University, College Station, TX, December 1993.

[Wall 93]   J. A. Wall, *Multilevel Abstraction of Discrete Models in an Interactive Object-Oriented Simulation Environment*, Ph.D. dissertation, Texas A&M University, College Station, TX, December 1993.

[Zyda 92]   M. J. Zyda, D. R. Pratt, J. G. Monahan, and K. P. Wilson, "NPSNET: Constructing a 3D virtual world," *Proceedings of the 1992 Symposium on Interactive 3D Graphics*, pp. 147 – 156, April 1992.

8

Modeling and Abstraction in Multilevel Simulation

Once the desired resolution of a simulation model is determined, it is still necessary to determine a level of *abstraction.* Abstraction is the separation of qualities and properties from particular instances. An analytical model measuring arrivals and departures in a simple system may not require any abstraction. Domains such as computer networks are sufficiently complex that some abstraction is required to make the simulation tractable. A network simulation with packet-level resolution may have several levels of abstraction. For example, packets may be simulated at the workstation level, the subnet level, or higher. The appropriate level of abstraction is dependent upon the objectives of the simulation run, the capability of the system, and the ability and interests of the researcher.

In many cases, the desired level of abstraction changes dynamically. This has led to the development of *multilevel simulation.* A multilevel simulation is able to accommodate multiple levels of abstraction. Levels of abstraction may be hierarchical, model-based, resolution-based, or hybrid constructions.

One way in which levels of abstraction may be changed dynamically is through *aggregation.* Unfortunately, aggregation is a one-way process unless lower level state information is saved. Deaggregation can only produce approximations of the components originally aggregated if the original components are not maintained. Therefore, deaggregation often results in some loss of fidelity. The aggregation/deaggregation problem is one of the major issues in simulation scalability.

8.1 Multilevel abstraction

The purpose of abstraction is to isolate aspects of the problem that are important and suppress those that are unimportant [Rumbaugh 91]. Multilevel simulation is based on multiple levels of abstraction and is a strategy to extend the utility of a simulation model. Levels of abstraction have several meanings, all of which may coexist in the same simulation.

A *base model* is capable of accounting for all of the input-output behavior of the real system [Zeigler 76]. The base model is a hypothetically complete explanation of the system behavior. For any non-trivial system, it is axiomatically impossible to fully specify the base model. Abstraction is used to specify a higher level representation of the system.

Model abstraction serves two purposes. First, abstraction may increase understanding of models and model behavior. Second, abstraction may increase the computational efficiency of the implementation of the model [Sevinc 91]. Understanding of the model can increase when we discard unnecessary model details. There are limits to this approach, of course. In textbooks we often see abstract communications models similar to that shown in Figure 8.1.

Figure 8.1. High-level abstraction of a communication channel.

This abstraction is useful for introducing students to communications models, but is not sufficiently detailed for useful simulation study. [Fishwick 88] offers specific points on why abstraction is useful in simulation:

- An abstract model is usually less computationally complex than the base model. As long as the trade-off between complexity and data sufficiency is a favorable one, then the abstract model remains useful. (We would further note that it is theoretically possible for an abstract model to be *more* computationally complex. However, the effective use of abstraction will reduce the computational complexity.)

- The abstract model is easier to understand than the base model in most cases. Since an abstraction involves a reduction in process component(s), the model is more easily created and modified.

- The creation of an abstract model permits us to build a library of different models which represent the same process. In many cases, the library of models for one process represents an evolutionary path for the modeling process. Processes often are modeled using simple methods at first and more complex methods later as more knowledge is gained by the simulationist. Additionally, validation helps to prune away inferior models.

We use Fishwick's terminology to describe movement through levels of abstraction [Fishwick 95]. We *abstract up* and *refine down*, as shown in Figure 8.2. In this example, a strict hierarchy is illustrated which implies a totally ordered relationship.

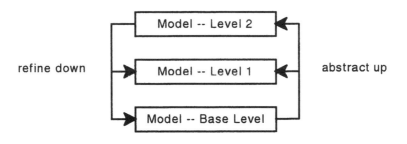

Figure 8.2. Abstraction hierarchy.

However, this need not be the case, as some models may simply be mapped to other models. Again, using Fishwick's terminology, the mapping relation shown in Figure 8.3 shows two models with different perspectives, but not different levels of abstraction.

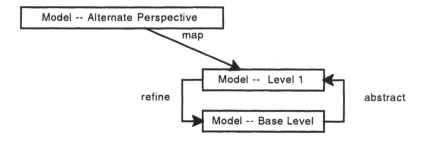

Figure 8.3. Abstraction network.

Abstraction passes essential information from a lower level model to a higher level model. Unnecessary information is not passed out. When additional information is required, then the model is refined to a lower level closer to the base model. We examine both hierarchical abstraction and abstraction networks in detail.

8.1.1 Hierarchical abstraction

Hierarchical modeling is a useful abstraction tool. [Iwasaki 92] offers four dimensions of abstraction:

Structural: Abstraction by lumping together a group of components that are physically close.

Functional: Abstraction by lumping together a group of components that collectively achieve a distinct, higher-level function.

Temporal: Abstraction by ignoring behavior over a short period of time.

Quantitative: Abstraction by ignoring small differences in variable values.

Iwasaki notes that these dimensions are neither complete nor necessarily independent of each other. Abstraction by ignoring behavior or small differences is akin to simplification strategies. Abstraction by lumping together denotes aggregation, which will be discussed in detail in section 8.2.

In discussing hierarchical abstraction, it is useful to recall the discussion of class hierarchies from Chapter 6. A manufacturing simulation of automobiles may have a resolution of stock numbered parts as illustrated in Figure 8.4. That is, specific parts with specific identification stock numbers are modeled. Common screws, molding clips, or any items without a specific stock number are not numbered.

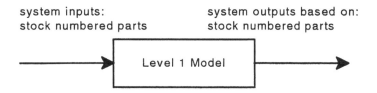

Figure 8.4. Defining resolution of a model.

The resolution of this model, the level of detail this model can input and output, is set. However there are many potential levels of abstraction. The base case occurs when there is no abstraction above the level of resolution. In such a case the simulation is designed to model the part-by-part assembly of an automobile.

It is often the case that the base level is unwieldy, hence we might want to model the assembly of an automobile in terms of assemblies and subassemblies. This is analogous to the whole-part relationships discussed previously. Figure 8.5 illustrates a partial hierarchy of automobile assemblies.

We can mask the part-by-part details of the base model and produce a model with a higher level of abstraction. Assuming the resolution remains fixed, the underlying simulation will still be executing with part-by-part detail. However, the information presented to the analyst will be at a higher level of abstraction.

We can apply this mask somewhat arbitrarily since we are currently working with a fixed-resolution model. We may wish to focus on brake pads and consider the rest of the simulation at the major assembly or sub-assembly level. Since the resolution of the model is part-by-part, we may focus on brake pads and consider the rest of the assembly process at higher levels of abstraction.

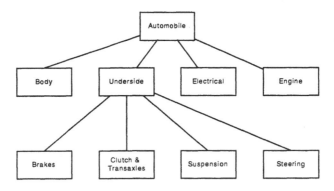

Figure 8.5. Hierarchical abstraction of an automobile assembly.

Abstraction hierarchies enable analysts to concentrate on particular parts of a complex model. Multiple levels of abstraction contribute to general purpose simulation models. A simulation created to study brake pads is unlikely to be easily extended for other study. However, a multilevel simulation model provides greater flexibility to allow analysts to focus on different parts of the model depending upon the current problem of interest.

8.1.2 Multimodels

Models that are composed of other models, in a network or a graph, are called *multimodels* [Fishwick 95]. Multimodels can combine the power of well-known modeling methodologies such as finite state automata (FSAs), Petri nets, block models, differential equations, and queuing models [Lee 93]. Multimodels may integrate different models at the same or varying levels of abstraction.

Typically, we abstract or refine models of the same type. If our base model was an FSA, we would expect abstractions from that model to also be FSA-based. Parts of a large system are often already well-modeled using various model types. For example, it might not be desirable to rewrite an existing Petri net model as an FSA model in order to use the models together. Multimodeling is often appealing since existing, validated models can continue to be used. In Figure 8.3 we illustrated an abstraction network in which one type of model could be mapped to another. Combining different *valid* model types in the same simulation can be very beneficial if we can maintain fidelity and if the resulting combined model can be validated.

Consider a simulation of a political campaign for President of the United States. (It is worth noting that simulation has recently become a very important part of American campaign strategies.) For our purposes, we are interested in gauging popular support for a candidate and how that may translate into electoral votes. Campaign managers are interested in a variety of predictive models. Polling is nearly continuous (although using a differential equation to model polling may be extreme) and there are a variety of models used to predict polling information. Some of the components for a political campaign multimodel are shown in Figure 8.6.

We can build several potential multimodels from the components shown in Figure 8.6. A campaign plan at any level of abstraction might make use of the fund raising, scheduling, voting booth, and polling models, thereby producing a multimodel. Such a multimodel may be constructed at a single level of abstraction or at multiple levels of abstraction. The multimodeling approach allows the integration of already existing (and presumably validated) models.

Some models are not easily combined. Continuing with our example in Figure 8.6, it may be difficult to assess how a county campaign plan is "more abstract" than a local campaign plan. This leads to difficulty in determining how to integrate the models. Well-defined data dictionaries for each model are required to determine what elements can be combined and which elements cannot.

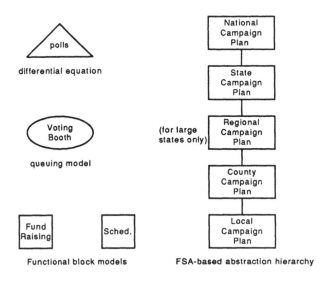

Figure 8.6. Components for a campaign multimodel.

When combining models at different levels of resolution, care must be exercised to ensure that the combinations occur at a common level. A polling model with a resolution at the individual voter level cannot be arbitrarily combined with a model at the county precinct level. Either the resolution of the county-level precinct model must be refined into an individual voter-level model or the polling model must be abstracted up to a precinct-level of resolution. This can be done by modifying the model or creating a transition function. A very useful alternative strategy is to design models with the built-in capability to operate at multiple levels of resolution.

8.1.3 Resolution and abstraction

Multilevel models incorporate components at multiple levels of resolution [Popken 96]. Resolution-based abstraction was discussed in detail in Chapter 7. To quickly review, in a multiresolution model, some entities may operate from event lists providing event-by-event detail while others may run based on PDFs.

When resolution is fixed at the base model level, a bound is placed on the ability to accept inputs at a level of abstraction finer than that specified. In designing a combat model, for example, we may specify inputs and outputs from a *resolution hierarchy* as shown in Figure 8.7. We may decide to set the resolution of the model at the company level. In this case, the model can neither accept input nor produce results at a resolution lower than selected without the assistance of some synthesizing function. A company-level model cannot directly accept individual soldier inputs nor provide results about individual soldiers. Higher levels of resolution may be approximated probabilistically, but with some possible loss of fidelity.

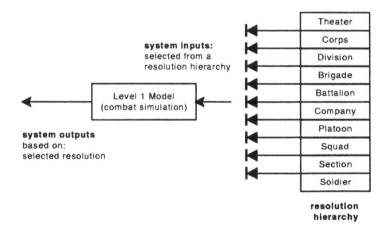

Figure 8.7. Resolving a hierarchy of inputs.

The simulation designer may wish to build base models which can accommodate multiple levels of resolution. Multiple

resolution is often desirable because of the flexibility it provides
to the analyst. The analyst is empowered to select one of the
provided levels of resolution that provides the information he or
she requires. This capability has been demonstrated by Wall and
was covered in detail in Chapter 7.

8.2 Aggregation and deaggregation

Closely related to levels of abstraction are the concepts of
aggregation and decomposition. Generally, to move to a higher
level of abstraction (less detail) involves aggregation, or the
representation of several more detailed components by a single
equivalent component. Grouping components and aggregating
variables is quite a well-known procedure. Conversely, to move
to a lower level of abstraction (more detail) the model has to be
further decomposed to adequately describe the modeled physical
entities. This procedure is more difficult and has largely been an
unsolved problem.

Aggregation is conceptually a subset of abstraction
[Fishwick 88]. Collecting lower-level entities and joining them
into a higher-level entity is certainly a form of abstraction.
Consider the system shown in Figure 8.8. If we collect and
combine the model elements of Figure 8.8(a) and replace it with
the single element in Figure 8.8(b), we have aggregated our
original model. When the original model elements are not saved
somewhere in the system, the aggregation is *destructive*. This is
not to be confused with representation issues. A network
simulation could present the analyst with a view of the model in
8.8(b) when in fact the simulation is continuing to execute with
the individual components of 8.8(a). This *representational
aggregation* is merely an aggregation of results. This can be
useful, but it does not produce any computational gains. The
computational cost of achieving high resolutions can be
prohibitive, so computational efficiencies must be achieved where
possible.

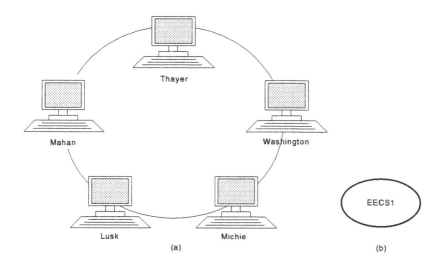

Figure 8.8. Aggregation.

Representational aggregation achieves complete consistency. This should not be surprising since only the outcomes of the lower-level components are aggregated. As long as the original, lower-level outcomes are saved in the system, loss of consistency may be avoided. In many cases this is not a feasible strategy. Simulations may have a very large number of entities. The U.S. Army's Prairie Warrior '94 simulation exercise had more than 50,000 entities, and that should not be considered close to an upper bound [MITRE 95]. It is very difficult and computationally expensive to constantly track so many individual entities.

Intuitively, we can think of consistency as similar to moving from one map scale to another in the same family of maps [Davis 91]. Model consistency may be more rigorously defined in the manner suggested by Hillestad and Juncosa [Hillestad 93]. Figure 8.9 illustrates consistency between two models at time 0 and time *t*. As mentioned previously, some sort of mapping or transition function may be required to compare the outputs of two different models.

We define the mapping function Z_A and mapping function Z_B to produce comparable output from models *A* and *B*, respectively.

Since the outputs can be represented as vectors, consistency may be defined in terms of a scalar norm of the differences [Hillestad 93]. Initially, consistency $\varepsilon(0) = \|Z_A(0) - Z_B(0)\|$ and at time t, $\varepsilon(t) = \|Z_A(t) - Z_B(t)\|$. Acceptable consistency may then be defined as the acceptable size of ε for all t in the range of interest. For example, inconsistencies occurring before steady state is reached in both simulations may be unimportant.

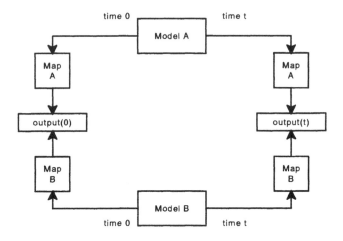

Figure 8.9. Consistency in terms of output measures.

Let model A be the historical event script which has recorded the number of packets on an Ethernet segment. Model B uses a probability distribution function to generate packets on an Ethernet segment. The functions Z_A and Z_B convert the outputs from the respective models into common units and map the output onto a common time interval. We can analyze the differences between the models by comparing the number of packets each model produces at discrete time points.

We often think of aggregation in terms of hierarchical structures, but this need not be the case. Consider two network simulation models. Model A has a resolution at the message level and model B has a resolution at the octet level. In order to evaluate the consistency of the two models, we need to map their output into common terms. Typically we are interested in packets which are composed of octets and constructed by a network's transport layer mechanism to move octets from one application to another. We could decide to map both model *A* and model *B* to produce packets and compare the consistency of the output as illustrated in Figure 8.9. We may choose to simply map one model directly to another, in which case only one mapping function is required. Model *B* could simply have its octets aggregated into messages. In this case no mapping function Z_A is needed for model *A* and map *A* would be null.

When *absolute consistency* is desired, that is, when $\varepsilon = 0$, then any destructive aggregation is strictly a one-way street, as shown in Figure 8.10. If we try to move from model *A* back to model *B*, the best we can achieve is an approximation of the expected state when the simulation resumes execution at the base level.

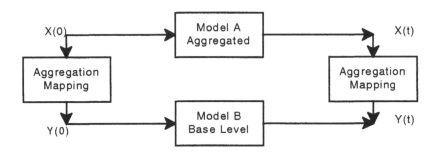

Figure 8.10. Absolute consistency.

Noted RAND researcher, Paul K. Davis [Davis 92], outlines the challenges associated with aggregating and deaggregating models:

- Getting concepts and names right.

- Defining the reference model.

- Determining relationships and mappings.

- Determining the form of reasonable aggregate equations relative to detailed equations.

- Finding conditions under which aggregation equations might be reasonably valid.

- Deciding on cases to be distinguished and how to make calibrations for each case − e.g., how to determine weighting factors over case and time so that the calibrations will be appropriate for the context of the larger application.

Most traditional simulation systems are limited because they are unable to handle models with different degrees of aggregation. As Wall observes, the appropriate level of aggregation may not be known when the simulation system is built [Wall 93]. It is necessary to be able to move dynamically through different levels of aggregation.

Current systems are fairly inflexible with respect to changing levels of aggregation. The difficulty arises from the problem of ensuring consistency among all active levels [Wall 93]. The use of an open architecture provides a means of constructing simulation models with the requisite flexibility to accommodate multiple levels of aggregation.

8.3 Architectural considerations

The practical development of non-trivial distributed simulations is bedeviled by complexity. It is impossible to fully specify the desired implementation on the first try. Iteration during the development stage is inevitable. Any useful simulation is likely to be modified and extended. A distributed system adds another dimension to simulation extensibility. The nature of a distributed system allows heterogeneous hardware to be added to the system.

A software system is said to be open if its behavior can be easily modified and extended [Wegner 92]. Openness can be achieved dynamically through reactiveness or statically through modularity. A *reactive* (interactive) system is one that can react to stimuli by modifying its state and emitting a response. A *modular* (encapsulated) system is one whose number of components and/or functionality can be statically extended by an external agent. Wegner goes on to note that most flexible open systems are both reactive and modular.

An open architecture is liberally defined as any design that has published specifications. A more useful definition of an open architecture is an architecture that allows for the interoperability of different systems [Sochats 92]. Published specifications are an important requirement but do not guarantee interoperability. An open system architecture is the combinational framework that supports the integration of multiple hardware and software systems.

In order to evaluate a simulation design on a distributed platform we first establish a framework which allows us to analyze the delays in the message transmission. Resulting issues are addressed in order to provide feasible solutions for distributed simulation applications. The following measurements provide some means of evaluating the distributed implementation.

Schedulability: This is a direct measure of the capability of meeting message delay requirements. There are two possible ways to measure it:

- The worst case achievable utilization. This is a threshold utilization below which the delay requirements are always met.

- The probability of meeting delay requirements for a given load. In both cases, the higher the measure, the better the performance is.

Complexity of schedulability testing: Sometimes it is necessary to know if a particular delay requirement can be met. This is done by schedulability testing. A lower level of complexity makes schedulability an easier evaluation to apply.

Buffer requirement: A message will be lost and never be delivered if a buffer overflows. Different network scheduling methods may result in different buffer requirements. An upper bound of buffer size must be derived for each scheduling method proposed.

Stability: This reflects the system's sensitivity to change in configuration. One would prefer that a small change in the system configuration (e.g., a slight increase on a node) have minimal impact on the system's capability of meeting message delay requirements.

These measurements may be obtained by rigorous mathematical analysis. One might argue that values of some measures could be obtained experimentally. However, there are two problems with the experimental approach:

- Usually these kinds of experiments are tedious and costly in terms of both time and resource.

- The measured values obtained are only correct for the limiting cases and may not apply to the general case of the simulated system.

We thus believe an analytical approach is necessary to establish performance bounds. Measurement strategies for such large systems are often difficult to formulate and even more difficult to execute.

Some special considerations are required during the verification and validation of a multilevel simulation. The implementation of different abstract levels makes it an intractable exercise to mathematically prove each level's equivalence to the other. An open architecture is most suited for statistical tests to establish the equivalence of the output data.

8.4 Summary

There is a fundamental need for variable resolution models (or families of models) in which there is true consistency across levels. Concepts and methods are needed to enable cross-resolution work, including work with models not originally designed to be compatible [Davis 91].

It is easy to confuse level of resolution with level of abstraction. In fact, both are closely related. Resolution is the level of detail a model can process. The same model may have multiple levels of abstraction. Aggregation is a powerful form of abstraction but can result in the loss of resolution and/or the loss of detail. When moving down an aggregation hierarchy, we can usually only approximate the expected state of the deaggregated components.

The ability to mix and match different forms of objects representing the same real entity is dependent upon the definition of appropriate classes of objects having the same interface. While the definition of these classes is ultimately in the application domain, the concepts and a basic set of class definitions are essential elements of the multilevel, multiresolution distributed simulation (MMDS) hierarchy.

Interfaces must be designed early and at all levels. It is well understood that physically connecting hardware isn't sufficient to achieve interoperability. Rather, the hardware must adhere to a common set of rules for defining their interactions [Rose 90]. This is the principle behind network protocols that provide the underlying connectivity in a distributed system. The software must be similarly defined. In an open systems structure the software must be modular. The interfaces must be built and then the underlying application built. The interfaces must be designed early in the process since a subsequent requirement to change the interfaces may require major modification of the underlying application.

In order to apply the power of integrating multiple models at multiple levels of abstraction with multiple resolution, a strong simulation infrastructure must underpin the design. Combining underspecified models will often lead to "patches" and one-time fixes, which will make the simulations inflexible and brittle. A clean architecture is an absolute requirement to bring distributed computing to bear on the problem.

8.5 Exercises

8.1   Detail the differences between an abstraction hierarchy and an abstraction network. Can an abstraction network exist within an abstraction hierarchy? Explain.

8.2   What is the difference between abstraction and detail?

8.3   In section 8.2 we state that the outputs of the models in Figure 8.9 will be vectors. Why is this the case?

8.4   Discuss the pros and cons of implementing a multimodel simulation on a distributed architecture.

8.5   More than twenty years ago, Zeigler claimed that in any realistic modeling and simulation area, the base model description can never be fully known [Zeigler 76]. Is this still true today? Why? What are the implications of this for abstraction hierarchies?

8.6   Under what conditions is absolute consistency required? What limitations does this impose?

8.7   When and how is representational aggregation useful?

8.8   Devise a detailed deaggregation management scheme and justify it. How would you measure the loss of information?

8.6 References

[Davis 91] P. K. Davis and D. Blumenthal, *The Base of Sand Problem, A White Paper on the State of Military Combat Modeling*, RAND Report N-3148-OSD/DARPA, The RAND Corporation, Santa Monica, CA, 1991.

[Davis 92] P. K. Davis, *An Introduction to Variable-Resolution Modeling and Cross-Resolution Model Connection*, RAND Report R-4252-DARPA, The RAND Corporation, Santa Monica, CA, 1992.

[Fishwick 88] P. A. Fishwick, "The role of process abstraction in simulation," *IEEE Transactions on Systems, Man and Cybernetics,* Vol. 18, No. 1, pp. 18 – 39, January-February 1988.

[Fishwick 95] P. A. Fishwick, *Simulation Model Design and Execution*, Prentice-Hall, Englewood Cliffs, NJ, 1995.

[Hillestad 93] R. J. Hillestad and M. L. Juncosa, *Cutting Some Trees to See the Forest, on Aggregation and Disaggregation*, RAND Report MR-189-ARPA, The RAND Corporation, Santa Monica, CA, 1993.

[Iwasaki 92] Y. Iwasaki, *Recent Advances in Qualitative Physics*, Faltings and Struss, ed., MIT Press, Cambridge, MA, 1992.

[Lee 93] J. L. Lee, W. D. Norris II, and P. A. Fishwick, *An Object-Oriented Multimodel Design for Integrating Simulation and Planning Tasks*, Technical Report 93-019, Department of Computer Science, University of Florida, Gainesville, FL, 1993.

[MITRE 95] *Aggregated and Deaggregated Estimates for a Corps-Level Exercise*, white paper, The MITRE Corporation, Washington C3 Division, McLean, VA, 1995.

[Popken 96] D. A. Popken and A. P. Sinha, "Object-oriented frameworks for multilevel simulation modeling," in *Object-*

Oriented Simulation, Zobrist and Leonard, ed., IEEE Press, Piscataway, NJ, 1996.

[Rose 90]   M. T. Rose, *The Open Book*, Prentice-Hall, Englewood Cliffs, NJ, 1990.

[Rumbaugh 91]   J. Rumbaugh, M. Blaha, W. Premerlani, F. Eddy, and W. Lorensen, *Object-Oriented Modeling and Design*, Prentice-Hall, Englewood Cliffs, NJ, 1991.

[Sevinc 91]   S. Sevinc, "Theories of discrete event model abstraction," *Proceedings of the 1991 Winter Simulation Conference*, Nelson, Kelton, Gordon, eds., Phoenix, AZ, pp. 1115 – 1119, 1991.

[Sochats 92]   K. Sochats and J. Williams, *The Networking and Communications Desk Reference*, Prentice-Hall, Carmel, IN, 1992.

[Wall 93] J. A. Wall, *Multilevel Abstraction of Discrete Models in an Interactive Object-Oriented Simulation Environment*, Ph.D. dissertation, Texas A&M University, December 1993.

[Wegner 92]   P. Wegner, "Dimensions of object-oriented modeling," *IEEE Computer*, Vol. 25, No. 10, pp. 12 – 20, October 1992.

[Zeigler 76] B. P. Zeigler, *Theory of Modelling and Simulation*, John Wiley & Sons, New York, NY, 1976.

9

Environments and Languages for Distributed Simulation

The software implementation of the simulation is sometimes considered only as an afterthought by simulation designers. Although software engineering is beginning to mature as a discipline, it still lacks much of the structure, practices, and associated formulae typical of most engineering fields. No project has the luxury of unlimited time. While some might prefer to have a completely specified and refined model prior to beginning the software engineering process, time constraints alone make this an ill-advised strategy. Many activities of simulation building and software engineering are complimentary. Performing these activities sequentially rather than in parallel at best is wasting time and at worst increases the difficulty in maintaining consistency between the simulation model and the software implementation. Therefore, the software engineering process should start concurrently with the beginning of the simulation effort.

Unfortunately, a casual attitude towards software development may greatly complicate the verification and validation of the simulation. Considerable time may be spent both debugging the software and fine tuning the model, so the choice of language platform and environment is important. The software implementation is important since a validated model incorrectly implemented in software is not likely to produce useful data until the software errors are corrected.

Distributed simulation is of interest because of the larger, more interesting, problem domains which may be feasibly executed with the increased computing power distributed simulation makes available. It is safe to presume that the power of distributed computing will most often be brought to bear on the most complex simulation applications. The software implementation of such systems is not trivial.

Programmers, like everyone else, tend to prefer familiar environments to new environments. The flexibility of software is such that there is rarely any one "right answer" when evaluating developmental environments and implementation languages. However, this is a decision that will be lived with throughout the development, experimentation, and maintenance cycles of the simulation, hence it should not be taken lightly.

As noted earlier in our definition of distributed systems, we are primarily interested in message passing as opposed to shared memory systems. Message passing systems need only two basic functions added to the standard language support: SEND and RECEIVE [Karp 87]. There are three general approaches to distributing programs. One is to build the needed instructions directly into the standard compiler, as in Ada 95. The second approach is to create special compiler versions which recognize inherent parallelism and add the necessary constructs at compile time. The special Cray FORTRAN and C compilers would be examples of this strategy. The third approach is to use remote procedure calls (RPCs) or system calls to a distributed operating system to execute the necessary SENDs and RECEIVEs.

Few mainstream languages exist in which the standard versions support distributed programming [Volz 90]. Most of the languages surveyed here will require RPCs or operating system support to be distributed. It is not our intent to detail parallel programming practices, this being a subject of several excellent textbooks already. For further reading on parallel and concurrent programming, we refer the reader to [Almasi 94] and [Andrews 91].

9.1 Simulation languages

There are many mature programming languages that were expressly designed to support simulation. Simulation languages typically provide specialized routines and libraries of special interest to simulation practitioners. As programming languages have advanced, it has become possible to add libraries of simulation routines to general-purpose languages. The continuing popularity and use of specialized simulation languages warrant their discussion, although they are not typically used in distributed implementations.

9.1.1 Characteristics of simulation languages

[Graybeal 80] lists the following common services provided by specialized simulation languages:

1. Generating random variates.
2. Managing simulation time.
3. Handling routines to simulate event executions.
4. Managing queues.
5. Collecting data.
6. Summarizing and analyzing data.
7. Formulating and printing output.

Almost any system of interest will exhibit stochastic behavior. Typical stochastic elements might include interarrival times in a queuing system or equipment maintenance requirements in production systems. Good, minimal standard pseudorandom number generators exist. Programming a random number generator is a straightforward exercise. Unfortunately, many systems use poorly constructed random number generators [Park 88] that superficially appear to produce random numbers. It is subtly difficult to build a generator that produces (for practical purposes) infinite, statistically independent random numbers uniformly distributed. It is very important that the output of any random number generator be carefully checked using several of the well-known means.

Later in this chapter we will present coded examples of a proven random number generator based on Lehmer's algorithm. Lehmer's algorithm is based on the careful choice of a modulus which is a large prime number and a positive integer multiplier. Random number generators based on this method are formally known as a prime modulus multiplicative linear congruential generator. For a detailed treatment of testing and validating random number generators, we refer the reader to [Pooch 93].

Time management is a major issue in simulation. The two general methods are to use fixed-time increments or event-based clocks with variable-time increments. A specialized simulation language would be expected to support both methods of time management to drive a simulation. Execution of a scheduled event requires changes in system state by invoking the appropriate program module. Not surprisingly, all three of the simulation languages profiled in this section have built-in time management routines. Simulation time can be managed by fixed-increment time advance (periodic scan) or variable-increment time advance (event scan). Fixed-increment schemes are generally easier to implement in a distributed system where clock synchronization is an issue. Ordering events that occur during each time interval may be problematic. [Law 91] observes that fixed-increment time advance is rarely used in discrete event simulation models when the times between successive events vary greatly. Variable-increment time advance schemes rely on the occurrence of events to determine when to update the clock.

Events are scheduled for execution. As an event is executed, the system must be updated to reflect any state changes caused by the event. State changes are effected by the program, often by calling a module such as `decrement_queue` or `fire_mission(parameter list)`. The complexity and number of the required state changes will determine the complexity of the supporting module. Simple queue updates may only require a few lines of code. The aftermath of a simulated artillery engagement may require several non-trivial routines to update ammunition counts and to effect state changes in targets.

Many models require efficient queue management. Whether the model is the classic queuing theory example of people waiting in line at a fast-food restaurant or a series of targets waiting to be "serviced" by attack aircraft, many systems involve competition for limited resources. The representation and manipulation of waiting lines can be accomplished in many ways. A straightforward way of representing queues is by a list because the primary operations in queue management are the addition and deletion of queue elements. The use of pointers and a list structure is one easy way to handle queues.

Considerable research and development have centered around new efficient list processing methods that include binary trees, indexed lists, multi–level indexed lists, and partitioned lists. The implementation of these techniques in a simulation model often results in an order of magnitude reduction in computation time. Thus a language with efficient list-processing capability offers a significant advantage in simulation.

Many simulation models are implemented to assess the effect on the system of varying certain conditions or parameters. This measurement and comparison requires the collection of data. There are two distinct philosophies for collecting data within a simulation: the classical approach and the total approach. In the classical approach we define precisely what information and statistics are to be collected prior to the simulation and use effective methods for collecting and calculating those within the simulation. In the total approach a database is created during the course of the simulation which consists of all the data and information that can be collected. An inquiry mechanism is used to extract any desired information from this database after the simulation.

There are many criteria for selecting a programming language. Specialized simulation languages offer significant advantages in simulation programming. Special-purpose simulation languages were developed (beginning in the late 1950's) because many simulation projects needed similar functions across various applications. Many, though not all, were derivatives of FORTRAN. The simulation languages shown in Figure 9.1 are all more than thirty years old but are still being modified and used.

Although many programming languages have been created, few have gained widespread acceptance and had such long lives as the languages shown in Figure 9.1. This section introduces three of the more important languages: SIMULA, an ALGOL60-based procedural language; SIMSCRIPT, a FORTRAN-based simulation language; and GPSS, which is both a simulation language and a computer program.

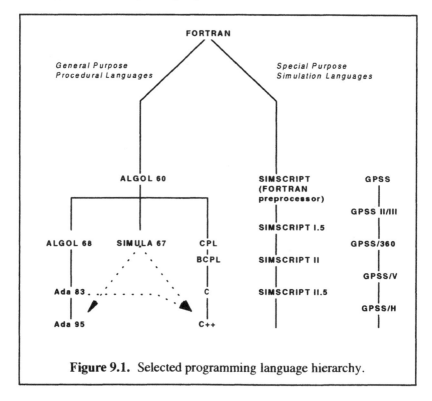

Figure 9.1. Selected programming language hierarchy.

9.1.2 SIMULA

As noted in Chapter 6, the object-oriented paradigm is rooted in SIMULA. The SIMULA language is closely associated with discrete-event simulation, and it is a mature procedural language. SIMULA is often best recognized for its simulation features, which is why we categorize it as a simulation language. However, SIMULA may also used for non-simulation applications. SIMULA is based on the ALGOL programming language [Kreutzer 86].

Although first developed thirty years ago, SIMULA is still in use, primarily in Europe and Australia [Sadiku 95]. Wegner listed the development of SIMULA as one of the major milestones in the evolution of programming languages [Wegner 87]. The implementation of the SIMULA class language construct was an important improvement over the ALGOL block language construct.

Example 9.1 Declaring a class in SIMULA [Kirkerud 89].

```
class Place;
begin
   real longitude, latitude;
   procedure read;
    begin
     latitude:=prompt_for_real("Degrees north? ");
     longitude:=prompt_for_real("Degrees east? ");
    end of Place'read
   procedure write;
    begin
     outfix(latitude, 2, 5);
     outtext(" degrees north, ");
     outfix(longitude, 2, 5);
     outtext(" degrees east. ");
     outimage;
    end of Place'write;
end of Place;
```

[Kirkerud 89] provides an example of declaring a simple class in SIMULA in Example 9.1. The class Place has four attributes: two real variables and two procedures. Thus we see the encapsulation of objects and the operations upon those objects, which are cornerstones of the object-oriented paradigm.

Coroutines in SIMULA are implemented in class structures. The use of coroutines is one way to control concurrent execution. The developers of SIMULA pioneered the concept of mutual control between procedures known as coroutines. As shown in Figure 9.2, control is passed from one coroutine to another by means of a RESUME statement. Coroutine A executes for some time and then passes control to coroutine B. Later, coroutine B executes RESUME A and control returns to coroutine A. As illustrated in Figure 9.2, order of execution is determined by the coroutines themselves. It is important to note that coroutines do not support true parallel processing but rather the execution of one process at a time. Synchronization is implicit since only one coroutine executes at a time.

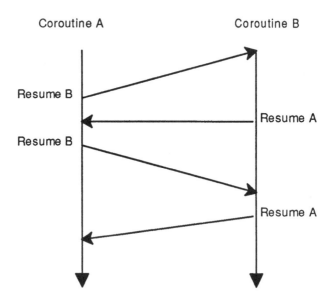

Figure 9.2. Coroutines.

Simulation languages typically use a general notion of coroutines to schedule events. Different subroutines switch from active to passive and from passive to active with control being passed to and from a scheduler, rather than directly between the coroutines.

[Kerr 89] summarizes the following strengths of SIMULA:

- Conventional general-purpose ALGOL-style algorithmic capability.

- Object-oriented programming (classes) encompassing encapsulation, inheritance, information hiding, autonomous activity, and strong typing supporting the concepts of modularity, generalization, specialization, abstraction, polymorphism, and pseudo-parallelism.

- Basic features for manipulating text strings.

- File concept supporting sequential and direct access methods for byte- and record-structured files.

- Large repertoire of utility functions.

- Features supporting two-way linked lists. More complicated list structures such as trees and lattices are easily constructed from the basic class facilities.

- Features supporting discrete event simulation in various styles including the object-oriented process view.

Although SIMULA never achieved widespread adoption, it is still available for many platforms and still in use. SIMULA was an important landmark in the evolution of programming languages. Although you may never program in SIMULA, it is likely that you will use the object-oriented and concurrent programming features pioneered in SIMULA.

9.1.3 SIMSCRIPT

SIMSCRIPT was developed by the RAND Corporation in 1962 by Markowitz, Karr, and Hausner [Markowitz 63]. The most current version of SIMSCRIPT is SIMSCRIPT II.5 which is proprietary. Originally, SIMSCRIPT was implemented as a FORTRAN preprocessor, but beginning with SIMSCRIPT I.5 in

1964 this was no longer the case. SIMSCRIPT executable files are created through the use of SIMSCRIPT compiler.

SIMSCRIPT was designed as a higher-order programming system [Kreutzer 86]. Thus, it may be used for applications other than simulation, as well as for a broad range of simulation applications. SIMSCRIPT programs consist of three parts:

1. Preamble:
   - Block where global variables are defined.
   - Precedes main program.
   - Contains no executable statements.

2. Main Program
   - Block where program execution begins.
   - Mandatory element for all SIMSCRIPT programs.

3. Event Routines
   - Subroutines written for each event.
   - Executed when simulated event is scheduled.

Experienced programmers will observe that the SIMSCRIPT program outlined above is similar to the program structure found in many programming languages. An example of a trivial SIMSCRIPT program which only has a main program block is shown in Example. 9.2.

Example 9.2 Main program in SIMSCRIPT.

```
main
  print 1 line
  thus
  HELLO WORLD
end
```

Routines in SIMSCRIPT are similar to subprograms in other languages and are declared after the main program block. There must be an event routine for each event named in the preamble. Event occurrences are modeled by calls to event routines from the main program block. Event routines update the system state when called for by the occurrence of the event. A simple initialization routine is shown in Example 9.3. As may be seen in the examples, SIMSCRIPT employs an English-like syntax.

Example 9.3 SIMSCRIPT routine example.

```
routine INITIALIZE
  define A,B as integer variables
  '' integers A and B are local variables
  let LOCATION = 1
  let A = 0
  let B = 0
  until A eq NUM.APCS
''APC stands for armored personnel carrier
  do
    let A = A + 1
    let B = B + 1
    create an APC
    if B > LO.INIT.APCS(LOCATION)
      let B = 1
      let LOCATION = LOCATION + 1
    endif
    activate this APC now
  loop
end
```

SIMSCRIPT includes standard functions to support statistical analysis. Random number generation is an essential simulation service. SIMSCRIPT supplies ten independent random number streams. Each stream is generated using the *multiplicative congruential method*. Each of the ten generators uses the same multiplier, $a = 14^{29}$, and the same modulus, $m = 2^{31} - 1$. The seed determines the differences in the generated streams. For a further discussion of random number generation in SIMSCRIPT we refer the reader to [Pooch 93] and [CACI 71].

The simulation clock is set by the double precision variable time.v. The default time quantum is a unit. Other time elements such as days, hours or minutes may be selected. The simulation clock advances when an event is scheduled for execution. The current simulation time is accessed in time.v. Typically, simulation time is started as soon as initialization routines complete.

There is no inherent simulation structure in SIMSCRIPT as in GPSS. Detailed problem analysis is required before any programming should begin. The structure for a specific simulation must be developed by the system designer. Model relationships are set up utilizing the entity-attribute-set relationships. An *entity* is an element of the simulation system that can be individually identified and processed. As the name implies, an *attribute* is a characteristic of an entity such as an identification number or color. A *set* is an ordered list of entities.

SIMSCRIPT has been extensively used for military simulations because it can handle large, complex models that are not queueing-oriented [Law 91]. SIMSCRIPT has much of the functionality of older third generation programming languages and remains in widespread use today.

9.1.4 GPSS/H

The General Purpose Simulation System (GPSS) is a non-procedural language designed to model queueing systems. GPSS was developed in 1961 by [Gordon 78] and was designed for the express purpose of simulating the operation of discrete systems. Interpreted and compiled versions of GPSS exist.

GPSS provides the analyst with predefined blocks to construct queueing-based simulation models. This may be viewed as advantageous in terms of easing the programming skills needed to use GPSS, but this ease comes at the cost of flexibility. The analyst lacks the means to significantly change the predefined blocks provided by GPSS.

The simulated system is represented by a set of blocks connected by lines. Each block represents some activity, and each line represents a path to the next activity as shown in Figure 9.3. Each block symbol is unique, thus providing a ready interpretation of the block diagrams. For a more complete description of GPSS, see [Schriber 91].

Consider the problem of simulating passenger train platform in the busy U.S. Northeast Corridor. The model is constructed to represent four types of passengers waiting for two types of trains. The passengers and trains are linked through two gates so that when the gates are open, passengers may board the train. When no train is present, the gates are closed.

The entire simulation program (not shown) consists of nine block segments. Segments 1 through 4 let the passengers enter the model. These segments share QUEUE - DEPART sequences which allow statistical data collection. Segments 5 through 8 generate the trains. The first eight segments share the SEIZE - RELEASE sequence for the appropriate gates. Segment 9 is the timer. The source code for Segment 1 is shown in Example 9.4.

Example 9.4 GPSS V source code, segment 1, commuter train model.
Courtesy of Lt.Col. A. S. Ruocco, U.S. Military Academy.

```
SIMULATE
*
*MODEL SEGMENT 1 (EXPRESS PLATFORM)
*
1    GENERATE    15,5    GENERATE EXPRESS PASSENGERS
2    QUEUE    TOTQ    ENTER TOTAL QUEUE
3    QUEUE    EXPLQ    ENTER EXPRESS PLATFORM QUEUE
4    QUEUE    EXQ    ENTER EXPRESS PREFERENCE QUEUE
5    SEIZE    GAT1    GAIN ACCESS TO THE TRAIN
6    DEPART    TOTQ    LEAVE TOTAL QUEUE
7    DEPART    EXPLQ    LEAVE THE PLATFORM
8    DEPART    EXQ    LEAVE PREFERENCE QUEUE
9    RELEASE GAT1
10   TERMINATE
*
*MODEL REMAINING SEGMENTS
*Additional platforms, Train access locks,
*Train runs, Timer
     START    1    START THE SIMULATION
     END    END THE SIMULATION
```

Segment 1 is easily understood. Passengers arrive, enter the QUEUES where statistics on their arrival are collected, board the train (via SEIZE), DEPART the QUEUES, RELEASE the gate and exit the model. The block diagram for this part of the program is shown in Figure 9.3.

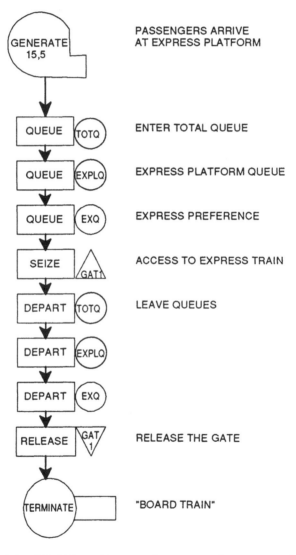

Figure 9.3. GPSS block diagram: Segment 1, Commuter train model.
Courtesy of Lt.Col. A. S. Ruocco, U.S. Military Academy.

GPSS has many advantages and disadvantages. It is easy to learn; coding from the block diagrams is straightforward. Basic simulation functions are built-in. Many statistics of interest are printed automatically. Subprogramming is not supported. User-defined extensions to GPSS generated statistics are often difficult to implement.

Simulation languages such as SIMSCRIPT and GPSS have proven themselves sufficiently robust to remain in widespread use in the third decade of their existence. Since compiled versions of both languages are available, it is possible to consider distributed implementations of both even though the languages themselves do not have parallel/distributed programming constructs provided. The continuing popularity and use of specialized simulation languages warrant their consideration for use in distributed implementations.

9.2 General-purpose languages

We distinguish a general-purpose language from a simulation language by characterizing the former as a high level language suitable for any programming task as opposed to a language specialized for simulation.

Introduced in 1957, FORTRAN (for IBM Mathematical FORmula TRANslation System) was the first high-level general-purpose language to be standardized and is still in use more than forty years after it was first specified. [Wegner 87] calls FORTRAN "the single most important milestone in the development of programming languages." FORTRAN has been widely used in simulation and is well surveyed in the literature [Graybeal 80][Pooch 93][Law 91].

FORTRAN remains the programming language of choice for many segments of the scientific community. A large amount of simulation software has been written and is being maintained in FORTRAN. For examples of FORTRAN routines in simulation, see [Graybeal 80]. FORTRAN is likely to continue in use through the 21st century. One reason for FORTRAN's staying power is the rich set of scientific program libraries that have been thoroughly verified and validated.

We cover two languages in detail here: Ada 95 and C++. Both languages provide full support for object-oriented programming which was not fully supported in either Ada 83 or C. Ada 95 and C++ are more modern general-purpose programming languages. In the next decade, we can expect to see more development in these languages and their descendants. Both Ada 95 and C++ support the development of external program libraries. This capability makes it eminently possible for a general-purpose language to provide the same kind of programming support provided in specialized simulation languages.

9.2.1 Ada 95

In 1975, the U.S. Department of Defense (DoD) began searching for a standard programming language that would support specific military requirements such as embedded real-time programming as well as general-purpose requirements.

In 1983, Ada was designated as military standard MIL-STD 1815a, which also became the ANSI standard. The most recent revision is ANSI/ISO/IEC-8562:1995, popularly called Ada 95. Many of the programming language innovations pioneered in Ada are now taken for granted. Interest in Ada has not been limited to military applications. It is also used in many commercial sectors, particularly those areas requiring high reliability.

Ada was designed from the beginning to strongly support software engineering principles. The design of Ada stresses the ease of reading code over the ease of writing code, thus greatly contributing to maintainability [Naiditch 95]. Modularity is an inherent part of the Ada language design. Ada packages are separately compiled modules that may be used and reused in various programs. Packages are generally divided into two parts: a package specification and a package body [LRM 95].

Packages are an important means of information hiding. Users without access to the source code of the package body may only pass the appropriate parameters to the functions or procedures listed in the specification. Private types provide a stronger form of information hiding. When a type is declared in a package specification, its implementation details may be hidden by declaring the type to be **private**. The implementation details follow later in the private part of the package [Ada 95]. A trivial example of a private type, casualty_factor, is given in Example 9.5.

Example 9.5 An Ada package specification.

```
with Ada.text_io;
use Ada.text_io;
with Ada.float_text_io;
use  Ada.float_text_io;
with Ada.Numerics.Elementary_Functions;
use Ada.Numerics.Elementary_Functions;


--Package casualty computes the casualty inflicting
--effectiveness of both force X and force Y.
--A thorough description of the computation can be
found on --pg 49 of "Numbers, Predictions & War" by
COL T. N. Dupuy.

package CASUALTY is


procedure Casualty_Effectiveness(
    Vulnerability_x,Vulnerability_Y,
    Numbers_x,Numbers_y,
    Strength_x,Strength_y,
    Casualty_x,Casualty_y: in float;
    Eff_Casualty_x,Eff_Casualty_y: in out float;
    Vulnerability_X_sqr,Vulnerability_Y_sqr: out
float;
    factor: in float);
end CASUALTY;
```

The full implementation of **procedure** Casualty_ Effectiveness declared in the package specification is shown in the package body that follows in Example 9.6.

Example 9.6 An Ada package body.

```
package body CASUALTY is

procedure Casualty_Effectiveness(
    Vulnerability_X,Vulnerability_Y,
    Numbers_x,Numbers_y,
    Strength_X,Strength_y,
    Casualty_x,Casualty_y: in float;
    Eff_Casualty_x,Eff_Casualty_y:in out float;
    Vulnerability_X_sqr,Vulnerability_Y_sqr: out
float;
    factor: in float) is

begin
    Vulnerability_X_sqr:= Vulnerability_X *
Vulnerability_X;
    Vulnerability_Y_sqr:= Vulnerability_Y *
Vulnerability_Y;
    Eff_Casualty_x:=
    Vulnerability_Y_sqr *
(sqrt((Strength_X/Strength_y) *
    (Casualty_x/Casualty_y))-(sqrt( factor *
Casualty_x) /
    Numbers_x) ));

    Eff_Casualty_y:=
    Vulnerability_X_sqr *
(sqrt((Strength_y/Strength_X) *
    (Casualty_y/Casualty_x)) - (sqrt(factor *
Casualty_y) / Numbers_y) ));
        put("Eff_Casualty_x--> ");
    put(Eff_Casualty_x, AFT => 4);
    new_line;
    put("Eff_Casualty_y--> ");
    put(Eff_Casualty_y, AFT => 4);
    new_line;
end Casualty_Effectiveness;   --procedure end
end CASUALTY; -- package body end
```

A major design goal of Ada 95 was to provide support for object-oriented programming. Ada 95 builds on the object-oriented design capabilities provided by Ada 83 and adds support for inheritance and polymorphism. A simple example of inheritance, known as programming by extension, is shown in Example 9.7. The tagged record `student_object` has four defined fields. The derived type, `doctoral_student` inherits the four components from `student_object` and explicitly adds the Boolean fields `prelims` and `thesis`.

Example 9.7 Objects and inheritance in Ada 95.

```
type year_type is (freshman, sophomore, junior,
senior,

                   master, doctorate);


type student_object is tagged
   record
    GPA:      FLOAT range 0.00..4.00;
    year:     year_type;
    hours:    INTEGER range 0..300;
    SSN:      STRING(1..9);
   end record;


type doctoral_student is new student_object with
   record
    prelims:    BOOLEAN;
    thesis: BOOLEAN;
   end record;
```

Simulation is usually difficult to extend to general purpose languages. Typically, when a procedural language not specifically designed for simulation is used, one of two approaches may be used to build the simulation: event-driven simulation or time-driven simulation [Cook 93]. Event-driven simulation is desirable from a design, implementation, and verification/validation standpoint; however, time-driven simulation is often easier to code. Time-driven simulation requires the system to perform a check of all possible events for each logical time tick. Although very easy to implement, this type of implementation typically leads to large, monolithic programs that are very difficult to verify.

Event-driven simulation allows closer modeling or abstraction of the real world. Each event from the real world that is being simulated is represented as a separate event within the program code. The scheduling and handling of these events, however, is difficult to program. Often, an interrupt-driven implementation is the only alternative. The resulting operating system overhead can be costly. In addition, the scheduling and handling of interrupts requires coding at the operating system level. This is difficult to program and even more difficult to test. Minor changes to an interrupt-driven program can cause major changes in performance. Because of the difficulty of using general purpose languages for event-driven simulations, specific simulation languages, such as SIMSCRIPT or SIMULA, are often used.

Ada, however, has constructs that allow event-driven simulations without resorting to operating system interrupts. The mechanism that allows this is the *tasking* model. The use of the tasking model in Ada to model the real world could best be called model-driven simulation. Ada easily allows each external event generator to be modeled as a separate task [Hamilton 95]. In this manner, each can be modeled as a task call or an `accept`. Adequate timing features in Ada 83 exist, permitting tasks to use physical timing for event simulation.

Each task can share common data with other tasks. This feature permits events to modify the state of the system without performing a task call or accept. In this manner, multiple tasks, each representing an event generator, can modify the system state quickly.

An example of the Ada tasking system is given in Example 9.8. `Procedure matrix_mult` declares four tasks, each of which compute one element of the product of multiplying matrix **A** with its transpose. For the purposes of this example matrix $\mathbf{A^tA}$ is assumed to be a 2×2 matrix. The computation of $\mathbf{A^tA}$

may be done in parallel. Each element of A^tA is computed by a separate task. Procedure mult11 computes $A^tA(1,1)$, etc.

Like many applications in linear algebra, this problem is inherently parallel. When the code in Example 9.8 is executed on a uniprocessor, the tasks execute in arbitrary order. This is perfectly satisfactory since the computation does not depend on the execution order of the tasks.

Example 9.8 Ada tasking.

```
with Ada.text_io;
with Ada.float_text_io;


--Procedure matrix_mult is the parent procedure for
--tasks which compute A transpose * A.


procedure matrix_mult(n: in INTEGER; ata: in out
atrana; a:in matrix; atran: in tran) is


--Once procedure matrix_mult is invoked, the tasks
may
--execute concurrently.  Each task invokes a
--procedure to calculate an element of atran * a.


  task mult11;
  task body mult11 is
  begin
      ata11(n,ata,a,atran);
  end mult11;
  task mult12;

  task body mult12 is
  begin
      ata12(n,ata,a,atran);
  end mult12;

  task mult21;
  task body mult21 is
  begin
      ata21(n,ata,a,atran);
```

```
end mult21;

task mult22;
task body mult22 is
begin
    ata22(n,ata,a,atran);
end mult22;

begin
    Ada.text_io.put_line("At * A is: ");
    Ada.float_text_io.put(ata(1,1),AFT => 3);
    Ada.float_text_io.put(ata(1,2),AFT => 3);
    new_line;
    Ada.float_text_io.put(ata(2,1),AFT => 3);
    Ada.float_text_io.put(ata(2,2),AFT => 3);
    new_line;
end matrix_mult;
```

Ada 95 contains additional support for both real-time and distributed simulation. The Distributed Annex (Annex E) of the Ada *Language Reference Manual* contains support for distributing code [LRM 95]. This annex defines the partitioning of a large system (including the partitioning of packages across nodes) and allows the designer to specify synchronous or asynchronous subprogram calls. In addition, predefined library packages exist to simplify communication between active partitions of a distributed program.

Ada is designed for reliable programming of large systems. The modular design of Ada promotes software engineering in general and reuse in particular. Packages that support discrete event simulation are available in the public domain. Such external packages provide Ada with many of the advantages found in simulation languages while retaining its general-purpose flexibility and portability.

9.2.2 C++

C++ was developed because its author wanted to write some event-driven simulations for which SIMULA67 would have been ideal, except for efficiency considerations [Stroustrup 91]. C++

is based most closely on the C language. C is described non-pejoratively as a relatively low-level language [Kernighan 88]. Stroustrup attached great importance to maintaining compatibility with C, which prevented him from cleaning up C syntax [Stroustrup 91]. However, given the large amount of C code in use today, it is hard to criticize the decision for C++ to maintain backward compatibility with C.

In direct contrast to Ada, C is not a strongly typed language. There are advantages and disadvantages to a weakly typed language. The essential point is that users of C/C++ need to be aware that C/C++ is a weakly typed language and defensive programming is appropriate. As with most programming language design issues, trade-offs are involved.

Example 9.9 demonstrates the terseness of C with the new stream IO feature of C++.

Example 9.9 Multiplicative congruential random number generator.

```
/* random.cc: Random number generation using the
multiplicative congruential method, wherein the
(n+1)th value of the sequence is calculated by:


        X(n+1) = lambda * [X(n) mod P]


lambda is the _multiplier_, and P is the _modulus_
of the sequence so generated. */

// Includes:
#include <math.h>
#include <stdlib.h>
#include <stream.h>

int main (int argc, char* argv[])
   {
// Establish values for the multiplier and modulus:
double lambda, P, Xtemp;
```

```
lambda = pow(7, 5);
P = pow(2, 31) - 1;
cout << "Lambda=" << lambda << ";P=" << P << "; ";

// Initialize the first value in the series:
Xtemp = drand48();
cout << "X(0) = " << form("%.25lf", Xtemp) << endl;

for (int dex= 0; dex < 250; dex++)
  {
  cout << form ("%.24lf", (1.0/Xtemp)) << endl;
  Xtemp = fmod (Xtemp, P) * lambda;
    }
  }
```

As object-oriented programming grew in importance in the 1980s, C was extended to support classes. This began the evolution that led to the development of C++. The OOP terminology used in C++ varies from that used in Ada 95. Whereas visibility in Ada 95 is either public or private, C++ has three levels of visibility: private, protected, and public. In C++, a private member is visible only within its own class, protected members are visible within the class, and any of its descendants in the inheritance tree. C++ directly supports multiple inheritance, unlike Ada 95. A simple demonstration of inheritance in C++ is given in Example 9.10. The **class** doctoral_student inherits the public attributes of **class** student_object.

Example 9.10 Inheritance in C++.

```
enum year_type {
    freshman,
    sophomore,
    junior,
    senior,
    master,
    doctorate
    };
```

```
enum boolean { false, true };

class student_object{
   public:
    float    GPA;
    year_type   year;
    int      hours;
    int      SSN[9];
};


class doctoral_student : public student_object {
    boolean prelims;
    boolean thesis;
};
```

C++ does not have pre-defined language constructs for distributing programs. Rather the low-level design of the language facilitates the use of system calls to distribute a program. In Example 9.11, the Cholesky factorization of a matrix is presented. For a positive definite matrix **A**, Cholesky factorization returns a lower triangular matrix **L** such that $\mathbf{LL^t} = \mathbf{A}$. The target architecture is a 64 node nCube hypercube, a distributed memory MIMD device. A master-slave model is used in which one node is the master and distributes parts of the problem to the slave nodes. nCube specific system calls typically have the letter "***n***" prefixed to a predefined C function, such as ***nread*** and ***nwrite***; they are noted in bold italics. It would be very convenient to have some of the Ada constructs available for a program of this nature. However, when main memory and memory buffer lengths are limited, the programming overhead associated with Ada tasking might be impractical, thus forcing the programmer to use low overhead features of the implementation language.

Example 9.11 Hypercube programming example.

```
#include <stdio.h>
```

```
#include <math.h>

#define min(A, B)   ((A) < (B) ? (A) : (B))
#define max(A, B)   ((A) > (B) ? (A) : (B))
#define DIMENSION 5

typedef struct mystruct
   {
   int msg_code;
   int originator;
   float value;
   int low_index;
   int high_index;
   int row;
   int col;
   } MSG_STRUCT;

/* Prototypes: */
void execute_message (MSG_STRUCT* arg, int node_id,
                      int num_procs,
                    float Lptr[DIMENSION][DIMENSION],
                    float Aptr[DIMENSION][DIMENSION]);

extern double amicclk(void);

main (int argc, char** argv)
   {
   int a, dex, i, j, k, k2, column_counter, flag,
offset;
   int type, any_node_id;
   float L[DIMENSION][DIMENSION];
   float A[DIMENSION][DIMENSION];
   MSG_STRUCT in_message, out_message;
   int node, proc, host, dim, nprocs;
   float result, temp;
/* 'A' is the original matrix, 'L' is the new lower-
triangular matrix.   Initialize A to be a positive
definite matrix:
     [  2    -1     0    ...]
     [ -1     2    -1    ...]
     [  0    -1     2    ...]
     [  ...   ...            ]
code to initialize matrix A and matrix L = 0.0 is
omitted */
```

```
/* Determine processor's identity: */
whoami (&node, &proc, &host, &dim);
nprocs = 1 << dim;
```

/* The "**if**" part insures that no MORE than DIMENSION nodes compute the entry; the "**for**" loop establishes the number of times that a particular node will compute an entry. */

```
if (node < DIMENSION)
  {
  j = 0;
  for (i = 0; i < (DIMENSION/nprocs)+
                ((DIMENSION%nprocs)>node); i++)
    {
    /* Calculate L00: */
    temp = sqrt(A[0][0]);
    L[0][0] = temp;
```

/* Calculate the remaining entries of column 0: */
/* Determine starting point in column zero. DIMENSION%nprocs != 0 means either that there are more than DIMENSION processors available, or that at least one processor, but fewer than all of them execute the task more than the others. In the case where there are fewer processors than tasks, the quantity DIMENSION%nprocs tells the number of processors which much do the task more than the others. */

```
    if ((DIMENSION%nprocs) != 0)
      {
      if (nprocs > DIMENSION)
        offset = node;
      else
        {
        if (node <= (DIMENSION%nprocs)-1)
          offset = node * ((DIMENSION/nprocs)+1);
        else
          offset = (DIMENSION%nprocs) *
                   ((DIMENSION/nprocs)+1) +
                   ((node-(DIMENSION%nprocs)) *
                   (DIMENSION/nprocs));
        }
      }
```

```
      else
        offset = node * (max((DIMENSION/nprocs),1));
      L[offset+i][0] = A[offset+i][0] / L[0][0];
      j++;
      }
    }

  /* Calculate remaining columns. */

  if (node == 0)
    {
    /* Ask for values in column 0, update node 0's
L-matrix: */
    out_message.msg_code = 4;
    out_message.originator = node;
    for (k = 1; k < min(nprocs,DIMENSION); k++)
      nwrite((char *) &out_message,
             sizeof (MSG_STRUCT), k, 0xFF, &flag);
/* Receive the values.  Node 0 should receive
DIMENSION values, less the number of entries it
computed itself: */

    for (k = 1; k <= DIMENSION-(DIMENSION/nprocs)-
       ((DIMENSION%nprocs)>0); k++)
      {
      type = -1;
      any_node_id = -1;
      nread((char*) &in_message, sizeof(in_message),
            &any_node_id,&type,&flag);
      L[in_message.row][in_message.col] =
                                    in_message.value;
      }

    for (i = 1; i < DIMENSION-1; i++)
      {
      /* Start with Lii, the main diagonal entry: */
      result = 0.0;
      for (k = 0; k <= i-1; k++)
        result += L[i][k] * L[i][k];
      L[i][i] = sqrt(A[i][i] - result);

      /* Calculate remaining entries in column i: */
      for (j = i+1; j < DIMENSION; j++)
        {
```

```
        /* Initialize some state variables: */
        out_message.msg_code = 3;
        out_message.originator = node;
        column_counter = 0;
        result = 0.0;
```

/* Send messages to the processors that are going
   to actually do the calculating. Outer loop
   controls which processor the message is sent to.
   Inner loop controls how many messages get sent to
   that processor. */

```
        for (k2 = 1; k2 <= min(nprocs-1,i); k2++)
           {
```
/* Indicate the base row and column in the msg
   structure: */
```
           if ((i%nprocs) != 0)
             {
             if (nprocs > i)
               k = 1;

             else
               {
               k = (i/(nprocs-1)) + ((I%
                                  (nprocs-1))>k2);
               printf("k = %d\n", k);
               }
             }

           for (dex = 0; dex < k; dex++)
             {
             out_message.row = i;
             out_message.col = j;
             out_message.high_index = column_counter;
             nwrite((char *) &out_message,
                     sizeof(MSG_STRUCT), k2,
                     0xFF,&flag);
             column_counter++;
             }
           }

        /* Accept their responses: */

        for (k2 = 1; k2 <= i; k2++)
          {
```

```
                  type = -1;
                  any_node_id = -1;
                  nread((char*)&in_message,
                        sizeof(in_message),
                        &any_node_id, &type, &flag);
                  result += in_message.value;
                  }

/* Calculate L[j][i] and update the other nodes: */
            L[j][i] = (1.0/L[i][i])*(A[j][i] - result);
            out_message.row = j;
            out_message.col = i;
            out_message.value = L[j][i];
            out_message.msg_code = 5;
            out_message.originator = node;
            nwrite((char *) &out_message,
                    sizeof(MSG_STRUCT), i+1, 0xFF,
                    &flag);
            end_com_time = amicclk();
            elapsed_com_time += end_com_time-
                                    start_com_time;
            }
        }

      /* Calculate Lnn: */
      start_comp_time = amicclk();
      result = 0.0;
      for (i = 0; i < DIMENSION; i++)
        result += L[DIMENSION-1][i]*L[DIMENSION-1][i];
      L[DIMENSION-1][DIMENSION-1] =
          sqrt(A[DIMENSION-1][DIMENSION-1] - result);

      /* Kill off all of the slave nodes: */
      out_message.msg_code = 0;
      for (k = 1; k < nprocs; k++)
        nwrite((char*) &out_message,
               sizeof(MSG_STRUCT), k,
               0xFF, &flag);

      }   /* End if (node == 0) */

   else
     {
     while (1)
       {
```

```
      type = -1;
      any_node_id = -1;
      nread((char*)&in_message,sizeof(in_message),
            &any_node_id, &type, &flag);
      execute_message (&in_message,node,nprocs,L,A);
      }
   }
}

void execute_message (MSG_STRUCT* arg,
                      int node_id,
                      int nprocs,
                      float Lptr[DIMENSION][DIMENSION],
                      float Aptr[DIMENSION][DIMENSION])
  {
  int i,j, dest, offset;
  static int flag, src, type;
  static MSG_STRUCT msg;

  switch (arg->msg_code)
    {
    case 0:                  /* NODE SELF-DESTRUCT */
        exit();

      case 1:
/* We have to notify the master node when the output
is written, so that it shows on-screen in the
correct order. */
        msg.msg_code = 6;
        msg.originator = node_id;
        msg.value = Lptr[arg->row][arg->col];
        nwrite((char *) &msg,
               sizeof(MSG_STRUCT), 0, 0xFF, &flag);
        break;

      case 2:        /* CALCULATE A PAIRED PRODUCT */
        msg.value = Lptr[arg->col][arg->high_index] *
                    Lptr[arg->row][arg->high_index];
        msg.msg_code = 3;
        msg.originator = node_id;
        nwrite((char *) &msg,
               sizeof(MSG_STRUCT), 0, 0xFF, &flag);
        break;
```

```
  case 3:                /* REPORT 0th COLUMN VALUE */
   msg.msg_code = 5;
   msg.col = 0;
   msg.originator = node_id;
    for (i = 0; i < (DIMENSION/nprocs) +
                  ((DIMENSION%nprocs)>node_id); i++)
      {
      dest = 0;
      if ((DIMENSION%nprocs) != 0)
        {
        if (nprocs > DIMENSION)
          offset = node_id;
        else
          {
          if (node_id <= (DIMENSION%nprocs)-1)
            offset = node_id *
                          ((DIMENSION/nprocs)+1);
          else
            offset = (DIMENSION%nprocs) *
                    ((DIMENSION/nprocs)+1) +
                    ((node_id-(DIMENSION%nprocs)) *
                      (DIMENSION/nprocs));
          }
        msg.row = offset+i;
        msg.value = Lptr[offset+i][0];
        if (dest != node_id)
            {
            nwrite((char *) &msg,
                    sizeof(MSG_STRUCT), dest, 0xFF,
                    &flag);
            }
          }
        }

    break;

  case 4:  /* RECEIVE AN L-MATRIX ENTRY UPDATE */
    Lptr[arg->row][arg->col] = arg->value;
    break;
    }
  }
```

C++ is a powerful language with many strengths. Because C++ is built on C, C++ provides the capability to add object-oriented or other software engineering related constructs to existing C code. C is closely associated with UNIX [Kernighan 88]. Both UNIX and many of its important programs are written in C. This can be very useful when programming in a UNIX environment. ANSI C and ANSI C++ are both characterized by low overhead and efficiency. However, the price of these features is terseness, a sometimes confusing syntax, and potential reliability problems. As noted earlier, C++'s complete backward compatibility with C has limited some desirable language improvements. However, C++ greatly enhances the ability to do good software engineering over C, while still retaining the original strengths of C.

9.3 Summary

Fifteen years ago the distinction between simulation languages and general-purpose languages was clear. Simulation languages such as SIMSCRIPT and GPSS as well as SLAM and GASP offered important simulation features that had to be explicitly and tediously developed in a general-purpose language.

As the software engineering discipline began to mature in the 1980s, software reuse received more attention. FORTRAN had long benefited from important software libraries to support scientific and mathematical programming. The development of simulation libraries for C++ [Fishwick 95] and Ada 95 [Tindell 94] are giving general-purpose languages the same capabilities as simulation languages while preserving the greater flexibility of the general-purpose languages.

Research is being done on C++ to Ada 95 translators [Uhde 95]. Although the design philosophies of both languages are radically different, in fact they have many similar capabilities. Language choice is often a matter of taste or driven by external requirements. Perhaps the single most consistent factor is the existence of legacy software and the familiarity and preferences of the programming staff.

The existing software libraries written in FORTRAN ensure that FORTRAN will continue in use for many more years to come. A survey of simulations in use in the U.S. Army show many simulations written in SIMSCRIPT, GPSS, and FORTRAN are still in use [Freeland 88]. The Army, as well as the field in general, are writing newer simulations in Ada 95, C++ and other languages. However, there is a wide body of experience and legacy code invested in the older simulation languages so we can expect them to remain in service for some time to come.

9.4 Exercises

9.1   It was noted earlier that SIMULA is a general-purpose language in its own right. Under what conditions might SIMULA be preferable to other general-purpose languages such as C++ and Ada 95?

9.2   What language characteristics do you think are most important in selecting an implementation language for a distributed simulation?

9.3   FORTRAN was mentioned in passing at the beginning of section 9.2. Why is FORTRAN still in use today? Why might you choose to use FORTRAN instead of SIMSCRIPT or C++?

9.4   When would it be advantageous to use a weakly typed language?

9.5   At what point in the simulation planning process should a programming language decision be made? Why?

9.6   Why might you choose to implement a simulation in SIMSCRIPT or GPSS instead of a general-purpose language?

9.7   Compare and contrast the utility of Ada 95 and C++ in distributed simulation.

9.8 How important a consideration is C/C++'s relationship with UNIX?

9.9 Why is standardization an important feature of a programming language?

9.10 Which programming language do you prefer to work in and why? Evaluate your choice against the criteria given in section 9.1.1.

9.5 References

[Ada 95] *Ada 95 Rationale*, Intermetrics, Inc., Cambridge, MA, 1995.

[Almasi 94] G. S. Almasi and A. Gottlieb, *Highly Parallel Computing*, Benjamin/Cummings Publishing Company, Menlo Park, CA, 1994.

[Andrews 91] G. R. Andrews, *Concurrent Programming Principles and Practice*, Benjamin/Cummings Publishing Company, Menlo Park, CA, 1991.

[CACI 71] Consolidated Analysis Centers, Inc., *SIMSCRIPT II.5 Reference Handbook*, Santa Monica, CA, 1971.

[Cook 93] D. A. Cook and U. W. Pooch, "Asynchronous simulation in a distributed real-time environment," *International Journal of Systems Science*, Vol. 24, No. 3, pp. 451 – 478, March 1993.

[Fishwick 95] P. A. Fishwick, *Simulation Model Design and Execution*, Prentice-Hall, Englewood Cliffs, NJ, 1995.

[Freeland 88] B. G. Freeland, *Inventory of TRADOC Models*, Headquarters, Training and Doctrine Command (TRADOC) Analysis Command, Fort Leavenworth, KS, 1988.

[Gordon 78]   G. Gordon, *System Simulation, 2d ed.*, Prentice-Hall, Englewood Cliffs, NJ, 1978.

[Graybeal 80]   W. T. Graybeal and U. W. Pooch, *Simulation: Principles and Methods*, Winthrop Publishers, Inc., Cambridge, MA, 1980.

[Hamilton 95]   J. A. Hamilton, Jr., D. A. Cook, and U. W. Pooch, "Distributed simulation in Ada 95," *Tri-Ada '95 Proceedings*, ACM Press, Anaheim, CA, 1995.

[Horowitz 83]   E. Horowitz, *Fundamentals of Programming Languages*, Computer Science Press, Rockville, MD, 1983.

[Karp 87]   A. H. Karp, "Programming for parallelism," *IEEE Computer*, Vol. 20, No. 5, pp. 43 – 57, May 1987.

[Kernighan 88]   B. W. Kernighan and D. M. Ritchie, *The C Programming Language*, Prentice-Hall, Englewood Cliffs, NJ, 1988.

[Kerr 89]   R. Kerr, Postings to USENET comp.simulation, FTP archive at the University of Florida at ftp.cis.ufl.edu/pub/simdigest/volume07.tar.Z, 1989.

[Kirkerud 89]   B. Kirkerud, *Object-Oriented Programming with SIMULA*, Addison-Wesley, Reading, MA, 1989.

[Kreutzer 86]   W. Kreutzer, *System Simulation Programming Styles and Languages*, Addison-Wesley, Reading, MA, 1986.

[Law 91]   A. M. Law and W. D. Kelton, *Simulation Modeling and Analysis, 2d ed.*, McGraw-Hill, New York, NY, 1991.

[LRM 95]   *Ada 95 Reference Manual*, Intermetrics, Inc., Cambridge, MA, 1995.

[Markowitz 63] N. M. Markowitz, H. N. Karr, and B. Hausner, *SIMSCRIPT: A Simulation Programming Language*, Prentice-Hall, Englewood Cliffs, NJ, 1963.

[Naiditch 95] D. J. Naiditch, *Rendezvous with Ada 95*, John Wiley & Sons, New York, NY, 1995.

[Park 88] S. K. Park and K. W. Miller, "Random number generators: Good ones are hard to find," *Communications of the ACM*, Vol. 31, No. 10, pp. 1192 – 1201, October 1988.

[Pooch 93] U. W. Pooch and J. A. Wall, *Discrete Event Simulation*, CRC Press, Boca Raton, FL, 1993.

[Sadiku 95] M. N. O. Sadiku and M. Ilyas, *Simulation of Local Area Networks*, CRC Press, Boca Raton, FL, 1995.

[Schriber 91] T. J. Schriber, *An Introduction to Simulation Using GPSS/H*, John Wiley & Sons, New York, NY, 1991.

[Stroustrup 91] B. Stroustrup, *The C++ Programming Language*, Addison-Wesley, Reading, MA, 1991.

[Tindell 94] K. Tindell, E-mail correspondence with the authors, ftp.cs.york.ac.uk from the University of York, 1994.

[Uhde 95] K. K. Uhde, *Translating C++ to Ada 95*, Technical Report 95-03, Vanderbilt University, Nashville, TN, 1995.

[Volz 90] R. A. Volz, P. Krishnan, and R. Theriault, "Distributed Ada – A case study," in *Distributed Ada: Developments and Experiences*, Cambridge University Press, Cambridge, UK, 1990.

[Wall 93] J. A. Wall, *Multilevel Abstraction of Discrete Models in an Interactive Object-Oriented Simulation Environment*, Ph.D. dissertation, Texas A&M University, College Station, TX, December 1993.

[Wegner 87]   P. Wegner, "Programming languages – the first 25 years," in *Programming Languages: A Grand Tour, 3d ed.*, E. Horowitz, ed., Computer Science Press, Rockville, MD, 1987.

10

Distributed Simulation Considerations

The implementation of a simulation is clearly an application of software engineering. The case that software engineering and simulation design processes should begin concurrently. Similarly, implementing a simulation on a distributed system requires consideration of distribution issues early in the design process.

The objective of the simulation is an overriding determinant in the design of the system. It is foolish to distribute a simulation merely because a distributed system is available for use. There is non-trivial overhead associated with distributing an application. The primary motivations for distributing a simulation are to reduce execution time and to increase the potential problem size. Additionally, in large interactive simulations, a distributed implementation can help solve representation issues [Hamilton 96].

The flexibility and extensibility of distributed systems means that the target architecture may vary from installation to installation. In this respect, writing an application for a distributed system is very different from writing an application for a parallel multiprocessor.

In this chapter we will focus on some of the specific issues associated with simulation on distributed systems. Of particular concern are the handling of clocks, synchronous and asynchronous execution, and logical process simulation. We will begin by addressing how to decompose a simulation for distributed implementation.

10.1   Decomposition of a simulation

The decomposition of a simulation for effective use by multiple processors is key to the successful implementation of a distributed discrete event simulation system [Pooch 93]. There are five fundamental approaches to simulation decomposition and a sixth which is a hybrid of the other five fundamental techniques [Righter 89]. Each approach has its own strengths and weaknesses with regard to the exploitation of concurrency and parallelism and each poses unique challenges for synchronization.

10.1.1   Parallelizing compilers

This method uses a parallelizing compiler to find sequences of code in a sequential simulation that can be processed in parallel and on separate processors on a multiprocessor. Compilers continue to improve both in terms of ease of use and the efficiency with which they generate executable programs. However, implementing efficient parallelizing compilers which make the vectorization of a program transparent to a code writer is very difficult. Under ideal conditions, parallelizing compilers are transparent to the user. In practice, it is often difficult to rely on compilers to partition and distribute the source code without explicit directives coded by the programmer.

Amdahl's law states that in any system having two or more processing modes of differing speeds, the performance of the system will be dominated by the slowest mode [Levesque 89]. What this means in terms of parallel processing is that if a computation has both parallel and serial components, execution speed will be dominated by the serial portion of the code.

We can derive a simple performance measure to show how the serial code dominates overall performance. We define the following terms:

-   T = time

- T_s = time to execute an operation serially

- T_P = time to execute an operation in parallel

- P_S = the proportion of serial operations

- P_P = the proportion of parallel operations

- N = the number of operations

- S = speedup = T_s/T_P

With these definitions, we have Performance = N/T, and $P_S + P_P = 1$. Then

$$\text{Time } T = N[(P_S T_s) + (P_P T_P)]$$

Recalling that $P_S + P_P = 1$ and substituting for P_S we get:

$$T = N[(1 - P_P)T_s + (P_P T_P)]$$

Substituting for S, our definition of speedup:

$$T = N[(1 - P_P) + (P_P/S)]T_s$$

Using Levesque's definition of performance = N/T [Levesque 89].

Thus performance = $\dfrac{1}{\left[1 - \left(\dfrac{S-1}{S}\right)P_P\right]T_s}$

For any given system, S and T_S are constants. Thus as the proportion of work that can be done in parallel increases (as P_P approaches 1), the denominator will become smaller and performance will improve. Significant speedup will not occur unless most of the problem can be parallelized. If there are

significant parts of the computation that must be executed
sequentially, then a fast uniprocessor will often outperform a
multiprocessor.

10.1.2 Distributed experiments

One way to apply the power of multiprocessing to a
primarily serial simulation is to run independent replications of the
same simulation on N processors and average the results. No
coordination is required among processors except for the
averaging. Since overhead is dominated by communication costs
between processors, this has some very desirable aspects. One
could expect to see a virtual acceleration of N with N processors
if the lengths of the experiments are approximately equal. The
individual replication of the simulation on separate processors is
most effective if the system quickly reaches steady state and if the
simulation run times are long. Otherwise, the start-up costs tend
to dilute the contribution of multiple distributed processors.

This approach would also allow simultaneous simulations,
each with different parameters. Low-level processors running the
same simulation with different parameters may provide valuable
data for optimization or factor screening. Although this method
is effective, no single simulation run is accelerated. Therefore,
any decisions about simulation model parameters that are to be
used for parallel simulation runs must be made *a priori* before
actual scheduling. This precludes interactive decision making,
especially important for optimization, and promotes sequential
decision making.

On many message-passing parallel processors, the amount of
memory on each node is often small. Thus this strategy for
distributing experiments may be better suited for distributed
systems where each processor may have significant independent
computational resources. Additionally, distributed systems
require far less synchronization than functionally equivalent
parallel systems.

10.1.3 Distributed language functions

As previously mentioned, tasks with minimal interdependencies are prime targets for execution on separate processors. This approach involves the assignment of simulation support tasks (e.g., random variable generation, event set processing, statistics collection, graphics generation, etc.) to various individual processors.

This is a very clean approach from a design standpoint. However, this offers no potential speedup of any one task. Further, in some cases, the synchronization costs of tightly coupled functions may eliminate any overall gain. Graphics generation to support event processing is going to be tightly coupled with event processing. If the objective of the graphics support is to provide near real-time video updates as simulation events are processed, considerable synchronization will be required. Since graphics can be computationally intensive, off-loading this function to another processor should reduce the load on the processor handling the event list processing. However, a very fast processor may be able to context-switch between event processing and graphics generation faster than distributing the computation across two processors.

This approach is appealing because it offers the opportunity to use off-the-shelf hardware components and to use an existing simulation language. None of the major simulation languages currently in use were designed for distributed execution. The fact that computer networks are now nearly ubiquitous makes this a considerable deficiency. The advantages of distributed language functions are that they avoid the deadlock problem and are transparent to the user. A disadvantage is that it does not exploit any inherent parallelism in the system being modeled [Krishnamurthi 85]. Related research has shown that significant simulation acceleration occurs when only a few processors are used and that the marginal speedup with additional processors drops off quite rapidly [Pooch 93].

10.1.4 Distributed events

The scheduling of events from a global event list may be distributed. Protocols that preserve consistency are required because currently processed events may affect the next event on the list. Therefore, event dependencies must be known prior to scheduling. This approach is particularly appropriate for shared memory systems because in such an environment the event list can be accessed by all processors [Righter 89].

The global event list is composed of all events sorted in chronological order. "Safe" events, that is, those events whose execution does not depend upon previously unexecuted events, must be identified and scheduled. A master processor is required to maintain the global event list. Each available processor queries the global event list for the next event to execute. The master processor updates the global event list. The master processor must maintain several copies of the event list due to the asynchronous execution of the events which may result in an event logically invalidating another event. [Cook 93] provides the following example which illustrates the invalidation of an event and the subsequent rollback to a previous state.

1. Processor i queries the master processor and simulates an event at time t.

2. After processor i begins execution, processor j simulates an event at time $t + x$.

3. Processor j completes the event and returns the result to the master processor.

4. Processor i returns a result to the master at simulation time $t + e$, where $e < x$, that affects other already executed events. Based on this result, the event that occurred at time $t + x$ no longer occurs.

The state of the system is now inconsistent. A rollback must occur to a state prior to step 2 above.

Distributed events are suitable for a small number of processes or when the components of the system require a large amount of global information. Additionally, this approach is suitable for problem domains in which a significant number of events have few, if any, dependencies. Earlier we asserted that distributed systems exhibited fault tolerance. In this case, where all state information is maintained in the master processor, failure of the master processor could create an unrecoverable failure. Because the master processor is so critical to this implementation, some form of hardware redundancy for the master processor would be advisable.

10.1.5 Distributed model components

The decomposition of the simulation model into loosely coupled components makes it possible for components to be assigned to a process, where several processes could be run on the same processor. This approach exploits the inherent parallelism in the model but requires careful synchronization. Depending upon the definition of the objects, an object-oriented program might decompose the simulation by assigning objects and the operations on those objects as independent processes. [Righter 89] observes that this approach requires a system which does not call for a great deal of global information and control.

Synchronization of the processes is usually controlled by message passing. The synchronization primitives required for message-based simulations are [Bagrodia 87]:

- **create** and **terminate** processes;

- **send** messages to processes;

- **wait** for messages and/or simulation time to elapse.

Such a system is usually modeled as a directed graph where the nodes represent processes and links represent possible interactions or message paths.

For a fixed topology, such as a queuing system, a good decomposition is to assign a process to each station and have the movement of customers be represented by message passing. Furthermore, the possible routes of customers may be fixed. Alternatively, both stations and customers can be modeled by processes with messages used to change the customers' states as required.

For a dynamic topology, such as a battlefield scenario, processes can be used to represent the components that are interacting, such as tanks and aircraft. In this topology, components can move in any direction and can interact with all other components. Messages are used to define the interaction taking place. A more efficient variation of this method is to divide the physical space into regions or sectors and assign a process to a particular region. Messages are then used to describe the interactions among the components in different sectors or the movement of components from one sector to another [Pooch 93].

Righter and Walrand rate this approach as having the greatest potential in terms of exploiting inherent parallelism in the system. This procedure is especially appropriate for systems that require little global information and control, since this tends to minimize the requirement for synchronization. Such systems often function in a highly asynchronous fashion.

10.1.6 Combined approach

The ideal decomposition of a simulation model may involve a combination of the above approaches. For example, in decomposing a simulation of a computer network we could distribute the event processing and graphics update functions of the simulation (distributed functions). We could further distribute the processing of the event list (distributed events) and have those events update distributed subnetwork objects (distributed components).

10.2 Time, clocks, and synchronization

To this point, we have stressed the desirability of minimizing interprocess communication. Interprocessor communication costs dominate the overhead of distributing an application. Chapter 7 contains strategies for reducing subsystem interdependence, simplifying models, and decomposing models. However, these strategies only allow us to manage timing and synchronization issues; they do not resolve them. Time, clocks, and synchronization are tough issues for simulations implemented on a distributed system. The execution time for a simulation often has little in common with the actual time it takes for the real-world event to complete. The network simulation run shown in Figure 7.2 simulated sixty seconds of network behavior. The same simulation took fifty-four minutes to execute. Those sixty seconds worth of data would be generated in the physical world in sixty seconds, not fifty-four minutes. In other cases a simulation may execute faster than the real-world event. Simulation execution time is often unrelated to actual execution time.

One of two approaches may be used to control a simulation: event-driven simulation or time-driven simulation [Cook 93]. Event-driven simulation is desirable from a design, implementation, and verification/validation standpoint; however, time-driven simulation is easier to implement.

Time-driven simulation requires the system to perform a check of all possible events for each increment of logical time. This type of implementation typically leads to large, monolithic programs that are very difficult to verify. Worse, there is significant communications overhead imposed by the continual requirement to poll the global clock. There is no possibility of a rollback since each event that is executed is safe. However, the synchronization costs of the global simulation clock often make this unsuitable unless the simulation time intervals are relatively coarse.

Event-driven simulation allows closer modeling or abstraction of the real world. Each event from the real world that is being simulated is represented as a separate event within the implementation. The scheduling and handling of these events, however, is difficult to implement. Often, an interrupt-driven implementation is the only alternative. The resulting operating system overhead can be costly. In addition, the scheduling and handling of interrupts requires explicit programming at the operating systems level. This is difficult to program, and even more difficult to test. Minor changes to an interrupt-driven program can cause major changes in performance [Hamilton 95].

The method used to advance the simulation clock can significantly impact on the performance of the simulation. Under different loads, one method may perform better serially and the other may perform better in parallel on a distributed system. Therefore, speedup, considered alone, may be misleading in comparing time-driven and event-driven clock advancement schemes. Galuscio, Douglass, Malloy, and Turner illustrate this in their implementation of an automobile traffic simulation over an asynchronous network of Sun workstations. For dense traffic flow in the network, the implementation of the time-driven approach achieved less speedup than the implementation of the event-driven approach. However, the execution time for the time-driven approach was significantly less than that of the event-driven approach [Galuscio 95].

10.2.1 Simulation state and time

The state of a system is usually expressed as a function of time. Two time references are involved in the simulation of a system: simulation time and run time. *Simulation time* is the period of time simulated by the model. Simulation time is usually set to zero at the beginning of the simulation run and acts as a counter for the number of simulation time units. The *duration* of a simulation run is the difference between the initial clock setting and the final clock setting at the termination of the run. *Run time* is simply the time that it takes the computer to simulate the period of interest.

Run time is influenced by the complexity of the simulation model and the number of events simulated, as well as by the duration of the run. In distributed simulations, the overhead required to distribute and synchronize the simulation as well as the ability of the simulation design to exploit parallelism will heavily influence run time. Run time in many cases is significantly different from simulation time. Using simple models, one can simulate the operation of this country's economic system over a period of years, in minutes on a computer [Pooch 93].

10.2.2 Time and clocks

Recall that in any message passing system, a global state cannot be assumed. Message passing must be used to create a coherent global state. While the communications might be reliable, messages may arrive out of order. Synchronization of physical clocks is impractical because message delivery times are not guaranteed. A master station sending time updates to multiple remote stations can expect the update messages to be delivered to different stations at different times. Thus any message such as "time now is..." will set clocks at remote stations to the same time, but since the updates will not occur simultaneously, the clocks will not be synchronized.

Every computer has a physical clock. A computer's clock is an electronic device that counts oscillations which occur at a certain frequency in the clock crystal. The oscillators are affected by environmental variations such as temperature. Although these variations are very small, the accumulated differences are measurable. Clock *drift* is defined as the difference between the clock and a theoretical perfect clock. For clocks based on a quartz crystal, the difference is approximately 10^{-6} seconds, resulting in a drift of one second every 11.6 days (1,000,000 seconds) [Coulouris 94]. Simulation time is usually defined in one of two ways:

- timer "ticks"

- the logical time when events execute

The issue for clocks in a distributed system is how to transmit the same time to all stations. On a local network, a clock watching program (such as **timed** in UNIX) may be used to constantly watch other clocks and synchronize the local stations as necessary. When there are significant geographical distances between stations, this approach fails because of the aforementioned difficulties of predicting message arrival times.

The network time protocol (NTP) uses multiple time servers across the Internet to broadcast time synchronization messages from the U.S. Naval Observatory [Krol 92]. NTP uses statistical techniques for the filtering of timing data to dampen the varying transmission delays experienced by Internet traffic. Atomic clocks, such as those used to calculate International Atomic Time and also used by the U.S. Naval Observatory, are accurate within nanoseconds. Transmitting the information over a network which measures delays in milliseconds degrades the accuracy of the transmitted time. Measuring physical time with an accuracy of ten milliseconds is insufficient to determine the relative order of many events in a distributed system [Coulouris 94]. Therefore other means must be used to ensure that ordered events are executed in the correct sequence.

The time and space problem is illustrated in Figure 10.1. Each processors generates events (E) that send requests to other processors and subsequently receive replies. Local time (T) advances but may not be advancing uniformly on each processor; hence, order of arrivals are not guaranteed. For example, when processor 3 receives event 1 from processor 1 and generates a reply at time (local to processor 3) 2, there is no way to know whether processor 1 will receive that reply before or after processor 1 receives processor 2's event 2 request.

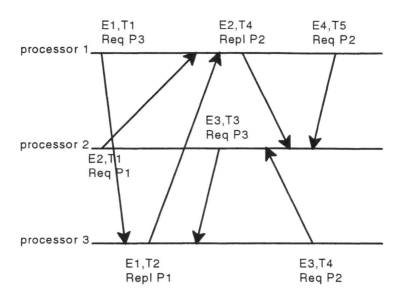

Figure 10.1. Time and space diagram.

The primary objective in event ordering is to ensure that events execute in the correct order. One way to do this is with "happened-before $\Rightarrow$" relations based on the law of causality [Lamport 78]. The relation is defined by [Goscinski 91] as follows:

- If a and b are events in the same process, and a was executed before b, then $a \Rightarrow b$.

- If a is a send event message from one process and b is a receive event message from another process, then $a \Rightarrow b$.

- If $a \Rightarrow b$ and $b \Rightarrow c$ then $a \Rightarrow c$.

Since we cannot synchronize the physical clocks of a distributed system, Lamport developed the concept of logical clocks. A logical clock is a monotonically increasing counter local to each processor. Three rules are applied to update logical clocks:

1. When a process initiates an event, it increments its own logical clock (generally by one).

2. When a process sends an event to another process, the sender appends the value of its logical clock to the message as a timestamp.

3. The receiving processor determines the maximum of its own logical clock and the timestamp from the sender and then increments the maximum by one to timestamp the received event.

In the example in Figure 10.2, the sender in (a) is running behind the receiver. Since the receiver's logical time is greater than the sender's timestamp, the receiver increments its logical clock for the received timestamp. In (b) the sender is running behind the receiver. The receiver determines that the sender's timestamp is greater than its logical time so the logical clock is reset to the timestamp and then incremented.

10.2.3 Synchronization algorithms

Distributed systems are not centrally controlled. The distributed computing model allows significant independent

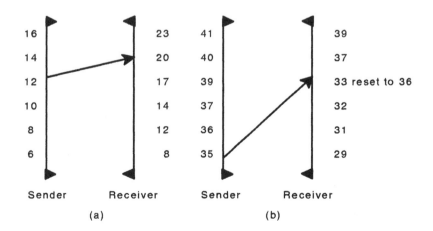

Figure 10.2. Lamport's logical time.

operations by each station. Eliminating the interactions between subsystems greatly eases the distributed implementation. One of the many reasons electronic mail has become so popular is that sender and receiver can exchange information asynchronously, unlike a telephone call which requires synchronization between the called and calling parties.

Minimizing the need for synchronization in a distributed system clearly eases the implementation issues. However, integrating work across remote sites is a main reason for building distributed systems. And integration of non-trivial applications will require synchronization.

There are three primary strategies for synchronization: time-based event ordering, token passing, and priority-based event ordering.

Time-based event ordering. This method uses timestamps to order events for execution across the distributed system. Synchronizing physical clocks via message passing is impractical since messages may be lost, delayed, or arrive in a different order than that in which they were transmitted. Timestamps are applied to events based on logical clocks rather than physical clocks. The lowest relative timestamp is used to schedule event execution.

Token passing. This concept is similar to that used in the IEEE 802.5 Token Ring and FDDI protocols. A specially formatted message is circulated around a logical ring. This scheme can be implemented by imposing a ring structure or by creating a virtual ring. Non-ring structured systems may implement token passing as long as the controlling algorithm ensures that each requesting process receives the token in a finite amount of time. The key component is a scheme that ensures that all stations get a chance to "take a ticket" and therefore the opportunity to execute.

Priority-based event ordering. Control is based on process priority rather than the time the processes initiate. This results in the elimination of problems associated with timestamp-based event ordering. This method is particularly applicable to real-time systems. Distributed synchronization algorithms using time-based event ordering are not fully suited to use in real-time distributed systems due to the unavailability of a common clock. Processes that execute in real-time environments have priorities attached to them and need to execute in priority order [Goscinski 91].

Distributed applications exhibit a greater degree of integration than a networked application. Integration requires some means of synchronization, which is why the above methods are important. The synchronization problem is a major challenge in implementing a distributed simulation.

10.3 Logical process simulation

The technique of partitioning a distributed simulation into logical processes was developed by Fujimoto [Fujimoto 90]. This approach is a means of distributing a simulation at the event level. The objective of logical process simulation is to partition a global simulation task into a set of communicating logical processes in order to exploit any inherent parallelism in the model components. An architecture for logical process simulation similar to that described by Ferscha and Tripathi is illustrated in Figure 10.3 [Ferscha 94].

A *logical process*, LP_i, has an assigned subsystem, SS_i, upon which a simulation engine, SE_i, operating in event-driven mode executes local (and generates remote) event occurrences. Each event executed by a simulation engine advances a local clock. A *set* of LPs is designed to execute events in parallel either synchronously or asynchronously. Each LP_i accesses only a statically partitioned subset of state variables. This subset is disjoint to state variables assigned to other LPs.

The *communications interface* provides for the propagation of effects across the system to remote LPs that result from the local execution of an event by an LP. This is done primarily by sending and receiving event messages with the sender's local time (timestamp) appended to the message.

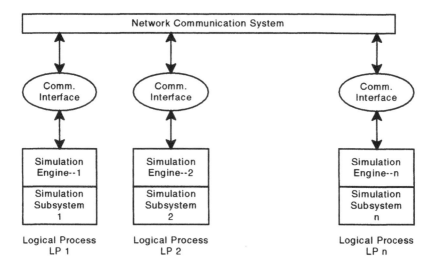

Figure 10.3. Logical process simulation structure.

10.3.1 Synchronous vs. asynchronous LPs

Synchronous LP simulations are time-driven simulations. Both centralized and distributed clocks may be used. Regardless of the implementation, the simulation proceeds according to a global clock since all local clocks appear as copies of the global clock value. Every LP must process all events in the time interval $[i\Delta, (i + 1)\Delta]$ before any LPs are allowed to begin execution of events occurring at time $(i + 1)\Delta$ or later [Ferscha 94].

As with any time-driven simulation, clock synchronization costs may be high. In order to avoid synchronization overhead, a time-driven parallel simulation may be better implemented on a shared memory multiprocessor. Since all processors can directly access a global clock in shared memory, the message passing required for a distributed implementation may be avoided. A time-synchronized simulation cannot enter into an unsafe or inconsistent state; hence, rollbacks are not necessary.

Asynchronous LP simulation is an event-based method which depends upon the existence of events which do not affect each other to accelerate the simulation.   Events with dependencies cannot execute correctly in an arbitrary manner. Correctness may be ensured if the total ordering of events produced by a sequential simulation is consistent with the partial event ordering. This is the inverse of Lamport's logical clock problem. A logical clock value is required for each event to order events in logical time.

No causality error occurs, that is, no effect being executed prior to its cause, if every LP processes events in timestamp order. This is the local causality constraint described in [Fujimoto 90] as:

> A discrete event simulation, consisting of logical processes (LPs) that interact exclusively by exchanging timestamped messages, obeys the local causality constraint if and only if each LP processes events in nondecreasing timestamp order.

Adherence to the local causality constraint is sufficient to ensure that no causality errors occur. In some cases, we may safely ignore this constraint.

Consider the events in Figure 10.4. Event 3 is caused by event 1; hence, we must ensure that event 3 is not processed prior to event

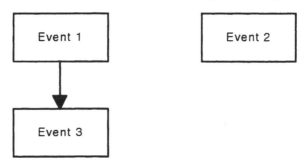

Figure 10.4. Event causality.

1. Event 2 is independent, however, and may safely execute before or after event 1. The manner in which events are processed in asynchronous LP simulation motivates a discussion of conservative and optimistic protocols.

10.3.2 Conservative vs. optimistic LPs

Conservative mechanisms first determine if an event is safe before processing the event. Given an event with a timestamp, the process must first determine that there can be no other event with a smaller timestamp. Otherwise, a possible violation of the local causality constraint may occur. Processes with no safe events to execute must block. It is easy to see the possibility of deadlock developing if all processes wait to confirm that there are no earlier timestamps. Additionally, the input buffers of deadlocked LPs may grow unpredictably and result in a memory overflow.

Both deadlock avoidance and deadlock detection algorithms exist which can solve the deadlock problem in conservative LP simulation [Chandy 79][Chandy 81]. Null messages may be used to avoid deadlock. When a process completes an event, it sends a null message on each of its outbound ports providing the other processors a lower bound on the value of the next timestamp. It can be shown that this mechanism avoids deadlock so long as there are no cycles in which the collective time stamp increment of a message traversing the cycle could be zero [Fujimoto 90]. Deadlock detection and recovery is a two-step process. The system is allowed to deadlock and a detection process is used to determine that all LPs have blocked. The recovery mechanism recognizes that the event with the lowest timestamp is always safe. The safe event is then executed and the simulation allowed to proceed.

Optimistic mechanisms do not prevent deadlock. Optimistic mechanisms allow the LP to advance the local clock as fast as possible, assuming that the *local virtual time* (LVT) will remain consistent. An event may proceed, and then later it may be discovered (via exchanged messages) that the event was *unsafe*. One obvious advantage is that the individual processors are free to advance whenever they can, thus taking full advantage of any potential parallelism that might be present in the simulation. The corresponding disadvantage is that *rollbacks* will occur to recover from unsafe events [Cook 91].

10.4 Summary

Partitioning is the heart of any distributed simulation. There are five well-established methods for partitioning a simulation for distributed execution. Combinations of the five methods are also possible. Synchronization is the most significant implementation issue. The concept of causality mandates the need for synchronization and is fundamental to the design and analysis of a distributed simulation. Logical time can capture the monotonicity property induced by causality in the simulation [Raynal 96]. Causality among events in a system is a powerful tool for analyzing the effectiveness of a distributed simulation.

10.5 Exercises

10.1   Discuss the pros and cons of using optimistic logical process protocols in conjunction with an implementation on a shared memory multiprocessor.

10.2   Are synchronous LPs inherently conservative?

10.3   Why would a distributed simulation require a global event list?

10.4   In section 10.1, we discussed five fundamental approaches to simulation decomposition and a sixth hybrid approach. Are any two of the fundamental approaches mutually exclusive? If so, why?

10.5   In what ways may a distributed implementation solve representation issues?

10.6 Does Amdahl's law lead to the conclusion that a completely serial computation may execute slower on a distributed system? Why or why not?

10.7 Why is the software implementation of a time driven simulation easier than event-driven simulation? Is this always the case? Why or why not?

10.8 If the time resolution of a simulation is greater than one second, would the network time protocol (NTP) be sufficient to synchronize the simulation?

10.9 When conservative LP mechanisms use null messages to avoid deadlock, a significant communications overhead is imposed. An alternative to null messages is to arbitrarily select an LP to process its next event if all LPs are blocked. Discuss the pros and cons of this alternative.

10.10 How can the simulation designer compare and evaluate the potential performance costs of optimistic versus conservative LP protocols?

10.6 References

[Babaoglu 93] O. Babaoglu and K. Marzullo, "Consistent global states of distributed systems: Fundamental concepts and mechanisms," in *Distributed Systems, 2e,* S. Mullender, ed., Addison-Wesley, Reading, MA, 1993.

[Bagrodia 87] R. L. Bagrodia, K. M. Chandy, and J. Misra, "A message-based approach to discrete-event simulation," *IEEE Transactions on Software Engineering*, Vol. 13, No. 6, pp. 664 – 665, June 1987.

[Chandy 79] K. M. Chandy and J. Misra; "Distributed simulation: A case study in design and verification of distributed programs," *IEEE Transactions on Software Engineering*, Vol. 5, No. 5, pp. 440 – 452, September 1979.

[Chandy 81]   K. M. Chandy and J. Misra, "Asynchronous distributed simulation via a sequence of parallel computations," *Communications of the ACM*, Vol. 24, No. 11, pp. 440 – 452, November 1981.

[Cook 91]   D. A. Cook, *Accelerated Time Discrete Event Simulation in a Distributed Environment*, Ph.D. dissertation, Texas A&M University, College Station, TX, August 1991.

[Cook 93]   D. A. Cook and U. W. Pooch, "Asynchronous simulation in a distributed real-time environment,", *International Journal of Systems Science*, Vol. 24, No. 3, pp. 451 – 478, March 1993.

[Coulouris 94]   G. Coulouris, J. Dollimore, and T. Kindberg, *Distributed Systems, 2e*, S. Mullender, ed., Addison-Wesley, Reading, MA, 1994.

[Ferscha 94]   A. Ferscha and S. K. Tripathi, *Parallel and Distributed Simulation of Discrete Event Systems*, Technical Report #CS-TR-3336, University of Maryland, College Park, MD, August 1994.

[Fujimoto 90]   R. M. Fujimoto, "Parallel discrete event simulation," *Communications of the ACM*, Vol. 33, No. 10, pp. 30 – 53, October 1990.

[Galuscio 95] A. P. Galuscio, J. T. Douglass, B. A. Malloy, and A. J. Turner, "Advancing time in parallel simulation," *Proceedings of the 1995 Winter Simulation Conference*, Washington, DC, pp. 650 – 657, Dec. 3 – 6, 1995.

[Goscinski 91]   A. Goscinski, *Distributed Operating Systems*, Addison-Wesley, Sydney, Australia, 1991.

[Hamilton 95]   J. A. Hamilton, Jr., D. A. Cook, and U. W. Pooch, "Distributed simulation in Ada 95," in *Tri-Ada '95 Proceedings*, ACM Press, Anaheim, CA, 1995.

[Hamilton 96]   J. A. Hamilton, Jr., B. D. Bachus, and U. W. Pooch, "Integrating distributed simulation into Force XXI training," *Proceedings of the 1996 SCS Simulation Multiconference*, New Orleans, April 8 – 11, 1996.

[Krishnamurthi 85]   M. Krishnamurthi, U. Chandrasekaran, and S. Sheppard, "Two approaches to the implementation of a distributed simulation system," *Proceedings of the 1985 Winter Simulation Conference*, San Francisco, pp. 435 – 444, Dec. 11 – 13, 1985.

[Krol 92]   E. Krol, *The Whole Internet User's Guide & Catalog*, O'Reilly & Associates, Inc., Sebastopol, CA, 1992.

[Lamport 78]   Lamport L., "Time, clocks and the ordering of events in a distributed system," *Communications of the ACM*, Vol. 21, No. 7, pp. 558 – 565, July 1978.

[Levesque 89]   J. M. Levesque and J. W. Williamson, *A Guidebook to FORTRAN on Supercomputers*, Academic Press, San Diego, CA, 1989.

[Pooch 93]   U. W. Pooch and J. A. Wall, *Discrete Event Simulation*, CRC Press, Boca Raton, FL, 1993.

[Raynal 96]   M. Raynal and M. Singhal "Capturing causality in distributed systems," *IEEE Computer*, Vol. 29, No. 2, pp. 49 – 56, February 1996.

[Righter 89]   R. Righter and J. C. Walrand, "Distributed simulation of discrete event systems," *Proceedings of the IEEE*, Vol. 77, No. 1, pp. 99 – 113, January 1989.

11

Enabling Technologies for Distributed Simulation

In a sense, this entire book is about enabling technologies for distributed simulation. The confluence of recent advances in computer architecture, software engineering, and simulation modeling techniques has made distributed simulation a reality.

Computer networks are the cornerstone of distributed systems. A central feature of distributed applications is providing users the illusion that they have sole, local access to the distributed application. Users are then freed from concerning themselves with the physical connections and communications details of the distributed system they are using.

No matter how seamless or transparent the distributed application appears to the user, the underlying network connections play a pivotal role in the execution of the distributed system. Networks are not only an enabling technology for distributed simulation, they are also a prime subject for simulation themselves.

Another enabling technology for distributed simulation is the use of knowledge-based systems to monitor and control distributed systems. Artificial intelligence (AI) applications are generally computationally intensive. Distributed systems offer additional computing power to expand the problem domains that AI methods may be applied to.

11.1 Network simulation

Distributed applications run over networks. An overloaded network, an intermittently operating network, and/or an improperly specified network precludes distributed execution of an application (simulation). Distributed systems are dependent upon the networks on which they are built. Automated tools to aid the network management process abound, but they are often very expensive.

Network management is often accomplished by trial and error, damage control, or other ad hoc methods. Some of the most successful network managers primarily rely on their past experience to make educated guesses about the networks they maintain. Using ad hoc methods it is almost impossible to determine the actual performance of contemplated network extensions, upgrades, or other network modifications prior to purchase. As the size, capability, and importance of local area networks (LAN)s continues to grow, something more than ad hoc management methods are needed. There are three methods for obtaining predictive data about networks: analytical modeling, monitoring/measurement, and simulation.

Analytical methods offer important performance advantages over simulation [Mouftah 90]. Unfortunately, analytical modeling using conventional queuing theory does not provide high-fidelity models. Some types of network activity are accurately modeled using Poisson processes. Other network activities are more accurately represented by hyperexponential distributions, and still others are not easily characterized by standard distribution functions [Paxson 95]. The next section will deal with network monitoring in detail, but we note here that monitoring in and of itself is not predictive. In practice, for non-trivial networks, simulation is often the only forecasting method available.

Many networks of interest are already constructed and in use. Through the use of network simulation, modifications to existing networks can be tested for performance and cost-effectiveness before they are implemented. This can save money by reducing unnecessary modifications and saving costly down time. In order to create an accurate network model, the performance of the existing network must be understood. Additionally, after modifications are made based on results from the model, the network manager must be able to verify that the changes had the desired effect.

Intuitively, the best way to check the operation and performance of a network is to observe and measure the results. There are two major drawbacks to this approach:

1. This is not predictive, as past performance provides no clues on how the network will react to previously unseen changes.

2. Experimenting on an operational network is very risky since the experimental changes may produce unforeseen problems.

Simulation offers a realistic alternative. The three major challenges in network simulation are: monitoring the network, modeling the network, and operating and maintaining the simulation.

11.1.1 Network monitoring

Network monitoring provides the measurements that may determine the face validity of the simulation. However, the monitoring process is neither easy nor inexpensive and requires the desired configuration to be already installed and operational.

An important objective of network monitoring is to collect operational data to find or derive the appropriate probability distribution functions to model the network traffic. These distributions could then be used to create an accurate representation of the network. The data collection objectives for constructing a network simulation are:

- Locate and test tools that might be suitable for network monitoring and network traffic analysis.

- Monitor the network of interest to determine the overall traffic pattern for each subnet.

- Monitor representative individual machines to determine the amount of traffic that individual machines produce.

As noted by Pooch and Wall [Pooch 93], the bottleneck of many simulation processes is the data collection step. Law writes that failure to collect good data is a major pitfall in simulation modeling and validation [Law 94].

11.1.2 Multilevel network modeling

A standard model that may be used to understand and explain networking principles is the International Standards Organization (ISO) Open System Interconnection (OSI) Reference Model. The OSI model was described in Chapter 5. Although many of the popularly used protocols do not use the same layers as the OSI reference model, the protocols have the same functionality.

Jain and Agrawala cite the following objectives of the OSI reference model:

- To identify the collection of functions that are fundamental to providing reliable, cost-effective, secure, and transparent communication between systems

- To give a precise definition of each function without necessarily providing details of how the functionality is to be achieved

- To define the concept of layered architecture in terms of services, functions, and protocols

- To specify the seven-layer OSI architecture in terms of the functionality of each layer [Jain 93]

The OSI reference model is important because it provides a common frame of reference for modeling interconnected networks with differing protocols. In Figure 11.1, the functionality of the IEEE 802.3 Ethernet layer is compared with the bottom two layers of the OSI reference model. Note that the OSI data link layer is implemented in Ethernet as a logical link layer and the media access control (MAC) layer.

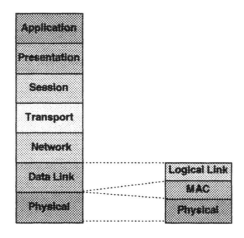

Figure 11.1. OSI reference model mapped to Ethernet.

It is not uncommon for an organization to interconnect heterogeneous subnets, some of which may be Ethernet-based, others Token-Ring-based, and still others using FDDI, as shown in Figure 11.2. Although FDDI is very different from the CSMA/CD-oriented 802.3, both protocols have the same functionality outlined in the OSI stack, even if the layer decomposition differs.

It is impractical to consider modeling all the elements of Figure 11.2 immediately. A multimodeling strategy is more realistic in which models are created for each particular network architecture. The various resulting models are unlikely to be integrated unless the interfaces are standardized. We may start with one of the "black boxes" in Figure 11.2, an 802.3 LAN. 802.3 refers to IEEE standard 802.3, which defines the network protocol popularly called Ethernet.

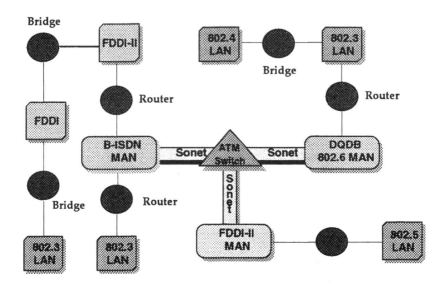

Figure 11.2. Heterogeneous interconnected networks.

First we model a single Ethernet node, as shown in Figure 11.3. Figures 11.3 – 11.6 were created using OPNET, a commercial network modeling and simulation tool [Mil3 95]. The dotted lines in Figure 11.3 represent statistic wires which provide dynamic inputs to the model. The solid lines represent packet streams. The primary module of this node model is the mac module. The mac module receives packets from the bus via the bus_rx module and transmits packets on the bus via the bus_tx module.

The defer module is a supporting module used to calculate a deference value for the mac module. The deference value is the amount of time to compensate for propagation delay. That is, a station must defer a certain period of time to wait for a signal to travel the full length of the bus in order for all stations to be warned that the bus is busy.

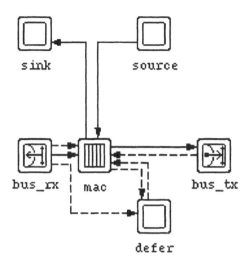

Figure 11.3. Ethernet MAC-level node model.

A more detailed model of the media access control layer may be achieved by defining state transition diagrams (STDs) for each module. Some STDs may be very simple and have only one state. Others, such as the one defining the mac module in Figure 11.4, may have many states and transitions. The other modules in the node model in Figure 11.3 also have defining STDs.

The functionality of an 802.3 Ethernet LAN at the (MAC) layer is modeled using a state transition diagram. The simulation infrastructure provided by OPNET uses state transition diagrams to define modules. This process model has packet-level resolution. Each state and their transitions are implemented in source code.

The queue is initially empty in the INIT state. Once packets arrive, their various states are modeled until FRM_END, when the current frames are completely processed. Other state transition diagrams support the Ethernet process model. The

deference value is computed by the supporting process model
that the defer module is defined by. When the Ethernet process
model enters the BACKOFF state the deference value determines
when a new transmission may be initiated by the Ethernet
interface.

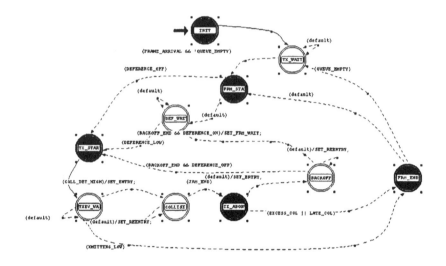

Figure 11.4. Ethernet modeled as a state transition diagram.

We know that every station on a segment will use the same
network protocol since some device such as a router is required
to interconnect segments with differing protocols. Since we now
have designed a model for an Ethernet node, we can proceed to
model a network segment of workstations based on the node
model. Figure 11.5 shows the individual stations on a segment.
Each station is based on the node model shown in Figure 11.3.

We are now ready to simulate the operation of a single
network segment. We have implemented the functionality of the
physical and link layers of the OSI reference model and that is
sufficient to model the operation of a single segment. At this
point we may customize the individual stations on the segment if
we desire a more detailed representation. Individual workstations
or types of workstations may be specially modeled. Special

characteristics could be implemented by modifying the individual modules of the station of interest.

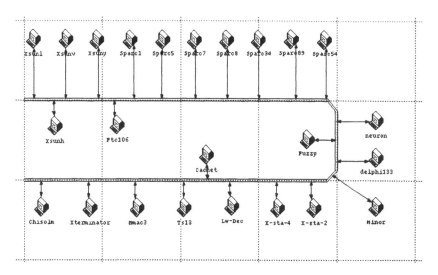

Figure 11.5. Network segment model.

If we desire to simulate the operation of more than one segment, we must add the functionality of the network and transport layer services to our model. The Internet protocol suite is one of the most widely implemented sets of network protocols. The TCP (transport control protocol) and IP (Internet protocol) protocols have the same functionality as the OSI model's transport and network although the layers and layer boundaries are different.

We can extend the node model of Figure 11.2 by adding modules to implement TCP, IP, and ARP (address resolution protocol). As is commonly done, we will incorporate the functionality of the upper three layers of the OSI in a single application module, two of which are defined by app1 and app2. The extended node model is shown in Figure 11.6.

Creating a model of the network architecture does not necessarily result in accurate traffic models. While the operation of network hardware and protocols is essentially deterministic,

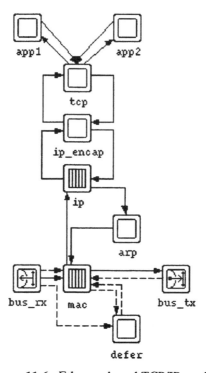

Figure 11.6. Ethernet-based TCP/IP model.

human-generated traffic is stochastic. Network simulations can exercise network designs through the use of event lists based on simple recording or the specific interests of the analyst. The needed fidelity of the traffic model will vary with the objective of the simulation.

By using a multimodel approach, the simulation designer can integrate other network protocols (see Figure 11.2) into the simulation. Different node models may be designed for token ring, FDDI, etc. Designing the simulation based on standard interfaces is essential to developing a maintainable and extensible simulation infrastructure. An open design for network simulation does not specifically require the use of the OSI model. The requirement is for an open model which can accommodate the different functions of network protocols in a robust manner, as the OSI model does.

11.1.3 Network simulation operations

Network simulation requires a high level of understanding of the particular network implementation that is being simulated. Analysts often require a set of tools that enable them to view the entire network. Individual devices must each be modeled. On large networks this is a tedious process. However, to get anything resembling a high-fidelity simulation requires a great deal of effort by the network administrator.

[Terplan 92] observes that network simulation models are very sensitive to:

- Workload descriptions

- Network configuration

- Software environments

Network configurations can be exercised with event lists generated from historical traffic (workload) data. Predictive data about the effects of configuration changes can be made based upon known usage. Predicting future workloads is much more difficult. Recent research has indicated that TCP/IP traffic may be self-similar [Willinger 95] [Leland 94]. This is an intriguing result.

A simple definition of self-similarity follows. An object may be partitioned and then a portion of the original object may be magnified. When the magnified portion closely resembles the original object, it is said to be self-similar. Self-similarity is an important characteristic of fractals, which are beyond the scope of this book.

However impressive the research progress, most system administrators need reasonably mature products and are not prepared to perform the mathematical analysis required to apply fractal geometry to derive traffic generation patterns. How precise the traffic generators must be depends upon the fidelity needs and operational requirements of the simulation.

Improved tools and methods are easing the challenges of network monitoring. However, data collection and analysis are still challenging issues. There is no network simulation package that is completely convenient and appropriate for all communications applications [Law 94]. Thus, organizations that do a large amount of simulation may want to consider using several different simulation packages.

A significant amount of up-front effort is required to initialize the network configuration. Often, many organizations lose track of the current configuration of their network. Network configurations tend to be very dynamic, which can produce a significant maintenance requirement once the simulation is initially configured. If the simulation model is not updated when the actual network configuration changes, then the simulation tool will rapidly lose its usefulness.

Another issue is the resolution of the network simulation. The vast majority of network simulation products operate at fixed levels of detail. Again this may necessitate the use of several simulation packages. For instance, a wide-area network (WAN)-oriented simulation package may be unsuitable for a detailed station-by-station analysis of a particular segment.

Simulation performance is a major concern. A simulation which takes one hour to run one second of simulation time is rarely of operational use. This is a major issue in limiting the level of detail which can be modeled in a large network. The minimum time interval for a simulation should be on the order of the duration of the shortest significant event of interest. For network simulation, significant events may be individual bits when studying physical layer phenomena; packets for most performance models; or messages for higher order traffic studies.

In the domain of computer networks a second is an eternity. A great deal can happen between one second and the next. It is not unrealistic to expect that modeling thousands of messages may require hundreds of thousands of programming instructions in the simulation. Once the physical network has been modeled and implemented in software, then analysis can be conducted by varying the configuration and/or the workload, as shown in Figure 11.7.

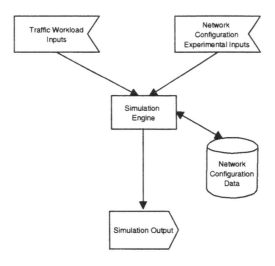

Figure 11.7. Network simulation operations.

The serious simulation developer would be well advised to investigate network monitoring and simulation tools developed in the research community. Generalizing a bit, we find that commercial tools are forced to trade off flexibility for ease of use. Network modeling and simulation tools in the research community provide important exemplar technology that has the potential for reuse. In many cases source code is readily available which provides the capability for extensibility and better understanding. Unfortunately, most mid-sized organizations cannot invest the time and personnel to adapt and extend simulators in the research community to their own use.

Some typical shortcomings of commercial network simulators include:

- Inability to input data to build a network topology from an external file produced by an existing topology building tool.

- High-level layers of certain protocols not implemented.

- Lack of source code makes it impossible to verify the implementation of the protocols or the random number generator.

- Inability to add custom or non-standard probability distributions.

Other useful tools to support network simulation are on the horizon. Such tools include reliability assessment tools, traffic generators, topology builders, and analytic modeling tools. In addition to their individual functionality, integration of these tools in an intuitive environment is becoming important as the complexity of network installations increases.

Many network simulation or modeling tools listed have the capability to capture and analyze packets. This presents a security challenge. Anyone who can download and run some of these programs may be able to capture passwords. Network managers should certainly not blithely allow the casual use of these tools.

Network simulation can eliminate much of the uncertainty involved in LAN planning and management. However, non-validated simulations may produce subtly erroneous data. Since simulation is the only tool that is really scaleable to handle large networks, validating a large network simulation is not easy. One strategy is to individually monitor manageable parts of the network and using that as input to validate the simulator. If the observed and the predicted data check out, then the simulator can be used to forecast topology/equipment changes and upgrades with some confidence.

11.2 Artificial intelligence

We noted in Chapter 4 that simulation is typically a complex process. Distributed simulation is even more demanding in terms of the resources required to implement and manage a given system. As the sophistication and power of the simulation increases, so does the difficulty of employing it. Often it is necessary to seek automated solutions to the problem of using a simulation which operates in a distributed computing environment.

Employment of a distributed simulation implies the use of various types of hardware and software for the purpose of exchanging information. Overseeing the operation of these components can be a challenging undertaking all by itself. There are a host of tasks associated with network supervision which until fairly recently seemed so complex as to resist automation and require the interface of a human manager. In particular, tasks such as traffic management, load balancing, system security, and troubleshooting have historically relied upon the special skills of a dedicated individual: the network administrator. The application of developments in the field of artificial intelligence, however, have shown that we are approaching a state of the art which will allow for the automation of many of these complex responsibilities.

11.2.1 Expert systems

An *expert system* (often referred to as a *knowledge-based system*) is a computer program that duplicates the problem-solving ability of a human expert in some domain. Fundamentally, it is an automated method for retrieving specific knowledge applicable to a particular set of circumstances, with the objective of changing those circumstances in a fashion which enhances or optimizes some cost function.

The development of expert systems is the most mature branch of the many subspecialties which comprise the field of computer science known as artificial intelligence (AI). The past decade has seen the fielding of dozens of expert system-related development tools, putting this branch of AI in an application domain almost on par with database and other information management applications. In part to make them more acceptable to a lay marketplace, modern expert systems development environments almost invariably sport a sophisticated visually oriented user interface.

We may distinguish the use of expert systems from a conventional or procedurally programmed application by several characteristics. First, the manner of performance of an expert system is intended to be truly expert; it must be capable of accommodating the majority of conceivable inputs that can arise when addressing a given problem. Second, the means by which a solution is achieved mimics in some fashion the manner in which a human would achieve the same result. While this distinction is of little importance to an end user, from a developer's point of view it is key, because the types of problems which employ the expert system approach are, in general, those in which a conventional approach is not economically feasible, or even impossible.

The use of expert systems, under appropriate circumstances, can be superior to the use of a conventional approach. From a technical point of view (i.e., software development), we can consider the following to be desirable results from the use of expert systems technology:

In general, the ways that knowledge is expressed in expert systems is very high-level, which means that we can think about the problem domain in a way that isn't as rigid as the syntax usually associated with procedurally programmed solutions. This creates the potential for increasing the speed of production of programs. This sort of environment lends itself well to a software development paradigm known as *rapid prototyping*, which can be explained essentially in terms of an iterative process of fielding software packages that are incrementally more and more robust. In fact, Noren suggests that given the dynamic nature of modern network topology and configuration, expert systems will quickly become tools which are as commonly used in network management as spreadsheet programs are used in accounting [Noren 88].

The high-level nature of most expert systems programming means that the code produced in the development of a knowledge base is self-documenting. This means that the intended functionality of the code is evident immediately from the code itself; little additional human-readable commentary is required. This is important from both a software engineering standpoint as well as a commercial one: programmers can concentrate more on the efficiency of the algorithms while preserving an acceptable level of documentation in their code.

Rule-based expert systems are highly modular. They depend upon a collection of rules in the form **if** *premise* **then** *consequence* to do their work. As such, each rule is a small chunk of problem-solving knowledge, having clear boundaries which are established by the premise of the rule. The bounded nature of a rule's applicability, coupled with other good software engineering practices, simplifies the maintenance and validation of an expert system. The actual validation of an expert system is an open research topic; this is something that is difficult enough to do for procedurally specified programs, let alone ones using alternative control paradigms, as expert systems do. Because humans structure their knowledge in the same if-then fashion, many people find it easier to learn to program using an expert system approach than using a conventional language such as Ada or C++. The familiarity of the rule-based paradigm, coupled with the intuitive nature of the language, often simplifies the programmer's task of implementing an automated solution to a problem.

All expert systems have some capability which allows them to explain themselves. Often, this ability is of equal importance as is the particular result of the consultation itself. As an example consider the first provably "expert" system, MYCIN [David 77].

MYCIN's purpose was to render a diagnosis of an infectious blood disorder based upon a consultation with an attending physician. The physician relying upon such a system for use in an actual medical setting would want to be very sure that the assumptions leading to the recommendations that such a system might make were valid ones. Thus the ability to explain why a particular conclusion was reached can be very desirable.

The explanatory abilities that all expert systems enjoy give rise to their use with a variety of user profiles. Sophisticated expert systems are able to tailor their explanations in a fashion which maximizes the use of the system by people that are totally unfamiliar with the domain, as well as near-expert users.

All expert systems have two major components:

- The *knowledge base* is a collection of rules and facts which captures the problem-solving heuristics of the problem domain. It is analogous to the source files a programmer creates using a high-level programming language.

- The *inference engine*, or *shell*, is a computer program whose purpose is to interpret the knowledge base and apply the rules in a fashion such that useful processing results.

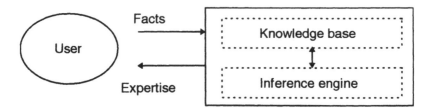

Figure 11.8. The basic structure of an expert system.

The structure of the knowledge base is a common means of classifying an expert system. There is naturally a strong correlation between the structure of the problem-solving information and the means used to apply it. The two most common techniques for achieving this structuring are structuring according to first principles (*rule-based* systems) and according to solution characteristics (*case-based* systems). A rule-based knowledge base describes information in the problem domain hierarchically and focuses on describing the relationships between forces, notions, or circumstances which produce an effect of some sort. The goal of any such system is to be able to describe these relationships so comprehensively as to have the equivalent of the human capacity of reasoning. A drawback of this approach is that in order to be able to draw inferences from loosely structured data, the number of conceivable paths from cause to effect which may explain the data can be enormous. Thus we can think of problem-solving in a rule-based system as being related to the problem of search in a structured state space, and consequently a major problem associated with the task of inference in such a space is the pruning of irrelevant or marginally important paths from the search. Depending upon the characteristics of the problem domain, it may be possible to perform this pruning laterally (focusing the search effort upon one or several of the most probable from among many competing alternatives) as well as vertically (bypassing conclusions which follow obviously from the presented facts and therefore need not be verified).

The case-based approach is the inferential inverse of rule-based systems. Here, the focus is on the cataloguing of previous solution vectors, each of which encodes the values of parameters that the final decision is based upon. In this way, solving a problem can be accomplished directly, by "looking up" the solution from a table of vectors whose decision variables correspond to the data which present themselves in the current problem. Naturally, in non-trivial domains one finds that there is rarely an exact correspondence in the first examination of the knowledge base; it is usually not the case that an exact match can be found between information which describes the current situation and a previous entry. Thus, a major component of the case-based approach is a means of measuring proximity between solution vectors and an efficacious way to extrapolate and interpolate values for parameters which do not relate identically.

11.2.2 Virtual participants

Some simulations are concerned with the analysis of entities that exhibit complex, dynamic behaviors.   One approach to dealing with the representation of such activities is to use a human being to provide the requisite intelligence needed to reproduce the behavior of the system at run time, and interface these inputs directly to the simulation. In other cases, the whole purpose of the simulation may be to provide a sensory backdrop against which a human participant can exercise a certain skill, e.g., a surgical procedure or operation of a motor vehicle.   This technique can be extended to include groups of participants as well.

It is usually undesirable to employ a human in the role of an input generator, unless it serves some additional useful purpose such as education. The cost in terms of the participants' time usually makes such an approach prohibitive. In simulations where the inputs of several intelligent entities are required, the use of artificially intelligent autonomous agents can be very useful. An illustrative example of this approach concerns SIMNET, which is a graphical, three-dimensional environment for the simulation of (primarily) ground combat [Miller 95].

11.2.3 Network management

The management of a network of automated systems is a laborious,   time-consuming   process   under   the   best   of circumstances. It involves a great deal of supervisory effort, as well as analysis and policy execution.   The task of network management in modern systems is often complicated by the fact that in order to obtain the greatest value-performance ratios, most network administrators employ equipment and software procured through multiple vendors. The interest in interconnected systems of computers has generated a proliferation of vendors offering network operating systems, interface cards, hubs, and the like. Since vendors generally feel no compulsion to standardize protocols and interfaces beyond the point where it is profitable to do so, there is a corresponding plethora of "standards" for the various technical issues which relate to the task of managing the network. Thus the problem of effectively managing the network can be troublesome indeed.

The explosion in numbers of different approaches to the same problem is a common one in the computer industry. The flexibility of modern hardware and software seems to especially encourage entrepreneurship, and of course it is true from a business point of view that creating a slightly different technology and patenting it can be a much more profitable approach than simply selling an existing technology; assuming that the newer technique is in some way better, and in fact sells better than the older one. Theoretically, the laws of supply and demand in a capitalist market would determine the best product (at least in terms of what was the most-purchased), and competing, less capable standards would die on the vine. This has certainly happened to many niche hardware and software standards in the past; ESDI hard drives and Hercules graphics adapters to name a few. The market for network hardware and software, however, seems to resist this mold somewhat. In this case, the situation is one where a number of corporations have been able to develop approaches with roughly equivalent functionality and at approximately the same rate. Thus the laws of supply and demand take a bit of a back seat to the marketing ability of the corporations concerned. Being unable to demonstrate a decisive difference in performance, the factor keeping these companies alive becomes one of providing better service, or training, or price. In the final analysis, though, the fact remains that there are a number of different approaches to implementing network connectivity. These approaches are often divergent, and it is not feasible for a network manager to become completely expert in every method employed.

The community of people concerned with such an issue, namely, the users, managers, and technicians involved with the provision of network service have not stood idly by in the face of the standards dilemma. The fact that such difficulties have arisen in other areas of computer application has suggested a solution which has worked with varying degrees of success in other domains: the development of a standard outside of any single commercial concern. The various standards-creating organizations were created for just this purpose. In fact, a standard for network management techniques themselves has been proposed by the Open Systems Interconnect (OSI) committee, known as the OSI Network Management Architecture (OSINMA). Briefly, this standard proposes the identification of five major functional areas concerning network management [Klerer 88]:

- Configuration management: Collecting and exercising control over information from the system needed to implement connectivity services. This would include tasks such as the assignment of machine addresses, establishment of physical connections with external service providers, maintenance of name servers, etc.

- Fault management: Detecting and correcting erroneous conditions in the network service.

- Performance management: Monitoring the efficiency of network services and adjustment of parameters as necessary to optimize efficiency subject to current policy constraints.

- Security management: Protection of network resources against unauthorized use.

- Accounting management: Enabling the collection of network resource usage information and the mapping of usage to cost.

Numerous authors have developed network management systems organized around the OSI management model [Mansfield 92] [Lai 89] [Sutter 88] [Liao 90]. Lo proposes an expert system approach to network management which includes an expert system per OSI functional area and an additional expert system which serves to coordinate the activities of the others [Lo 91]. His structure is appealing because it is symmetric with respect to the functional areas. It would require no additional expertise outside the domain area to maintain either one of the functional area expert systems, as they will be expressed with the same logical constructs as every other one in the system. The integrator serves as a buffer between the actual interface and the individual functional areas, providing guidance and feedback to the user according to predefined criteria. Ideally, the integrator functions in the manner of a high-level filter, limiting the flow of information to the user to that data which is necessary for the network manager to accomplish the mission, neither more nor less than that. The functional area expert systems function as autonomous agents, carrying out the supervisory and data collection functions necessary to perform the requisite tasks in that functional area.

11.2.4 Neural networks

An intriguing alternative to the rule-based expert system is the neural network approach. A *neural network* is a computational structure that is controlled by a "learning" process very similar to the fashion in which humans learn, rather than being controlled by explicit programming. The means by which an artificial neural network functions is inspired by an analysis of how such behavior is produced by the brains of higher creatures. One convenient way to think about neural nets is in terms of a "black box" analogy. In an application, a neural net is presented with some set of inputs and produces a set of outputs. If the neural network is operating properly, then the outputs are appropriate, given the inputs and the intended behavior of the system.

Artificial neural networks (ANNs) can be implemented in either hardware or software. The fundamental theoretical concepts necessary to understand neural processing were developed between 1940 and 1960. The first implementations of these theories were accomplished in the early 1960s.   Just as actual implementations were starting to be developed, however, Minsky and Papert [Minsky 69] pointed out what appeared to be a huge flaw in the foundation of the neural net approach – single-layer neural networks were incapable of solving a major category of problems (in particular, recognizing the "exclusive or" of several inputs).   This has ramifications such as being unable to recognize simultaneity or coincidence in digitally rendered patterns.   However, in 1974, it was proven that with some modification, the original approach could be made to form any non-linear function of the inputs.   The modification required the use of at least three layers of neurons in the network.

An ANN is a network of computing nodes which are connected to one another in some fashion.   It is usual to organize these nodes into layers, each of which can have any number of nodes.   The orientation and usual naming of the layers is shown in Figure 11.9.

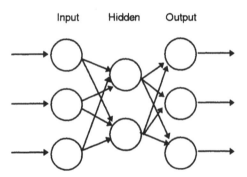

Figure 11.9. General structure of artificial neural networks.

Every node in the network has two defining characteristics: a *threshold* and a *transfer function*.   The threshold is a value which determines whether or not a node will fire at a given moment. When a node's inputs equal or exceed its threshold, then the neuron fires – it transmits a signal to be received as inputs at whatever other neurons it is connected to. The transfer function determines exactly what value is propagated through the neural network.   In addition, each link connecting to artificial neurons has an identifying characteristic, known as the link *weight*. The link weights give a particular node's output its strength and character (either excitatory or inhibitory).

We classify neural networks according to several characteristics:

- The number of layers in the network

- The direction of the connections allowed in the network (the example in Figure 11.9 is a *feedforward* network, since every connection proceeds from the input side toward the output side).

- Whether or not connections must proceed from one layer to the immediately adjacent layer.

- The means by which a network "learns."

The architecture and function of a neural network require the representation of data to be numerical. This is so that it can duplicate the notion of summing inputs and being able to compare that sum to a threshold. Ideas like an object's color and shape can't be "added" without first encoding that information numerically.

The *training* of neural networks is the process of finding a combination of thresholds and link weights such that for every combination of inputs, it produces an acceptable combination of outputs when propagated through the network. From an intuitive perspective, this is achieved by making a change to the weights and thresholds, then evaluating the performance of the network. We then compare the network's actual performance to the desired performance and use the difference between the two to adjust the weights and thresholds again. This process continues iteratively until the maximum performance level has been obtained; at this point, we say that the network has been trained.

This technology is incorporated into the management of the defense switched network (DSN). Shah and Arellano report the use of a neural network in conjunction with a rule-based system to monitor and detect network faults and to implement controls necessary to compensate [Shah 90]. The flexibility of the neural network in adapting its responses to a wide range of continuous inputs makes it especially well-suited for use in this domain. The network uses output from switch sensing units which report data such as the number of restarts, call-completed statistics, and delay. Having been trained to recognize patterns indicative of error conditions, the network constantly filters data received from the switches and alerts the console operator if it senses difficulties. In concert with the neural network, a rule-based system prepares a plan to implement responses to the sensed faults and observes the results. The sense-plan-observe cycle is repeated until the fault is corrected or the console operator advises the system that the pattern does not require adjustment.

11.3 Summary

Future networks with higher speed and greater bandwidth may require even higher levels of precision. As new networking technologies are introduced, there is little reason to expect a significant reduction in complexity. Simulation has a better chance of scaling up to meet the challenges of these new technologies than either direct observation or analytical methods. As networking capabilities increase, we can expect that to translate into greater capabilities for distributing applications.

11.4 Exercises

11.1   What is the difference between a network model and a network protocol?

11.2   In section 11.1, the typical shortcomings of commercial network simulation packages are outlined. Why might a network administrator want to make use of a commercial package anyway?

11.3   When would activity at the physical layer be of primary concern to a network administrator?

11.4   From a distributed systems standpoint, what level of the OSI model is of the greatest interest?

11.5   Identify the stochastic elements of a network simulation.

11.6   Discuss the major components of an expert system and explain the usefulness of making a distinction between them.

11.7   Describe an application of artificial intelligence to the task of network topology discovery.

11.8   Discuss advantages and disadvantages of the rule-based approach to expert system development.

11.5 References

[David 77]   R. David, B. Buchanan, and E. Shortliffe, "Production systems as a representation for a knowledge-based consultation program," *Artificial Intelligence*, Vol. 8, No. 1, pp. 15 – 45, February 1977.

[Giarratano 89]   J. Giarratano and G. Riley, *Expert Systems: Principles and Programming*, PWS-KENT Publishing Company, 1989.

[Hamilton 95a]   J. A. Hamilton, Jr., G. R. Ratterree, and U. W. Pooch, "A toolkit for monitoring the utilization and performance of computer networks," *Simulation*, Vol. 64, No. 5, pp. 297 – 301, May 1995.

[Hamilton 95b]   J. A. Hamilton, Jr. and U. W. Pooch, "An open simulation architecture for Force XXI," *Proceedings of the 1995 Winter Simulation Conference*, Washington, DC, pp. 1296 – 1303, Dec. 3 – 6, 1995.

[Innis 83]   G. S. Innis and E. A. Rexstad, "Simulation model simplification techniques," *Simulation*, Vol. 41, No. 1, pp. 7 – 15, July 1983.

[Jain 93]   B. N. Jain and A. K. Agrawala, *Open Systems Interconnection*, McGraw-Hill, New York, NY, 1993.

[Klerer 88]   M. Klerer, "The OSI management architecture: An overview," *IEEE Network*, Vol. 2, No. 2, pp. 20 – 29, March 1988.

[Lai 89]   E. Lai, "A knowledge-based approach to intelligent network trouble analysis," *Proceedings of the IEEE Global Telecommunications Conference*, pp. 512 – 516, 1989.

[Law 94] A. M. Law and M. G. McComas, "Simulation software for communications networks: The state of the art," *IEEE Communications*, Vol. 32, No. 3, pp. 44 – 50, March 1994.

[Leland 94] W. E. Leland, M. S. Taqqu, W. E. Willinger, and D. V. Wilson, "On the self-similar nature of Ethernet traffic," *IEEE/ACM Transactions on Networking*, Vol. 2, No. 1, pp. 1 – 15, January 1994.

[Liao 90]   T. Liao and D. Seret, "Toward the intelligent integrated network management," *Proceedings of the IEEE Global Telecommunications Conference*, pp. 1498 – 1502, 1990.

[Lo 91]   C. Lo, "An expert integrator for communications networks management," *Proceedings of the 16th Conference on Local Computer Networks*, pp. 369 – 374, 1991.

[Mansfield 92]   G. Mansfield, M. Murata, K. Higuchi, K. Jayanthi, B. Chakraborty, Y. Nemotoo, and S. Noguchi, "Network management in a large-scale OSI-based campus network using SNMP," *Proceedings of the SUPERCOMM/ICC Conference*, pp. 179 – 185, 1992.

[Mil3 95] *OPNET Modeler 2.5.B*, Mil3, Inc., Washington, DC, 1995.

[Miller 95] D. C. Miller and J. A. Thorpe, "SIMNET: The advent of simulator networking," *Proceedings of the IEEE*, Vol. 83, No. 8, pp. 1114 – 1123, August 1995.

[Minsky 69] M. Minsky and S. Papert, *Perceptrons, An Introduction to Computational Geometry*, MIT Press, Cambridge, MA, 1969.

[Mouftah 90] H. T. Mouftah and R. P. Sturgeon, "Distributed discrete event simulation for communication networks," *IEEE Journal on Selected Areas in Communications*, Vol. 8, No. 9, pp. 1723 – 1734, December 1990.

[Nemzow 92] M. A. W. Nemzow, *The Ethernet Management Guide*, McGraw-Hill, New York, NY, 1992.

[Noren 88] C. Noren, "Rapid prototyping network management systems," *Proceedings of the of the 1988 Conference on Military Communications*, pp. 891 – 895, 1988.

[Paxson 95] V. Paxson and S. Floyd, "Wide area traffic: The failure of Poisson modeling," *IEEE/ACM Transactions on Networking*, Vol. 3, No. 3, pp. 226 – 244, June 1995.

[Pooch 93] U. W. Pooch and J. A. Wall, *Discrete Event Simulation*, CRC Press, Boca Raton, FL, 1993.

[Shah 90] S. Shah and P. Arellano, "AI-based network management for the defense switched network," *Proceedings of the 1990 Conference on Military Communications*, pp. 1058 – 1061, 1990.

[Sutter 88] M. Sutter and P. Zeldin, "Designing expert systems for real-time diagnosis of self-correcting networks," *IEEE Network*, Vol. 2, No. 5, pp. 43 – 51, September 1988.

[Terplan 92]   K. Terplan, *Communication Networks Management, 2e*, Prentice-Hall, Englewood Cliffs, NJ, 1992.

[Willinger 95] W. Willinger, M. S. Taqqu, R. Sherman, and D. V. Wilson, "Self-similarity through high-variability: Statistical analysis of Ethernet LAN traffic at the source level," *Proceedings of ACM SIGCOMM '95, Computer Communication Review*, Vol. 25, No. 4, pp. 100 – 113, 1995.

12

Distributed Battlefield Simulation Design

Simulation has deep roots in the study of warfare. Chess has often been described as the first war game. Distinguished historian and military analyst Colonel T. N. Dupuy notes that the Prussians began adapting chess as a form of wargaming in the eighteenth century. In the 1820s, Prussian officers in the Guards Artillery shifted their play from a chessboard to a map [Dupuy 84]. In 1824, *Instructions for the Representation of Tactical Maneuver Under the Guise of a War Game* was published by the Prussian General Staff.

Set-piece war gaming as a planning tool has continued to increase in importance. The advent of the Cold War and the invention of the computer revolutionized war gaming and led to intense interest in battlefield simulation. The long-term stability of the Cold War gave analysts years to prepare detailed warfighting simulations. The U.S./U.S.S.R. battle in Germany's Fulda Gap may be the most intensely studied battle that never happened.

The dynamic nature of the post-Cold War world does not give military analysts and planners the luxury of years to analyze, model and simulate future contingencies. In order to be of any significance, modern military simulations must provide high-fidelity representations with flexible plug-and-play modules which will allow the creation and execution of battlefield simulations on very short notice.

12.1 Background

Operations research came into its own during the Second World War. The roots of the American military requirement for operations research can be traced back well before the war. In 1934, then Colonel George C. Marshall supervised the preparation of *Infantry in Battle*, which stated the following on page 1:

> The art of war has no traffic with rules, for the infinitely varied circumstances and conditions of combat never produce exactly the same situation twice. Mission, terrain, weather, dispositions, armament, morale, supply, and comparative strength whose mutations always combine to form a new tactical pattern. Thus, in battle, each situation is unique and must be solved on its own merits [Marshall 39].

Clausewitz noted that the art of war is based upon "a play of possibilities, probabilities, good and bad luck, which spreads about with all the coarse and fine threads in its web, and makes War of all branches of human activity the most like a gambling game" [Clausewitz 88]. The web of possibilities referred to by Clausewitz is based upon the complex interactions of combat that when unraveled appear to be simple and deterministic. Unraveling those threads is non-trivial because there are so many interdependencies on the battlefield [Hamilton 96]. Advances in technology have made it much more plausible to model the uncertainties outlined by Marshall. Decomposing the fine threads of combat makes it possible to create high-fidelity simulations. Such simulations can serve as an unequaled peacetime as well as a wartime training tool.

Computers, with their capacity to handle large volumes of information, have been a critical aid to the military analysis community. Today, increased processing power can be further augmented by linking powerful heterogeneous computers into distributed computing systems. The Defense Department is working to integrate the varied training and simulation tools of the services through distributed interactive simulation (DIS) [DIS

93]. In the DIS world, simulations are classified in one of three ways:

- **Live:** simulations involving soldiers exercising on instrumented ranges.

- **Virtual:** aircraft or vehicle simulators.

- **Constructive:** automated war games.

The seamless integration of live, constructive, and virtual simulation is a major objective in devising common DIS standards.

Distributed systems offer the potential to implement very high-fidelity combat models. The same computing power and speed that promises to increase the problem domain bounds that can be represented also threaten to overwhelm a user with details. This problem is not an artificiality imposed by the raw power of computers. Rather it reflects the ability to devise ever higher fidelity models of combat − the most chaotic of all human activity. The U.S. Army is the world's leader for ground combat operations. Capt. J. R. FitzSimonds, U.S.N, writes eloquently on this point:

> The most critical drag on high-tempo system performance is the cognitive limit of the human mind, the rate at which an individual can assimilate information and act. An information-intensive battle space may work to our advantage only if humans can be largely removed from the command loop. The need for speed will likely force today's hierarchical command structures to become very flat, with automated analysis and decision-making largely replacing time-consuming and error-prone human deliberation. More profoundly, technical limitations of communications and data fusion may mean that humans will have to forego a traditional "picture" of the battle space. The question then becomes whether future U.S. military commanders can accept a continuing reduction in their real-time battle information as the price of an increasing pace of activity [FitzSimonds 95].

The mobile strike force concept recently tested during the U.S. Army's Prairie Warrior 95 exercise featured a flattened command and staff hierarchy. While the Army of the 21st century is likely to feature a flatter hierarchy, span of control limitations will prevent a flat hierarchy. More probable is a dynamic hierarchy that can collapse and expand as needed. Modern military communications has already made this possible. During the 1973 Arab-Israeli War, an Israeli lieutenant and his platoon were personally directed around Suez City by the Israeli theater commander [Dupuy 78]. This kind of zooming in on a critical area by senior commanders will be the norm rather than the exception in 21st century warfare. This dynamic hierarchy must be represented in any high-fidelity simulation.

Battlefield simulation of the 1990s is far removed from the map table scenarios used to train the victorious leaders of the Second World War. Nor is participation limited to a room full of staff officers. Advances in technology have made it possible to integrate individual soldiers and their equipment into the same training simulations with commanders and staffs at all echelons of command.

12.2 Battlefield system analysis

The essential premise of military training is to train as you fight. In the past decade, battlefield automation of combat, combat support, and combat service support has grown tremendously. Unit standard reports, long the mainstay of transmitting administrative, operational, and logistical information, are now being digitally transmitted. The bulk of artillery fire support is accomplished digitally.

Integrating the numerous stovepipe systems currently fielded is no small task. Manual integration, that is, staff officers collecting data from one system and feeding that data into another system, has often been necessary to support constructive simulations. Enterprise-wide integration of these stovepipe systems is essential to ensure that a coherent view of the battlefield is presented to all simulation participants.

Additionally, this systems integration is shooting at a moving target – the systems continue to change dynamically. Therefore, it is critical that any integration effort be designed to accommodate new systems being developed without any assurance that the new systems will adhere to any predefined standards. These predefined standards provide a simulation infrastructure. Such an infrastructure provides the "building codes" for model development, since the developers know how and where the models must interact with the rest of the simulation structure. DIS is an example of a simulation infrastructure. The reason for developing a simulation infrastructure is to provide a framework for the integration of different simulation models.

An object-oriented decomposition of the battle space is an important and non-trivial first step. A "clean" representation of the battlefield functional areas will first be developed unconstrained by currently fielded automation systems. Next, DIS-compliant object interfaces will be designed. Finally, simulation interface gateway objects (SIGO) will be added to support current tactical MIS systems.

Traditional simulation environments limit user access to the simulation objects at run-time [Vidlak 93]. Vidlak showed that user access to simulation objects during execution reduces the length of time required to run credible simulation experiments. In a dynamic battlefield environment fidelity can be significantly enhanced by allowing dynamic simulation modification at run-time. Dynamically reconfiguring a system is much less abrupt than initializing a simulation, so steady-state is likely to occur sooner. Moreover, dynamic reconfiguration better models the real world. Many complex systems are never shut down even when configuration changes are made.

Consider division/brigade operations simulated against a formidable enemy's land army. As commanders, staffs, and soldiers become engaged in their synthetic environments, be they constructive, live, or virtual simulation based, it is not feasible to call a halt to the simulation and restart it to accommodate changes. A senior commander may want to observe the effects of an enemy initiating employment of a weapons system not previously modeled. Unless previously planned for in the simulation design, adding new, not previously defined classes of weapons to the enemy inventory is non-trivial. It is quite possible that an expert system controlling the enemy forces would require a doctrine change to reflect enemy employment of the new weapon. In order to provide real-time support for what-if analysis, it is clear that the simulation objects must be able to be accessed and modified at run-time.

As the pace of technological change increases, the research and development costs and challenges also increase. Military R&D must be part of any defense-wide enterprise integration effort. Integrating systems still on the drawing board into constructive and virtual simulations can provide important insights into the acquisition process. The acquisition process includes determination of design requirements as well as determining the quantity required for procurement. Simulation provides the opportunity to compare the developmental RAH-66 Comanche helicopter with existing AH-64 Apache helicopters. Dynamically re-equipping constructive simulations with weapons on the drawing board provides measures of the relative advantages of one system over another. Further up-front evaluations early in the engineering process can be generated by reconfiguring an Apache virtual simulator as a Comanche simulator. The key to this flexibility is simple and effective object interface design.

Distributed simulation can support force planning and development. By modeling current and evolving threat arrays, it can be determined if current capabilities are sufficient and what deficiencies require priority of effort. General strategy questions, such as force mix, could be addressed and then specific design issues, such as precise system capabilities (140mm main gun versus 152mm missile launcher as main armament, for example), could be dealt with. Finally, simulation can support efforts to fine-tune force structure. Force structure issues involve determining how many units of a particular type are required. Questions such as these are both system specific and project life cycle stage dependent [McHaney 91].

Constructing a synthetic theater of war will often require more participants than can be provided or accommodated in live or virtual simulations. Hence the need for constructive simulations to fill the void. It will be much more efficient if the constructive simulation can be distribution-based while the live and virtual players are running in an event-driven environment. The basic procedure is then the following:

1. Decompose and model each battlefield functional area. This is clearly a non-trivial task. Building a simulation infrastructure that can represent levels of abstraction from an individual soldier to theater of operations is by necessity very complex. Transitions between constructive, live, and virtual simulation must be enabled across all levels of abstraction. A bottom-up methodology is envisioned with soldiers and vehicles as the lowest level objects. Naturally these objects will be aggregated into higher level objects. However, the implementation of a multilevel simulation strategy will require extensive verification and validation at each level in order to ensure consistency across the entire object hierarchy.

2. Design and build DIS-compliant interfaces. The real issue here is to ensure that current DIS compliance is not the only consideration. Sufficient flexibility must be built in so that extensions to DIS as well as other emerging standards may be supported.

3. Overlay existing and projected tactical MIS systems and translate their inputs and outputs so that they may be directly linked into the synthetic environment. The critical first step here is to recognize the lack of standardization in currently fielded tactical automation MISs. Already existing tactical information systems will likely require modifications in order to fit into the simulation infrastructure.

It will be essential not to make system-wide changes to accommodate the integration of a particular system. Therefore, the core simulation infrastructure will be designed to accommodate custom-built simulation interface gateway objects (SIGOs). These SIGOs will accept inputs from an existing battlefield MIS and deliver simulation outputs to update the MIS.

4. Identify essential tasks and information not currently automated by a tactical MIS system and build support for them into the synthetic environment. Once the simulation infrastructure is complete and existing tactical automation systems tied-in, then any remaining unsupported functions must be built. It should be recognized that as the military services continue to progress with their tactical automation systems, these systems will be connected to the simulation infrastructure. Previously unsupported functions that are part of these emerging tactical automation systems will then be removed.

12.3 System decomposition

A multilevel simulation strategy is necessary to integrate different echelons and services into the same simulation. If a corps commander wants to focus on the progress of a platoon fighting as part of the covering force, he needs to see that part of the simulation in considerably more detail than other parts of the corps battle. However, a corps commander will not always be monitoring/fighting platoon battles. He/she must be able to quickly move back up to the corps level. Combat imperatives based upon the current tactical situation will determine the appropriate level of detail. It is clear that such changes must be accomplished accurately and very quickly.

Scaling multiple levels of command requires methods to deal with the potential combinatorial explosion that representing a division at the vehicle level would impose. A single vehicle object is simple to understand. As vehicles (nodes or objects) are added, the complexity of the interobject communication model grows almost exponentially. An armor company with seventeen tanks has 272 different possible communications paths just within that company.

Fortunately a matrix of tank-to-tank communications would be sparse. Military doctrine dictates that most communications are hierarchical. Rather than simply heuristically limiting communications paths, a more flexible approach would be to apply a multilevel simulation strategy. While virtual and live simulation participants would continue to be represented by event-driven simulation, constructive elements could be represented by process-oriented (distribution-based) simulations. Constructive units could be represented at the highest possible level of abstraction unless it was desired to "zoom in" on the activities of a particular element. Such higher level objects would still generate and receive the appropriate events and state changes but its intraobject-level events would be transparent to the other participants.

The large domain of service-varying requirements need multiple levels of abstraction of the base model [Walczak 88]. An object-oriented model is a logical framework for a multilevel implementation. Trade-offs always exist between complexity and data sufficiency [Popken 96]. Abstract model components have the advantage of great flexibility at the cost of specificity. Concrete implementations can provide more detail but less flexibility. From a software engineering standpoint, it seems clear that flexible abstract components must be developed before implementation. Generic howitzer objects could then be instantiated as specific, concrete models. Thus the same framework can be reused over and over for actual or planned models. A Swedish FH-77 howitzer may not be available for live testing. An abstract howitzer object could be instantiated to represent the FH-77. This would allow for interoperability rehearsals between U.S./Swedish forces on short notice.

For a variety of contingencies, it is not practical to rehearse long-term international interoperability. Being able to instantiate generic equipment objects would make it possible to represent a wide range of unit-types on short notice. A distributed simulation environment would allow for international joint exercises without forces having to leave home station.

The fundamental level of simulation is that of an object. The object will have a state that evolves with time or the occurrence of certain events. The simulation must determine and record the evolution of the state. The objects in the system are interrelated, i.e., the outputs of one object will influence the state of other objects. The state of an object can take many forms, depending upon the nature of the real entity it represents. The state may include variables having discrete values (e.g., alive or dead), variables evolving continuously in time (e.g., the location of the entity represented by the object), or statistical parameters (e.g., distribution of the strengths of the platoons in a battalion). Since objects may be composed hierarchically, their state may be some form of aggregation of the state of component objects (e.g., the total ammunition left in a platoon).

Abstraction is not synonymous with the formation of object classes. Abstraction is the selective examination of certain aspects of a problem. Its goal is to isolate those aspects that are unimportant. The formation of object classes is the identification of classes whose members share some set of properties. The functional or state-preserving characteristics of the properties shared will be propagated to each member of the class by means of the inheritance mechanism.

The component objects form the basis for aggregation, inheritance, naming, abstractions, attributes, time management and resolution, and encapsulating state and behavior. The ability to define, incorporate, change, and map objects that represent elements and components at different levels of abstractions is essential.

12.4 Distributed implementation

An army in the field is spread over a large geographic area. Dispersion, the distance between units, has been increasing dramatically in the last one hundred years. The military command structure is hierarchical and characterized by both dependent and independent simultaneous behaviors. Two direct strategies to represent these characteristics are a multilevel simulation as discussed in the previous section and the implementation across distributed heterogeneous platforms.

Consider the notional Army corps hierarchy represented in Figure 12.1. The 10th U.S. Corps is composed of the 201st Armored Cavalry Regiment, the 25th Armored Division, the 52nd Mechanized Infantry Division, and the 54th Infantry Division. In addition, the corps has the 10th Corps Artillery, the 440th Air Defense Brigade and other corps troops assigned. A U.S. Army Corps may often be composed of more than 100,000 soldiers.

The DIS paradigm was discussed earlier in Section 12.1. To simulate a corps, it is likely that a combination of live, virtual, and constructive simulations will be required. Figure 12.1 illustrates

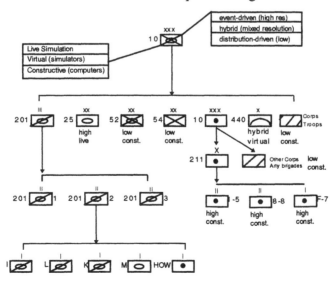

Figure 12.1. Decomposition of a notional Army corps.

one possible combination of live, virtual, and constructive simulation. It should be stressed that the decomposition of the notional 10th Corps is *extremely* high level. In order to avoid the combinatorial explosion that will occur as the 10th Corps is modeled at lower levels of command, a complexity management strategy is required. It is not unreasonable to model actions at the platoon level (approximately 40 soldiers) or lower. A corps of 100,000 or more soldiers is a complex domain.

There is an obvious trade-off between fidelity and complexity. However, complexity can be managed by running a simulation with varying levels of resolution. This is also illustrated in Figure 12.1 and discussed in detail in the next section.

12.4.1 Multiresolution simulation

One of the major challenges of building a large multilevel simulation is the requirement for scalability. Computation and communication techniques that work well for small systems often become totally unusable for large systems. Simulations of large numbers of low-level individual units (e.g., tanks or foot soldiers) can swamp computational capabilities, while transmission of large numbers of high-resolution images can swamp communication channels. We are concerned with identifying relationships between models described at different levels of detail.

Traditionally, researchers have been interested in processes deriving more abstract relationships from more detailed ones. However, the multiresolution simulations we seek, and the ability to dynamically view them at different levels of resolution, requires that we be able to move in the reverse direction as well. That is, we must be able to extend a single abstract relationship into a number of more detailed ones.

In Figure 12.2, Company A and the scout platoon of the brigade's armor battalion may be the units of interest. The simulation might then only use process-oriented simulation to model the battalions and the brigades, while the units of interest are running a more detailed event-driven simulation.

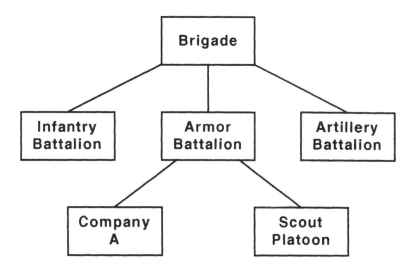

Figure 12.2. Simple decomposition of a combat brigade.

In process-oriented simulation, the focus is on abstraction with respect to individual model components or processes [Wall 93]. Process abstraction can be described as the transformation of one process to another occurring at a different level of abstraction. Moving to different levels of abstraction during the simulation provides the analyst different views of the "running" model. Such access can provide the key to the model's behavior and provides the opportunity to change lower level processes so the impact can be assessed at some higher level [Wall 93]. It is closely tied to the multiresolution issue described above.

As noted earlier, the fundamental problem in adding greater levels of detail is the problem of ensuring state, time, and event consistency among all active elements. For example, if one is interested at one point in time in a tank platoon level of information, and, at another time, individual tank information, how are these two kept consistent? One way, of course, is to always carry out the full simulation at the individual tank level and aggregate information at the platoon level when needed. This solution, however, will require prohibitive amounts of computation when utilized throughout a full simulation. Our approach, which avoids unnecessary computation, is to evolve summary statistical information at a high (e.g., platoon) level and deaggregate this information into initial conditions for lower levels (e.g., individual tanks) when one wishes to examine the situation in detail.

The multiresolution simulation described earlier provides the capability to simulate only at the level needed, suppressing unneeded low-level details. Similar support is needed to reduce the impact of computational and network bandwidth limitations for various forms of information that must be distributed, e.g., images, maps, graphics. We approach this in two ways.

First, we extend the multiresolution concept to representation of information, as well as the simulation resolution, and develop techniques to provide only the resolution of information needed for the task at hand. Data at the proper resolution must be delivered to destinations in real time without causing perceptive distortion to maintain meaningful connectivity between communicating parties. The resolution of information needed by varying levels of command and control provide a natural assist to this process since higher command levels often need higher levels of abstraction in the information they use. Consequently, as the level of information abstraction increases there is typically a decrease in the information resolution.

To accomplish multiresolution data management, data is divided into multiple resolution versions, which will be achieved by incrementally adding detail to lower resolution data. When an inquiry needs to retrieve data of some resolution, the decomposed information can be transmitted incrementally and reassembled to the required level of resolution. The criteria in determining information resolution increments include the total information demand, available system resources, presence of urgent events, and the computing ability of the receivers. For certain kinds of information, such as images, advanced compression techniques have yielded compression ratios of 100 to 1 with little loss of resolution, and approaching 200 to 1 with only modest loss of resolution [Lee 94], [Chan 95]. The combination of these techniques results in acceptable utilization of computational and network resources.

12.4.2 An open architecture for distributed simulation

Distributed objects for this problem domain will navigate through various levels of mixed (live, virtual, constructive) simulation components in a consistent manner. Multilevel/multiresolution abstractions provide interfaces to command echelons that provide varying views and details, from the individual component object, such as an instrumented vehicle or soldier, through aggregation to the brigade and/or corps level and beyond.

Dividing the problem space into layers promotes modularity. The separation and encapsulation of the various issues involved through well-documented interfaces and well-designed abstractions, and the application of the object-oriented design principles at every step, is essential to building an easily reused simulation infrastructure [Konas 96].

Interface specifications: Very precise and well-defined interface specifications are needed to co-mingle live, virtual, and synthetic environments – which may exist at differing levels of detail at different nodes in a distributed simulation. These then need to communicate via a well-defined message protocol. Strict adherence to interface standards is critical to allow for custom tailoring of the component applications. If interface standards are ignored in the short term, then the ability to subsequently modify the applications will be seriously compromised.

Seamlessly integrating live, virtual, and constructive simulation requires an object decomposition of the problem space with well-documented interfaces. As noted earlier, an armor battalion commander should be able to direct any combination of units in the field doing live simulation, others parked in their vehicles using them as virtual simulators, and the remaining units represented by a constructive simulation.

Finally, all interfaces must be backward compatible with DIS. It must be recognized that DIS standards are likely to be modified; considerable care must be exercised in designing interfaces for known present requirements as well as accommodating future DIS standard revisions.

Timing and synchronization: Time management is essential to distributed simulation. Without near real-time performance, seamless integration of the virtual and constructive simulation with the live simulation will not be practical. You cannot halt a moving tank platoon while you wait for the rest of the simulation to catch up. Thus, real-time communication is central to the success of distributed simulation.

Real-time communication deals with transmitting delay-sensitive messages in a distributed system. Minimizing the delays of messages communicated among the nodes will reduce the impact of rollbacks and hence improve the scalability of the system. Further, in a hybrid simulation system (i.e., one that consists of not only simulated devices but also actual ones) message delays must be carefully controlled in order to achieve desired (e.g., synchronized) effects. Thus, a successful distributed simulation system must have the support of real-time communication.

12.5 Employment of a distributed multilevel simulation

Force XXI is the designation for America's Army in the 21st century. Simulation is playing a crucial role in designing the Army of the next century. The U.S. Army is the world leader for distributed simulation research. As might be expected, much of the existing experience in distributed simulation is found in the Army and its research partners.

A multilevel simulation is required to support varying numbers and types of players at multiple levels of command. A multilevel simulation approach allows different echelons of command to view objects at varying levels of detail consistently and seamlessly. A task force commander would be able to view the position and movement of a tank platoon on a map, or a virtual view of the battlefield as seen from the platoon leader's hatch, or a real-time live video from an actual tank on the ground. Each view must be logically consistent with each other, so that the mountain on the map sheet affects movement in the same manner as the virtual mountain and the actual mountain seen via live video. In other words, a real-world mountain must have the same effect on movement as a virtual mountain does in the virtual world.

As shown in Figure 12.3, parts of the same simulation may operate at various command echelons. Because one platoon is being simulated at the platoon level, other platoons in the brigade may be aggregated into higher command levels in the same simulation. Transparently breaking down higher level units into smaller units is a major research area. Platoons may be easily aggregated into larger units. However, deaggregating a brigade into platoon-sized elements cannot easily be done unless the simulation maintains and updates separate state information about each platoon.

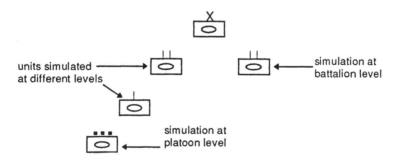

Figure 12.3. Multilevel simulation.

DIS classifications are the foundation for Force XXI simulation concepts. The synergy required for a synthetic environment requires integrated live, virtual, and constructive simulations at multiple echelons of command. A plug-and-play design is necessary to allow for both automated players and human-in-the-loop players at various friendly force and opposing force echelons. Various combinations of live, virtual, and constructive simulations will run concurrently in the same simulation. Expert systems will control simulation nodes lacking human players. At any level in the simulation, human players and expert systems may be interchanged. The opposing force will be similarly configured.

In the training/rehearsing cycle, the operations staff will load the digitized information to set up and drive the custom simulation. Digitized data will come from the rest of the staff to include personnel status, logistics status, enemy forces, maintenance status, etc. If the battalion is conducting a virtual simulation, then the crews will have their vehicle information systems switched into simulation mode, which will control the video inputs and vehicle status information. This training can take place in a motor park. If the battalion is conducting a live simulation (field training exercise or FTX), then their live training can still provide DIS-compatible inputs to constructive and virtual simulations. At the battalion level, an entire maneuver area could be devoted to one company conducting live simulation while the rest of the battalion conducts virtual training in their motor parks. Higher level and adjoining units could be represented by a constructive simulation to provide the battalion staff training as part of brigade and division level operations.

Consider a Force XXI armor battalion conducting simulation-based training (Figure 12.4). Company A is conducting live simulation training on a maneuver range. Digitized information from Company A is transmitted to the battalion tactical operations center. The remaining companies are conducting virtual simulation training in their vehicles in the motor park. Thus, Company A has the full use of the training range. All companies are exchanging digital information with battalion operations and each other. To exercise the battalion staff, a constructive simulation (computer war game) is used to represent the rest of the brigade.

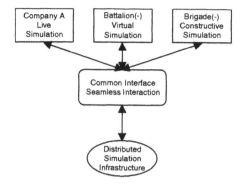

Figure 12.4. Integrating live, virtual, and constructive simulation.

The battalion operations officer (S3) receives digital inputs from the live simulation from Company A, the virtual simulations of the remaining companies, and the constructive simulation of the brigade. Ideally, the battalion operations staff will be unable to tell which units are live, which are virtual, and which are constructive. If the digital input formats from each type of simulation are indistinguishable, we can consider the live, virtual, and constructive simulations to have been seamlessly integrated.

Several things need to noted regarding the discussion of seamless integration. While this concept resembles a Turing Test in some ways, there are important differences. It is certain that an operations officer will always know which subelements are live, which are virtual, and which are constructive. Further, the many stochastic elements ensure that the probability of any virtual simulation exactly matching the performance of live participants is close to zero. Over time, we can reasonably expect the performance of virtual and constructive elements to approximate the performance of the live elements.

The command headquarters that has the capability to digitally communicate with any arbitrary combination of DIS-compliant live, constructive, and virtual simulations, can create custom synthetic environments for specific contingency planning and rehearsal. If the simulations are seamlessly integrated, then it will be impossible for the command headquarters to tell whether the units they are controlling are on field maneuvers (live), in their vehicles command post exercise-style (virtual), or notional with inputs and actions coming from a computer war game (constructive). The best synthetic environment can be transmitted immediately to the computers mounted in individual fighting vehicles as well as on maneuver, fire support, and combat service support computers at all levels of command from company/battery to echelons above corps (EAC).

Major enabling technologies for distributed simulation include simulation integration, expert systems, and stochastic modeling. The seamless integration of different simulation methods is the key to creating a synthetic environment. Expert systems will allow for the automated replacement of human participants. Stochastic modeling will provide the means to drive the various scenarios.

Expert system technologies play a critical role in supporting the plug-and-play strategy of interchangeable human and machine participants, allowing for the horizontal and vertical substitution of human players and automated players. After development of an appropriate expert system engine, variant attributes to model U.S., Allied, and Threat doctrine would be developed. Once the expert system is fielded, then deviations from expected doctrine and performance can be developed. It is not unreasonable that when good intelligence exists, specific enemy commanders may be modeled. For example, a task force simulation could have both humans and expert systems leading companies. Thus training could occur even when all key players are not available. Similarly, opposing force units could be played by human opposing force commanders at some levels and appropriate expert systems at other levels.

An emerging technology is the integration of stove-piped databases and data repositories into integrated information systems [Miller 94]. The implementation of SIGOs will facilitate access to already existing databases and provide integration capability across numerous platforms. It is feasible to consider the implementation of a virtual meta-database in which distributed data is seamlessly integrated via the direct translation capability of the SIGOs. By stove-piped we refer to a system lacking vertical or horizontal systems integration. If a word processor was unable to share data with a spreadsheet application, then we would consider this word processor to be a stove-piped system. In the same vein, current and proposed systems must be able to share data. A major contribution of DIS is the defining of common interfaces.

The information to drive a distributed simulation will come from the ongoing effort to digitize the battlefield. Army digitization efforts are placing computers in tactical vehicles and in command posts at all levels. The way to make the transition from a simulation exercise to an operational rehearsal is to turn a unit's organizational equipment into virtual simulators.

A forward deployed armored division anticipating the onset of hostilities is unlikely to have had the luxury of bringing along dedicated simulators. Operational and logistical constraints may limit or eliminate the opportunities for live simulation. However, an operational unit deployed for combat could rehearse using virtual simulation in their organic equipment. Combat information would be processed and recorded in the Army Battle Command System (ABCS, formerly ATCCS) or its successor system. Fighting vehicles would receive video feeds in their sights and appropriate command and control information over their combat vehicle information systems.

12.6 Summary

As the Army transitions to Force XXI, there will be several generations of technology represented in the operational units. Increased emphasis on joint and coalition warfare will add additional systems and levels of sophistication to an already heterogeneous environment. In order to operate in this fast-moving environment gateways must be constructed that can integrate new systems into the simulation infrastructure.

The rapid evolution from a bipolar to a multipolar world environment as well as the ever increasing pace of technology make the U.S. Army's transition to Force XXI a complex effort to hit a rapidly moving target. The transition to Force XXI will be incremental. Doctrine, weapons systems, and force structure are progressing at different rates. An open simulation architecture is required to support the evolving structure. Multilevel, multiresolution distributed simulation is a means for American commanders to continue to control the tempo of combat operations and to avoid being controlled by information-driven decision cycles.

Multilevel simulation is a critical enabling technology for a Force XXI simulation infrastructure. Multilevel simulation is directly applicable to the area of computer network simulation and other distributed simulation applications. Any large, multilevel domain is difficult to model and simulate at a fixed level of abstraction. Fielding a multilevel simulation capable of driving synthetic environments at multiple levels of command provides a basic architecture for simulating complex distributed systems. Most important, multilevel simulation provides a viable means of training Force XXI, America's Army in the 21st century.

12.7 Exercises

12.1 Describe another problem domain that would be appropriate to utilize a MMDS strategy.

12.2 In the problem domain that you selected to answer 12.1, illustrate and describe in detail the envisioned object hierarchy.

12.3 Describe and differentiate the dependencies between levels of the object hierarchy you described in 12.2.

12.4 Discuss the issues involved in porting a simulation designed for a uniprocessor implementation to a distributed system.

12.5 What are the advantages and disadvantages of implementing a simulation on a distributed system?

12.6 How does an expert system engine differ from a simulation engine?

12.8 References

[Chan 95] A. Chan, C. Chui, J. Lemoigne, H. Lee, J. C. Liu, and T. El-Ghazawi, "On the performance impact of data placement for wavelet decomposition of two dimensional image data on SIMD machines," *Proceedings of the Frontier 95 Conference on Massively Parallel Processing*, February 1995.

[Clausewitz 88] C. von Clausewitz, *On War*, Penguin Books, London, 1988.

[DIS 93] DIS Steering Committee, *The DIS Vision, A Map to the Future of Distributed Simulation*, Comment Draft, University of Central Florida/Institute for Simulation and Training, Orlando, FL, 1993.

[Dupuy 78] T. N. Dupuy, *Elusive Victory: The Arab-Israeli Wars 1947–1974*, Harper & Row, New York, NY, 1978.

[Dupuy 84] T. N. Dupuy, *A Genius for War, the German Army and General Staff, 1807–1945*, Hero Books, Fairfax, VA, 1984.

[FitzSimonds 95] J. R. FitzSimonds "The coming military revolution: Opportunities and risks," *Parameters*, U.S. Army War College, Carlisle Barracks, PA, Summer, 1995.

[Hamilton 96] J. A. Hamilton, Jr., G. B. White, and U. W. Pooch, "Towards a concurrent theory of combat: A parallel processing approach," to be published in *Military Review*, U.S.

Army Command & General Staff College, Fort Leavenworth, KS, pp. 30 – 36, November-December 1996.

[Konas 96]   P. Konas, "Object-oriented parallel siscrete event simulation," in *Object-Oriented Simulation*, Zobrist and Leonard, ed., IEEE Press, Piscataway, NJ, April 1996.

[Lee 94]   H. J. Lee, J. C. Liu, A. K. Chan, and C. K. Chui, "Parallel implementation of wavelet decomposition/reconstruction algorithms," *SPIE Wavelet Application Conference*, Orlando, Florida, pp. 248 – 259, April 1994.

[Marshall 39]   G. C. Marshall, *Infantry in Battle*, The Infantry Journal Inc., Washington, DC, 1939.

[McHaney 91]   R. McHaney, *Computer Simulation, A Practical Perspective*, Academic Press, San Diego, CA, 1991.

[Miller 94]   J. A. Miller, W. D. Potter, K. J. Kochut, and D. Ramesh,   *Object-Oriented   Simulation   Languages   and Environments*, Artificial Intelligence Program, University of Georgia, 1994.

[Popken 96]   D. A. Popken and A. P. Sinha, "Object-oriented frameworks for multi-level simulation modeling," in *Object-Oriented Simulation*, Zobrist and Leonard, ed., IEEE Press, Piscataway, NJ, April 1996.

[Vidlak 93]   M. D. Vidlak, *User-Object Interfaces in an Object-Oriented Discrete Event Simulation*, Ph.D. dissertation, Texas A&M University, College Station, TX, December 1993.

[Walczak 88]   S. Walczak and P. Fishwick, "A centralized methodology for multilevel abstraction in simulation," *Simuletter*, Vol. 19, No. 2, pp. 25 – 31, June 1988.

[Wall 93]   J. A. Wall, *Multilevel Abstraction of Discrete Models in an Interactive Object-Oriented Simulation Environment*, Ph.D.

dissertation, Texas A&M University, College Station, TX, December 1993.

Index

– D –

– E –

T - #0081 - 101024 - C0 - 234/156/22 [24] - CB - 9780849325908 - Gloss Lamination